Comedy and Cultural Critique
in American Film

Comedy and Cultural Critique in American Film

Ryan Bishop

EDINBURGH
University Press

Edinburgh University Press Ltd
22 George Square, Edinburgh EH8 9LF

www.euppublishing.com

Typeset in Monotype Ehrhardt by
Servis Filmsetting Ltd, Stockport, Cheshire, and
printed and bound in the United States of America

A CIP record for this book is available from the British Library

ISBN 978 0 7486 4307 3 (hardback)
ISBN 978 0 7486 7780 1 (webready PDF)
ISBN 978 0 7486 7782 5 (epub)
ISBN 978 0 7486 7781 8 (Amazon ebook)

Contents

Acknowledgements

Working on a topic such as this one has been an endless source of pleasure, surprise and spirited interactions. In the long list of people to whom gratitude is owed, the many students at the National University of Singapore who took the course that forms the base of this book, and whose many contributions and discussions have helped shape my views on the critical capacities of comedic work, deserve special mention. Thanks for dialogue, inspiration and support need to go to my colleagues and friends at the Winchester School of Art (WSA), University of Southampton, including Bashir Makhoul, Jussi Parikka, Jonathan Harris and August Davis. Former WSA colleagues, Sean Cubitt and Stefanie van de Peer, provided constant insights and help. The many friends and colleagues whose work and conversation have assisted me throughout include John Phillips, John Armitage, Steve Graham, John Beck, Tania Roy, Doug Kellner, Michael Fischer, Tim Barnard, Mike Featherstone, Couze Venn, Jordan Crandall, Joy Garnett, Caren Kaplan, Benjamin Bratton, Greg Clancey, George Marcus, Ingrid Hoofd and Sorelle Henricus. I am deeply indebted to Gillian Leslie, Jackie Jones, Jenny Daly, Michelle Houston and the entire editorial and production team at Edinburgh University Press, for their kindness and help throughout the process.

I would especially like to thank my father, Steve Bishop, for his boundless humour and for likely having sparked off this book the moment I could hear; my fabulously funny daughters, Sarah and Sophia; and Adeline Hoe for her patience, surreal sensibility and ability to make me laugh more than anyone else. Finally, this book is also dedicated to the many comedic artists who have enriched my life so thoroughly that I do not know where I leave off and they begin.

CHAPTER 1

American Film Comedy and Cultural Critique: Glitches in the Smooth Running of the Social Machine

To a joke, then, I owe my first gleam of complete consciousness – which again has recapitulatory implications, since the first creatures on earth to become aware of time were also the first creatures to smile.

Vladimir Nabokov, *Speak Memory* (19)

Contrary to what it seems, comedy was in reality the most serious genre in Hollywood – in the sense that it reflected through the comic mode the deepest moral and social beliefs of American life.

André Bazin, 1948 film review

One does not yet know what the image will give or show, but the interval must be objectively *calculable*, a certain technology is required, and this is perhaps the origin or the essence of technology.

Jacques Derrida, *Athens, Still Remains* (19)

If tragedy is about the fact that people are mortal, then comedy is about the fools we make of ourselves on the way to the grave. The traditional distinction between Tragedy and Comedy, however, has always been difficult, at best, to maintain, especially when any moment or statement, depending on context, has the potential to be funny. In fact, comedy has been able to perform a great deal of analytic work that typically was the domain of tragedy or drama, especially since the end of the First World War. The emergence in the twentieth century of a host of literary and cultural figures, from James Joyce to Samuel Beckett to Eugène Ionesco to Flannery O'Connor to Joseph Heller to Günter Grass to Gabriel García Márquez to Salman Rushdie to Don DeLillo to Martin Amis and many others, reminds us of the great traditions of comedic cultural critique often ceded to other expressive arts. These are but a handful of the large number of writers who turned to comic, and often darkly comic, modes to address the horrors of existence in times of war, trauma and upheaval wrought by culture, ideology, politics, race and technology. The powerful thrust of comic critique has long held sway in the Western intellectual tradition, certainly dating back to Aristophanes, and the early part of the twentieth century provides a temporal moment of initial and important impetus for comic engagement with large, socio-economic-historical–technological forces, most especially in and through film, an engagement that continued with a precipitous momentum throughout the century.

One of the major social and cultural issues that comic film took up was cinema itself, thematising its relationship to its audience and to the increasingly important status of the mechanically produced and moving image: that is, what cinema was doing to the collective understanding of the Real as it was understood in relation to technologies of representation as well as production. The trends begun early in comic film have continued with variations and different emphases throughout the century and into the next. Comic cinema in the early part of the twentieth century played a central role in cinema's history as an industry, in narrative development and, more pertinently, its role in complicating the distinction between tragedy and comedy as it concerns social relations, issues all at play within film. The forms of comic cinema, how they worked and how the images shape our sense of collective and individual selves, as well as its content, mirrored crises of knowledge production and legitimisation under way within a host of national institutions, including the university, at the same moment.

Essentially following a chronological arrangement while also making synchronic connections, this book examines, in a simultaneously historical and conceptual fashion, the central role comedic films have played in cinema history, in terms of narrative, the construction of specific comic modes, and the rapidly growing import of visual culture in the public discursive and political spheres: all related to the problematic of popular culture and / as cultural critique. Some ways of delimiting the very large brief of studying American comic film as performing cultural critique include: film comedy within cultural, historical, economic and theoretical contexts; film comedy and its traditions within cinema history; important innovators in American film comedy; the positioning of cinema within a larger technological field and mediascape, as well as the longer trajectories that constitute these larger contexts of cinema's emergence and changes; and the role of visual technology within cultural politics, self-reflexive examination of the status of the image, and cinema's engagement and thematising of its own power and influence in the changing nature of visual and aural representation/production. Though the book uses all of these as touchstones for analysis, the major portion of its engagement with the field comes with the role of cinema in the emergence of visual technology's specific ascendancy during the twentieth century, and cinema's reflexive engagement with visual culture and the various scopic regimes and technologies that constitute it.

The Maltese Cross: The Flickering Shutter of Auto-technological Education

The films produced today are merely the visible allegory of the cinematic form that has taken over everything – social and political life, the landscape, war, etc. – the form of life totally scripted for the screen. This is no doubt why cinema is disappearing: because it has passed into the hands of reality. A lethal transfusion in which each loses its specificity. If we view history as a film – which it has become in spite of us – then the truth of information consists in the post-synchronization, dubbing and sub-titling of the film of history.

Jean Baudrillard, The Intelligence of Evil (125)

So long as we represent technology as an instrument, we remain held fast in the will to master it. We press on past the essence of technology.

Martin Heidegger, 'The Question Concerning Technology' (32)

The hypnotic movements of the Sioux ghost dance could not be more aptly named, at least in the footage shot by W. L. K. Dickinson in 1894 in Edison's famous Black Maria studio. The performers are indeed performers, ethnographic examples from Buffalo Bill's Wild West Show. Philippe-Alain Michaud writes of them that

the performers in the two photo-printed strips escape from the circus world employing them and recall, in their spectral apparition, the reality of their disappearance. And while they entered the film in borrowed guise, they appear there for their own sakes, since, in fact, the set depicts nothing except the event of their vanishing and the litany of their return. (66)

Destruction in the name of preservation can be found in numerous cultural endeavours throughout history, not the least of which is documented in the act of documentation, in the representation of the cultural and technological regime that is replacing that which it preserves in representation. An early example resides at the very heart of Western secular literature with Homer's oral performance jotted down by a skilled amanuensis (as posited by Albert Lord and his student Milman Parry) – Homer's ghostwriter, as it were. Buffalo Bill's Wild West Show had been parked in New Jersey at the time of filming with Edison's Black Maria studio nearby. The Wild West Show itself was an endangered form of performance, whilst Native American nations such as the Sioux had been all but destroyed.

The techno-scientific capacity to document what a given technology's existence is erasing and destroying can be discerned in these brief film clips. The many links between film and gun technologies (as found in Etienne-Jules Marey's photographic gun from the early 1880s) lend an especial resonance to these haunting images of the ghost dance, for the gun in North America proved instrumental in the destruction of the native population and its cultures. Friedrich Kittler notes the linkages between the two technologies, with the history of the movie camera simultaneous with and influencing the history of automatic weapons. 'The transport of pictures', he writes, 'only repeats the transport of bullets' (124). Kittler brings these to Dickinson's footage through the Colt revolver and the Gatling gun that cleared the West of its 'nonhumans' (124). The Western as a genre that moved from the dime novel to become a foundational element of the new entertainment form of cinema is ironically and tragically prefigured in Dickinson's film clip. However, what has made it on to the film stock has already been mediated by performance and rendered fully decontextualised, for it is a circus show, a vaudeville version of Sioux cosmology that we see flickering before our eyes, simultaneously adding to and detracting from its poignancy. It is both better and worse that, through the technology of reproduction and representation found in this film, we are not necessarily witnessing some lost cultural expression. It would already have disappeared, been erased before Dickinson's specific camera arrived, and the camera documents merely a ghost of the ghost dance.

At many levels – the cinematic technology, its cultural influence and its ability to document, as well the conditions of possibility it produces – Dickinson's film footage embodies and exemplifies what Virilio calls 'the aesthetics of disappearance'. The gaps in perception caused by technologically produced movement and speed result in 'picnolepsy', a form of perception emergent from absences and lost snippets of time. Finding overlaps between the fundamentally different philosophical positions of René Descartes and Henri Bergson, Virilio claims that, for both thinkers, consciousness or thought emerges from duration. It is 'our duration that thinks, the first product of consciousness would be its own speed in its distance of time, speed would be the causal idea, the idea before the idea' (32). Virilio's preoccupations with speed in relation to temporality and its influence on apperception and consciousness direct us to cinema's position within and contributions to the vastly larger domain of material and immaterial changes resultant from technological prosthetic extensions of the senses and systems of thought that so dominated the late nineteenth and early twentieth centuries. The cinematic image fused with locomotion, motorised systems and movement, to become a standard, or normative, vision of the world: a default and 'natural' mode of seeing.

Tom Gunning argues that we need 'to theorize film's place synchronically within the wider system of interlocking technologies which compose the terrain of modern experience' (Calling 19). Making explicit connections to telephony and railroad transportation with and through cinema, Gunning suggests that 'cinema teaches us about technology not only through an examination of its own mechanics, modes of production and expression, but through its representation of, and interactions with, other technologies' (Calling 19). Cinema not only furthered the training of viewers to engage with moving images in specific ways, he continues, but it also showed viewers how to interact with and understand the host of technologies emergent at the turn of the twentieth century that transformed sounds, images and movement – and thus time and space – within a system of interconnected and mutually influential technologies (Calling 20).

One technology that was cinematic from its inception, even as it predated cinema, is the railway, and early cinema clearly enjoyed a fascination with train travel, starting with the Lumière Brothers' first public screenings. Early film screenings included what became known as 'phantom rides', simulations of train journeys that allowed audiences vicarious travel at speeds unimagined and often unexperienced. The sites and the locales on offer were often of the exotic stripe but even more so was the sheer technological splendour on display: speed, mobility and viewing-at-a-distance. Hale's Tours took phantom rides to another level by offering audiences visual travel to all parts of the world ('without the luggage!'), all augmented with haptic and aural effects such as shaking bleachers, hissing steam whistles and clanging bells. The Hale's Tours, like the panorama, provide early examples of immersive simulated environments. Striking in these early travelogues is the symbiotic glorification of the train and cinema (both movement machines) that, importantly, provided a view of the rail trip from the train's point of view, with one machine speaking to and being documented by the other. In essence, audiences were mere bystanders to a kind of early machine-to-machine communication, rather like seeing footage of a fighter plane through the cross-hairs of a gun aiming to bring it down, with the camera and gun speaking to each other and both agonistically engaging yet a third machine (the aeroplane). This kind of machinic communication and interaction, of course, gains a rapid momentum and undergoes exponential growth throughout the twentieth century, but finds an early and influential incarnation in the phantom rides.

Cinema, as a latecomer in this field, not only displayed its affinities with these other technologies but also became the vehicle for an interpretive mastery of them, a technology to contain and control other technologies, to show viewers how to understand themselves in relation to them and to the alterations of time and space they bore witness to in their daily lives. In much the same way some half a century later, the computer combined numerous extant machines to colonise and appropriate them, rendering their previous incarnations almost unrecognisable (the calculator, the typewriter and so on). Walter Benjamin argues, in 'The Work of Art in the Age of Its Technological Reproducibility', that *'the function of film is to train human beings in the apperceptions and reactions needed to deal with the vast apparatus whose role in their lives is expanding almost daily'* (27, emphasis in original). This training provides a kind of existential equilibrium between media technologies and the world they produce, within which humans must function. The equilibrium Benjamin hints at, though, is fundamentally a simulacrum manufactured by all media in their mediation between the Real and humanity (the Real as real and human- ity as human, as opposed to machinic). To continue an expanded sense of Gunning's suggestion, we can usefully understand cinema, or media, functioning along with and in reaction to many other discursive and material practices, such as the shift from rural and agrarian production to urban and industrial manufacturing, the organisation of urban space and the built environment, the movement of people on small and large scales, the exponential growth of science and technology to order and explain life, instrumental reason as dominant, bourgeois culture and those cultural and economic forces that sought to resist it (including the avant-garde).

Cinema mostly taught viewers how to understand cinema, constantly thematising its addresses and relationship to its audience: the broadcast monologue of cinema speaking to, not with, viewers. And comic cinema, perhaps consciously and perhaps knowingly, provided a self-reflexive critique of this auto-technological or auto-medial training, allowing audi- ences to glimpse the many ways in which they were being conditioned, shaped and articulated in the newly advanced mechanical era by this quintessential example of art form become industry. Comic cinema, then, returns us self-reflexively and through its own medium and medial rela- tions to the kinds of questions about the construction of human perception and consciousness (or aesthetics) that Benjamin raises in his meditation on art and mechanical reproduction.

Comedic film plays a central role in cinema's transformation from visual special effect and novelty device to art form and viable commercial product, especially through its centrality in the emergence of standardised narrative patterns, the early constitution of genres, and formalisation of cinematic grammar. It also explored the changing relationship between

mechanical visualisation and the constitution of the Real, a relationship it manipulated and perpetuated in specific ways. Visual culture's
ascendancy accelerated in and through early comedic cinema, and so did
the potential for the medium to question the very transformations it exacerbated. Through the manipulation of time and space, combined with an
apparently precise mimetic replication and indexicality (which is debat-
able), film contains the possibility to cause shifts in visual culture that are
capable of critique. Yet it can also be mobilised, and perhaps more easily so
in the perpetuation of that which it sought to challenge: culpability in the
conditions of crisis rather than critique of them. The vision machines of
entertainment had long been the vision machines of business enterprises,
urban control and military power too, but it took the early film comedians
to make this invisible usage of visual culture visible to the audiences who
were subject to popular entertainment, industrialised labour and warfare
all at the same time. The extent to which this intervention has continued
or not, as well as the metamorphoses of comedic film in questioning larger
cultural forces, remains in question.

Gunning has argued that the earliest audiences came to see not film
per se but the cinematograph, thus joining a long line of inventions that
people paid to watch or hear in operation. Their interest in film actually
revealed an interest in how the apparatus worked and what it did (Crazy
Machines 88). While this is certainly true, an equally important element of
the general fascination with the machine, as Virilio and others have noted,
is a fascination with its potential for failure. This possibility of failure or
disruption, Gunning further suggests, provides the appeal of the gag film,
which proved important for early cinema's viability. In a profound way,
the content of these early gag films depended on, while also contradicting,
the appeal of the apparatus: the self-negating appeal of machinic functioning and failure. The avant-garde in the early part of the twentieth century
seemed especially enthralled with technological potentials for shaping
consciousness and articulating modes of thought that resided outside the
rational systems of bourgeois culture, while also concentrating on the
ways in which the very *techne* underpinning the values and economy of
this culture could and did work against itself (cp. Bishop and Phillips).
Marcel Duchamp, for example, was especially interested in pursuing
logics, systems and technologies to their logical ends, which means their
breaking points, their failure – not their realisation. The comedic in film
operates in a similar fashion, as a form of disruption working to unsettle
and critique its very own conditions of possibility while drawing attention
to its dependent and contrary status. To update and expand this claim,
we can consider the comedic in cinema as an extension and manifestation

of contemporary glitch aesthetics operative at all levels. The comedic is the glitch writ large, the spanner in the works that is the working of the works itself. Thus the comic performs a kind of epistemic break in its very being while also highlighting the continuity that makes any kind of break possible.

Comedy, Cinema, Critique

Only comedy, with its conceits, makes it possible for the anonymous audience to become a public – a reality that must be reckoned with, but which can also be calculated upon. A humorous conceit easily turns the crowd of theatergoers into a mass that can be attacked, seduced, beguiled to listen to things it would otherwise not readily listen to. Comedy is a mousetrap in which the public is easily caught and in which it will get caught again and again. Tragedy, on the other hand, presupposes a community, the existence of which cannot always be presumed without embarrassing results.

Friedrich Dürrenmatt, 'Theater Problems' (156)

It is humor which makes language stammer, which imposes on it a minor usage, on which constitutes a complete bilingual system within the same language.

Gilles Deleuze, *Dialogues II* (51–2)

Aristotle asserts that a child becomes 'human' when s/he laughs because the child understands a specific combination of reality and fantasy, an awareness of rules, codes, values and the Law, and the pleasure derived from the imagination and creativity to manipulate them. The child's laughter emerges from the deep pleasure and giddy insight that the order of the world can be *otherwise*, which becomes the basis for critical engagement with it. Comedy provides a space of suspension, when the rules are momentarily revealed as rules, when form yields to content's brutal manipulation of it. Following Aristotle's insight that a child becomes 'human' when s/he laughs, the child then understands a specific combination of reality and fantasy, an awareness of rules/codes/values/Law and the pleasure derived from the imagination/creativity to manipulate them. Thus comedy can be and often is serious business because it is based on, works with, comments upon and critiques all that has the potential to be, or that is presented as, serious. As Dürrenmatt suggests in the epigraph attached to this section, comedy might well work better than tragedy or drama for addressing the serious demands and quandaries of existence, exposing the constructedness of values and culture, power and liberty, fear and hope. A kind of doubling and a nod towards audience awareness of this doubling are essential to the comic text. Similarly, because of the 'double vision' needed for the comedic to work, or the double modality with which it addresses its audience, the potential for an ethical gesture of explicit co-creation of meaning proves essential for the functioning of the comedic text.

However, important questions emerge. Does comedy reinforce the power it apparently overturns? Is the Law (the logos, the phallus, the father) reinscribed and reinforced by that which comments on it, even if done critically and derisively? That is, beyond the basic question of whether or not a popular culture product can critique effectively the systems that produce it, at a deeper epistemological level, can comedy effect meaningful change and insights with regard to the very conditions that make it possible? The ambiguous, even aporic, terrain that these questions constitute provides the ground for any examination of comedy's potential or capacity to perform cultural critique or cultural politics. Add to that the medium and industry that constitute cinema as emergent art form and cultural product, as well as collaborator in a rapidly shifting mediascape, and the questions become more complex, layered, nuanced and difficult.

Less difficult but no less nuanced or complex is the integral part that comedy played in film's movement from sheer visual effect to a consumer product that is a delivery system of narrative, thus saving the fledgling technology from the fate that befell a whole host of other optical manipulation devices. As the crowds began to tire of seeing trains enter a station, workers leave a factory or people sneezing, the Lumière Brothers struck on 'the single shot narrative', as Gunning productively named it, found in *L'Arroseur arrosé* (1895), or 'The Sprayer Sprayed' (Crazy Machines 89). The Lumière film is a gag film documenting the comic situation of a hoax being perpetrated on an unsuspecting victim. In this particular instance, a man is watering a lawn when a young scamp steps on the hose stemming the flow of water. When the sprayer looks curiously at the mouth of the hose, the boy releases the stream, thus spraying the sprayer. These single-shot narratives proliferated in the first decade of cinema's existence and remained the dominant genre in terms of sheer quantity until around 1903 (89). The single-shot narrative had the initial advantage of continuous time and space, rendering all of the action understandable in the physical world, and needing no knowledge of the emerging yet inchoate grammar of cinema and editing. Therefore the gag films did not avail themselves of cinema's infinite capacity to manipulate time and space: the metaphysics of cinema.

To realise the narrative capacity of film more fully, filmmakers needed to understand the implications of the camera eye replacing the audience's eye. The cinema camera frees our biological organ from its time–space and corporeal constraints, which had a profound impact on visual culture and how we view viewing (or see seeing). Editing clearly exemplifies this capacity to alter and play with time and space, and thus 'the shot' became the building block from which cinematic narrative could be constructed. As a visual literacy and cinematic grammar quickly established itself with regard to techniques for story telling, the medium's ability to render elastic the constraints of the physical world similarly increased. This had a huge appeal for magician filmmakers (from Méliès to Orson Welles) and comedians. Comedic filmmakers also added their own angles to what quickly solidified, under D. W. Griffith's tutelage, as stock elements of cinematic narrative. Mack Sennett's massively influential and successful Keystone studios helped establish speed as an important dimension of cinematic narrative, and of course film technology generally; indeed, the phrase 'cut to the chase', which has long been a part of daily parlance, resulted from Sennett's cure-all for narrative slack or obscurity as he cranked out films (literally) by the hundreds.

At the same time that the pace of films and the relationship of shot-to-scene gained complexity, genres codified narrative constraints and possibilities further, establishing a kind of story-telling *techne* that film comedians used and abused, parodied and kicked against. Doug Kellner and Michael Ryan argue that Hollywood genre films promote dominant American values and ideologies, such as the import of money and success; the proper social forms and institutions of heterosexual love, marriage and family; the legitimate sources of power and authority found in the state, police and legal system; the threat posed by violence to the American system (a threat met by even greater violence in the control of the state); and American values and institutions as largely correct, beneficial and benevolent to society as a whole. Cinematic comedy at times challenges these, while at other times it merely reinforces them. Again, we return to the dilemma of whether or not comedy reinstates the power it apparently overturns by choosing specific elements of culture to target for humorous engagement. Althusser's famous argument that 'ideology is a "representation" of the imaginary relationship of individuals to their real conditions of existence' (153) might well provide a way to work the ever-apparent inconsistencies in filmic cultural critique. Further, the insight that all ideology is in service of maintaining the status quo would have profound implications on film's (in)ability to function as critical engagement at all.

Regardless of its efficacy as cultural critique, comedic film does have social and cultural effects. The Dürrenmatt epigraph leads us to the possibility of the ethical, or rather the potential for the ethical, operative within comedy that emerges through a collective conversion of the anonymity of the crowd into the identity of audience through the double modality of the address upon which comedy relies. The playfulness essential to the comedic emerges from the explicit need for the addressee to 'get' the humour and interpret it as humour. If this fails, then the humour fails. Similarly, having to explain humour obliterates the effect that results from the splendid moment of 'getting it' and thus the shared insights that comedy allows. While reader-response and reception-based theories of meaning have long been in circulation with regard to all manner of textual address, they are perhaps more relevant with comedy than with other types of texts, for there is the tacit and unstated assumption from the addressor that is akin to saying 'I know you know what I am saying, and I am signalling to you that I know you know.' The result, then, can be a camaraderie of likeness, a shared sensibility about the working of the world. The profound inter-relatedness of addressor, message and addressee, most especially with regard to an awareness of the level of the address and its self-referentiality, makes the comedic communicative act possible. The comedic text, then, functions like a discursive glitch, or linguistic stammer, in the smooth-running machine of the social order. Miriam Hansen argues that 'film has the potential to reverse, in the form of *play*, the catastrophic consequences of an *already failed* reception of technology' (Benjamin and Cinema 52). Comedic film perhaps engages this general potentiality of film more fully than any other enunciative mode of the medium.

Animation and Automation: Technics of Vision, War and Entertainment

I have said that it is a quality, not a defect, of the photoplays that while the actors tend to become types and hieroglyphics and dolls, on the other hand, dolls and hieroglyphics and mechanisms tend to become human. By an extension of this principle, non-human tones, textures, lines, and spaces take on a vitality almost like that of flesh and blood.

Vachel Lindsay, *The Art of the Motion Picture*, writing in 1915

Walt Disney, along with Ub Iwerks, created Oswald the Lucky Rabbit for Universal Studios, an animated character deeply attuned to the vast range of technological developments and film comedians of the era. In her excellent study of animation's central position within the development of, and in dialogue with, the avant-garde, Esther Leslie links the character to a range of film comedians, including Charlie Chaplin, Harold Lloyd, and Laurel and Hardy, but especially Buster Keaton because of his consistent interactions and playful encounters with technology, including cinema (24). A 1927 cartoon featuring Oswald, entitled 'Great Guns', emerges in the interwar year era and examines the continued appeal of military action and its capacity for stoking nationalist fervour in spite of the exponentially powerful weaponry developed for the First World War. These weapons figure strongly in the film in both comic and horrific ways that bind the technology of cinema and its capacity for altering perceptions and images of the world, as well as our corporeal integrity, with those rapidly developing and changing technologies of warfare that do the same. The cartoon includes anthropomorphised and animate cannons (the eponymous great guns) and munitions, with the former having mouth-like barrels that consume cannon shells like food and the latter taking pleasure in destruction as well as heeding the neutrality of Red Cross medics – making a mockery of the international ideal of humane warfare in the age of modernist industrial production.

Leslie argues that 'Great Guns' parodies a then-popular educational film touting the wonders of a new 'silent great gun' fired by electromagnetic power, with its innovative firing mechanism seen as an improvement over more combustible methods (25). In the cartoon, the animate shells leap of their own volition into the outstretched mouths of the great guns they feed, with the entire system of battle being humanless in its conduct, if not in its results or effects. In fact, the battle scene depicted ranks high in carnage, with decapitations littering the screen. As early as 1900, Nikolas Tesla predicted warfare in the future being waged by machines and directed towards machines – rather like the machine-to-machine vision and communication discussed earlier – and solely a battle of technological supremacy. The closed loop of technology operating in and on the world without apparent human influence anticipates the fully automated weapons systems of the present, as well as numerous automatic systems such as elements of financial markets, but is also embodied by cinema in so far as human agents are not present, except through the medium of representation. An auto-technological awareness of cinema's relation to the other technologies with which it is engaged runs throughout 'Great Guns', and as always, cinema becomes its primary interest.

After Oswald is literally blown to bits, swept up and taken back to the hospital, the nurse (who, conveniently enough, is the love interest Oswald impresses by strutting around in his uniform early in the film) puts the rabbit pieces into a martini shaker, shakes it up and pours out a black liquid that forms into Oswald. The inky pouring out of the rabbit protagonist provides an allusion to the self-reflexive referencing in the Fleischer Brothers' Ko-Ko the Klown shorts, in which the character emerges from an inkwell, showing the material base of both his static and his animated self. Ko-Ko interacts with his animators in the 'Out of the Inkwell' productions and in one film – 'A Trip to Mars' (1924) – involuntarily journeys to space because of the animator's enthusiasm for astronomy. His trip and his experiences there thus provide yet another allusion to even earlier cinema, Edison's 'A Trip to Mars' (1910) and Georges Méliès's 'A Trip to the Moon' (1902) with direct references to Méliès's exploding moon demons. In fact, the films in Ko-Ko's 'Out of the Inkwell' series always begin with the animator Max Fleischer's hand, which is holding an ink pen that brings shape to the clown and manipulates him until he becomes animate; this could well be seen as an allusion to Emil Cohl's 1908 innovative animation short *Fantasmagorie*, which also features Cohl's hands drawing a clown that eventually begins to move. The 'Out of the Inkwell' series features extended interaction between animation and live action while foregrounding the cinematic manipulation required for each to materialise on the screen. In this way, the Fleischers' shorts offer a contained sense of human agency in the form of the illustrator and film technicians, but in each the animator falls prey to the antics of his animated character. The ghost in the machine is the genie in the bottle – or the klown in the inkwell – and, once loosed, can only momentarily be contained.

Mixing live action and animation, the film fully exploits the capacity of the cinematic image to offer windows on a type of reality that visual technologies make possible and can generate, harnessing the kinds of optics that also allow for prosthetic tele-viewing (telescopes), targeting (for guns and rockets) and perspectival projection and manipulation. The film ends with both the animator and Ko-Ko returning to the inkwell, with the heavens as background of the image crumpled up and also stuffed into the inkwell by a pair of metacinematic hands, revealing the image beneath the image that is always an image – the ground of the image as a technological and material necessity for the image to function as an image.

Both 'Great Guns' and 'A Trip to Mars' offer reflections on cinematic auto-technological education operative in film in relation to other technologies but also with regard to how its viewers, its addressees, might engage it. These films, as with any text, do not operate alone but rather within their level of address, and an awareness of the novelty of moving images as a unique mode of address is apparent in early cinema. Not only are the addressees far removed in space and time – potentially as distant as readers of written texts –but also they are in need of acquiring a grammar necessary for understanding the message. In general, any level of address includes some self-referential aspects, referring to itself as an act of communicative engagement. With cinema, the self-referential dimensions operate at the level of enunciation and are often about the means or media of enunciation, laying bare the host of technologies and institutional apparatuses that allow the film to articulate its message. Cinema's relationship to its audience has been the content of that address essentially from the outset, as soon as filmmakers started making films about the audience's confusion or wonderment at seeing a film, such as Edison's *Uncle Josh at the Moving Picture Show* (1902) and many others.

The relationship between addressor and addressee has been a long and complex one, as many film critics, historians and theorists have discussed. Vivian Sobchack, discussing movement and speed in film as considered through Tom Gunning's work on the cinema of attractions, asserts that cinema's self-reflexive consideration of its images is less to do with *the illusion of transparence* (or mimetic indexicality) and more to do with *the experience of revelation* (304, emphases in original). Sobchack's argument makes a productive move towards Heidegger's essay on the essence of technology as a means of instrumentalist control, in contrast to its potential for being a vehicle of revelation. Heidegger's term for this is 'enframing', in so far as the essence of technology is not its material influence but rather the way it shapes thought, perception, evaluation and understanding of the world (thus keeping thought within a specific kind of frame). The Fleischers' 'Out of the Inkwell' series allegorises cinematic enframing in relationship to the audience as Ko-Ko interacts in playful and malevolent ways with his animator, much as cinema does with its viewers, to interrogate (with humour) the silent, invisible operation of the technics that deliver the entertainment of the cinematic message. The audience is embodied by Fleischer, who believes he controls the animated entity, much as we believe we control our engagement with cinematic content. Each time, Ko-Ko as metonym for cinema's message simultaneously cooperates with Fleischer's desires and overturns them to express his own. The frame of the page and the frame of the cinematic image are broken repeatedly at the level of content while being maintained at the level of performance and enunciation: that is, the physical screen that is the ground of the image. The mode of presentation and representation inescapably dominates the film's relationship with the audience, though comedy provides a moment of breakage to reveal the mechanism at work, as well as in its failure, which is perhaps a moment of hope. If cinema provides us with 'a virtual encyclopaedia of modernity's tropes: agency, control, technological prowess, speed, intelligence (both human and machine), the power to render the invisible visible, and the intimate connections between aesthetics and technology' (Bishop and Phillips 50–1), then comedic cinema provides us with a means for swapping around the entries of modernity's encyclopaedia, changing its taxonomies and revealing their arbitrary yet determinate divisions.

In What Follows . . . and Other Caveats, Frames and Contexts

By doing so, Benjamin recast the more orthodox Marxist question of false consciousness in terms of his un/timely theory of 'anthropological materialism': How is consciousness, whether false or critical, produced and reproduced in the first place? What is the effect of industrial–capitalist technology on the organization of the human senses, and how does it affect the conditions of experience and agency, the ability to see connections and contradictions, remember the past, and imagine a (different) future?

Miriam Hansen, 'Why Media Aesthetics?' (393)

The restructuring of human work and association was shaped by the technique of fragmentation that is the essence of machine technology. The essence of automation technology is the opposite. It is integral and decentralist in depth, just as the machine was fragmentary, centralist, and superficial in its patterning of human relationships.

Marshall McLuhan, *Understanding Media* (23)

A large and influential body of work on comedic cinema exists, and these texts have proven to be invaluable interlocutors for this book. As far as film comedy goes, few address comedy with relation to cultural criticism, and when they do, the focus tends to be tightly on specific aspects of the social domain, e.g. gender, class, race and discourse. Clearly, these are all essential concerns; however, the larger cultural critique examined in the text that follows is that of technology and visual culture, the formation of the Real through media technologies, the changing status of the image in relation to other scopic and medial regimes, and self-reflexive engagement of the larger cinematic machinery (material and immaterial) in shaping culture. Books that plough the social and cultural terrain of film comedy and that have informed this one include: Christopher Beach's *Class, Language and American Film Comedy*, Dan Harries's *Film Parody*, James Harvey's *Romantic Comedy in Hollywood, from Lubitsch to Sturges*, Nora Henry's *Ethics and Social Criticism in the Hollywood Films of von Stroheim, Lubitsch, and Wilder*, Elizabeth Kendall's *The Runaway Bride*, Michael North's *Machine-Age Comedy*, William Paul's *Laughing Screaming*, Kathleen Rowe's *The Unruly Woman* and Steve Vineberg's *High Comedy in American Movies*, to name a few. Each of these texts contributes greatly to the discussion of the potential cultural critique that comedy and cinema afford, though they do so within some delimitations; the work that follows would wish to open this up and expand it, specifically with regard to the technological self-reflexivity of much comic cinema.

Works on film comedy more generally, which the current work relates to but differs rather widely from, include: James Agee's 'Comedy's Greatest Era', Alan Dale's *Comedy is a Man in Trouble*, Tom Gunning's groundbreaking articles and chapters, Andrew Horton's *Comedy / Cinema / Theory*, Henry Jenkins's *What Made Pistachio Nuts?*, Kristine Brunovska Karnick and Henry Jenkins's edited volume, *Classical Hollywood Comedy*, Geoff King's *Film Comedy*, Gerald Mast's *The Comic Mind*, Steve Neal and Frank Krutnik's *Popular Film and Television Comedy*, Jerry Palmer's *The Logic of the Absurd* and Lisa Trahair's *The Philosophy of Comedy*. Many of these more general texts are either genre-driven or cultural–historical (or industry-centred) analyses, providing overviews and documentation of a field without necessarily making arguments. A good number of these excellent works also analyse a specific temporal moment or desire to give a large overview of the entire terrain, thus presenting a detailed list rather than a sustained argument.

Comedy and Cultural Critique in American Film adds to the conversation of film comedy in three primary and inter-related ways. One is that the book argues for the centrality of comedy in film as a means for staging (or attempting) cultural criticism. Another focuses on the cultural formations emergent from cinema itself: that is, the powerful and sustained shifts in visual culture emergent in the twentieth century that cinema helped generate, foster and question. As a result, comedic film often addresses technology (industrial, mechanical, visual, digital, military and so on) and *techne* generally, which constitute the grounds of possibility for cinema itself that fall into its purview of self-reflexive cultural criticism. The ways in which cinema further amplifies concerns that reach back to antiquity about mimesis and its simultaneous capacity for imitation and production form part of this self-reflexive or self-staging interaction with its technology and various *techne*. Cinema, thus, becomes an important site for producing and critiquing visual technology within US and global cultural politics, examining the status of the mechanically produced and reproduced moving image, and the thematising of its own power. In so doing, cinema simultaneously represents itself as a unique medium that is also part of a larger trajectory of visual and audiovisual technologies that have not only contributed to cinema's formation but also created the media environment in which it must function. The final way in which this work adds to the current discussions about cinema comes through the role of critical theory outside the usual bounds of Bergson or Freud for addressing comic film, though these authors will be considered too. Other theorists brought into play include Baudrillard, Eco, Bakhtin, Virilio, Derrida, Kittler, Hutcheon and Elsaesser, to name a few. This larger theoretical canvas provides scope for a strategic placement of comedic cinema in the critical discursive sphere while also examining cinema studies in ways that differ from phenomenological, psychoanalytic or gender-based studies, and yet acknowledging the import of these theoretical contributions and indeed drawing on them. The book that follows provides both genre analysis as well as cultural–historical contextualisation for the areas and arguments detailed above and offers a strategically selective angle on US comedic film: neither a broad overview nor a narrow temporal / cultural focus, but something that mobilises both simultaneously. Through these three areas of inquiry and the set of inter-related arguments in combination with one another, this book hopes to contribute to the conversations about comedy and film generated by the titles listed above.

As always, a surfeit of potential films for discussion unfolds before the comedic film commentator, and one must make hard choices. An economy of excess exists when it comes to American film comedy and coverage of periods and genres is not really possible. Yet it is this very fecundity that creates the imperatives behind the kind of study this book attempts, knowing that it will unavoidably be incomplete, leaving much that is suggestive for potential further development in this work's gestures and engagements. Aiming for breadth and depth of canonical and mostly mainstream fare, though occasionally going outside the Hollywood norms, the book includes a wide range of filmmakers and films to be discussed in detail: Charlie Chaplin's *City Lights* (1931) and *Modern Times* (1936); Hal Roach/Laurel and Hardy's 'Finishing Touch' (1928); Buster Keaton's *Sherlock Jr.* (1924); Leo McCarey/Marx Brothers' *Duck Soup* (1933); Ernst Lubitsch's *To Be or Not to Be* (1942); Woody Allen's *Zelig* (1983); Mel Brooks's *Blazing Saddles* (1974); Barry Levinson/David Mamet's *Wag the Dog* (1997); Trey Parker's *Team America* (2004); and Albert Brooks's *Looking for Comedy in the Muslim World* (2005). Along with a handful of very early and contemporary animation shorts, ranging from Oswald the Lucky Rabbit (Disney), Ko-Ko the Klown (the Fleischers) and *The Dinosaur vs. The Missing Link* (Willis H. O'Brien; all dating from the first two decades of the twentieth century) to *Wall-e* (Andrew Stanton) and *The Fantastic Flying Books of Mr. Morris Lessmore* (William Joyce; from the first two decades of the twenty-first century), other films that are perhaps unusual for a book on American film comedy are examined in some detail, including the World War I documentaries 'War Neuroses' (1917 and 1918), Orson Welles's *Citizen Kane* (1941) and *F is for Fake* (1972), Spalding Gray's/Jonathan Demme's *Swimming to*

Cambodia (1987) and Michael Moore's *Bowling for Columbine* (2002). The animated films, especially but not exclusively the early ones, bespeak a studied engagement with the animated nature of the image that cinema mass-produced, and thus offer a thinking through and experimentation with cinema's machinery in operation and explicitly on display. The other oblique films – the ones not often represented in film comedy works – are deeply engaged with the various technologies that allow to them to exist, circulate and operate as films, while also serving as an important intertexts for a number of comic films. These films are comedic, in that they show the workings of the various systems that allow them to exist as films, as well as the effects and indeed failures of these systems – the glitches that invariably occur but which are often glossed over are rendered bold and underscored.

This book also takes up several cinematic genres to show how they work together in relation to cultural criticism, technology, the status of the moving image, and cultural politics. These genres include: the mockumentary and documentary, the parody, and the political satire. That genre functions as a kind of representational technology has been part of narratology for decades, especially amongst formalists, and has been an integral element of critical theory, as exemplified by Derrida's analyses of law (*nomos*) as genre and genre as a kind of law. Such an approach to genre is codified, though not necessarily intentionally, in the touchstone work of David Bordwell and Kristin Thompson in their own classic categorisation of Hollywood production that they call 'Classic Hollywood Narrative' (CHN); this has sparked a flurry of discussion not taken up here, but which proves useful for considering the machinic production of narrative within the Hollywood factory system.

Further, the book places film within a set of theoretical writings that have import for thinking comedy and technology as enunciated through film, especially the writings of Jean Baudrillard, Paul Virilio, Friedrich Kittler and Jacques Derrida in relation to repetition, automation, complexity, material systems of information media, the level of address in a communicative act, and the shifting role of the image as the bases for considering comedy as integral for a critical engagement of the constructs of culture and identifying them as such. Many of these theoretical works, though, have no direct connection to comedy or film, but rather consider the conditions for the production of knowledge: the oppositional poles of the machinic and the event, which constitute both epistemology generally and cultural production specifically. The material (technological, existential, sensory) and immaterial (ideological, conceptual, systemic) roles played by cinema writ large, and the inevitable but not necessarily predictable disruption of their functioning (the comic), form the main topics of inquiry of the study that follows.

Sources Cited

Agee, James. 'Comedy's Greatest Era', in *Agee on Film, Criticism and Comment on the Movies*, Martin Scorsese (ed.). New York: Modern Library, 2000, pp. 391–412.

Althusser, Louis. *Lenin and Philosophy and Other Essays*, Ben Brewster (trans.). London: New Left, 1971.

Baudrillard, Jean. *The Intelligence of Evil, or the Lucidity Pact*, Chris Turner (trans.). Oxford and New York: Berg, 2005.

Beach, Christopher. *Class, Language and American Film Comedy*. Cambridge: Cambridge University Press, 1998.

Benjamin, Walter. 'The Work of Art in the Age of Its Technological Reproducibility', in *The Work of Art in the Age of Its Technological Reproducibility and Other Writings on Media*, William Jennings, et al. (eds). Cambridge, MA, and London: Harvard University Press, 2008, pp. 19–55.

Bishop, Ryan and John Phillips. *Avant-Garde Modernist Aesthetics and Contemporary Military Technologies: Technicities of Perception*. Edinburgh: Edinburgh University Press, 2010.

Bordwell, David and Kristin Thompson. *Film Art: An Introduction*. New York: McGraw-Hill, 1997.

Dale, Alan. *Comedy is a Man in Trouble: Slapstick in American Movies*. Minneapolis and London: University of Minnesota Press, 2000.

Deleuze, Gilles and Claire Parnet. *Dialogues II*, Hugh Tomlinson and Barbara Habberjam (trans.). New York: Columbia University Press, 2007.

Derrida, Jacques. *Athens, Still Remains*, Pascal-Anne Brault and Michael Naas (trans.). New York: Fordham University Press, 2010.

Derrida, Jacques. 'The Law of Genre', Avital Ronnell (trans.). *Critical Inquiry*, 7:1, 1980, pp. 55–81.

Dürrenmatt, Friedrich. 'Theater Problems', in *Selected Writings: Vol. 3 Essays*, Joel Ageed (trans.) and Kenneth J. Northcott (ed.). Chicago and London: University of Chicago Press, 2006, pp. 137–62.

Gunning, Tom. 'The Cinema of Attractions: Early Film, its Spectator and the Avant-Garde', in *Early Cinema: Space, Frame, Narrative*, Thomas Elsaesser (ed.). London: BFI, 1990, pp. 56–62.

Gunning, Tom. 'Crazy Machines in the Garden of Forking Paths: Mischief Gags and the Origins of American Film Comedy', in *Classical Hollywood Comedy*, Kristine Brunovska Karnick and Henry Jenkins (eds). New York and London: Routledge / AFI, 1995, pp. 87–105.

Gunning, Tom. 'Fritz Lang Calling: The Telephone and the Circuits of Modernity', in *Allegories of Communication*, John Fullerton and Jan Olsson (eds). Rome: John Libbey, 2004, pp. 19–37.

Gunning, Tom. 'Non-continuity, Continuity', in *Early Cinema: Space, Frame, Narrative*, Thomas Elsaesser (ed.). London: BFI, 1990, pp. 86–94.

Hansen, Miriam. 'Benjamin and Cinema: Not a One-Way Street', in *Benjamin's Ghosts: Interventions in Contemporary Literary and Cultural Theory*, Gerhard Richter (ed.). Stanford: Stanford University Press, 2002, pp. 41–73.

Hansen, Miriam. 'Why Media Aesthetics?', *Critical Inquiry*, 30:2, Winter 2004, pp. 391–5.

Harries, Dan. *Film Parody*. London: BFI, 2000.

Harvey, James. *Romantic Comedy in Hollywood, from Lubitsch to Sturges*. New York: Da Capo, 1998.

Heidegger, Martin. *The Question Concerning Technology and Other Essays*, William Lovitt (trans.). New York: HarpersTorchbooks, 1977.

Henry, Nora. *Ethics and Social Criticism in the Hollywood Films of von Stroheim, Lubitsch, and Wilder*. Portsmouth, NH: Greenwood, 2000.

Horton, Andrew. *Comedy / Cinema / Theory*. Berkeley and Los Angeles: University of California Press, 1991.

Jenkins, Henry. *What Made Pistachio Nuts? Early Sound Comedy and the Vaudeville Aesthetic*. New York: Columbia University Press, 1992.

Karnick, Kristine Brunovska and Henry Jenkins (eds), *Classical Hollywood Comedy*. New York and London: Routledge / AFI, 1995.

Kellner, Douglas and Michael Ryan. *Camera Politica: The Politics and Ideology of Contemporary Hollywood Film*. Bloomington: Indiana University Press, 1988.

Kendall, Elizabeth. *The Runaway Bride: Hollywood Romantic Comedy in the 1930s*. New York: Knopf, 1990.

King, Geoff. *Film Comedy*. London: Wallflower, 2002.

Kittler, Friedrich. *Gramophone, Film, Typewriter*, Geoffrey Winthrop-Young and Michael Wutz (trans.). Stanford and London: Stanford University Press, 1999.

Leslie, Esther. *Hollywood Flatlands: Animation, Critical Theory and the Avant-Garde*. New York and London: Verso, 2002.

Lindsay, Vachel. *The Art of the Moving Picture*, 1915. Available at http://www.gutenberg.org/files/13029/13029–h/13029–h.htm.

Mast, Gerald. *The Comic Mind*. Chicago and London: University of Chicago Press, 1973.

McLuhan, Marshall. *Understanding Media: The Extensions of Man*, 2nd edn. New York: Mentor, 1964.

Michaud, Philippe-Alain. *Aby Warburg and the Image in Motion*, Sophie Hawkes (trans.). New York: Zone, 2004.

Nabokov, Vladimir. *Speak Memory*. London and New York: Penguin, 2000.

Neal, Steve and Frank Krutnik. *Popular Film and Television Comedy*. London and New York: Routledge, 1990.

North, Michael. *Machine-Age Comedy*. Oxford and New York: Oxford University Press, 2009.

Palmer, Jerry. *The Logic of the Absurd*. London: BFI, 1997.

Paul, William. *Laughing Screaming: Modern Hollywood Horror and Comedy*. New York: Columbia University Press, 1995.

Rowe, Kathleen. *The Unruly Woman: Gender and Genres of Laughter*. Austin: University of Texas Press, 1995.

Sobchack, Vivian. '"Cutting to the Quick": *Techne, Physis*, and *Poesis* and the Attractions of Slow Motion', in *The Cinema of Attractions Reloaded*, Wanda Strauven (ed.). Amsterdam: University of Amsterdam Press, 2006, pp. 337–51.

Trahair, Lisa. *The Philosophy of Comedy: Sense and Nonsense in Early Cinematic Slapstick*. Albany: State University of New York Press, 2007.

Vineburg, Steve. *High Comedy in American Movies: Class and Humor from the 1920s to the Present*. Lanham, MD: Rowan & Littlefield, 2006.

Virilio, Paul. *The Aesthetics of Disappearance*, Philip Beitchman (trans.). New York: Semiotext(e), 2009.

CHAPTER 2

The Feeding Machine and Feeding the Machine: Silence, Sound and the Technologies of Cinema

I think everybody should be a machine.

Andy Warhol, Art News, 1963

Charlie Chaplin as the Tramp stands at the assembly line where he mechanistically turns two screws every few seconds for hours on end. He falls behind, rushes to catch up and loses his sanity in the process; he snaps right there on the line, eventually following the screws into the workings of the machinery of the automated assembly-line belt. As his body threads over the gears of interlocking parts, it looks like nothing other than celluloid film being threaded into a projector. His body become film, Chaplin's movie on mechanical assembly-line production proves an allegory for the film industry, his reflections engaging the technologies that provide him with his art. Buster Keaton plays a projectionist in a slightly earlier film and falls asleep beside the projector. Understanding cinema's deep pull on the unconscious, Keaton's character enters the stuff of dreams by entering the film itself, and once having done so, becomes subject to the manipulations of the editing table and film's capacity to change chronotopes in a flash: the character-as-object within the *mise-en-scène*. Both iconic films, *Modern Times* (1936) and *Sherlock Jr.* (1924) respectively offer different engagements with the visual *techne* of cinema and its by-then decades of manipulation of visual representation, as well as of time, space and corporeal constraints, while also providing uniquely nuanced engagements with the visual technologies of their craft.

If Chaplin enters the mechanical age by being fed into a machine, Keaton enters it by feeding himself into a camera/projector/screen cinematic apparatus and exploring how electric mass media will forever change our sense of self, reality and fantasy. These two films provide a fulcrum around which this chapter turns, films that explicitly engage in the cultural critique of cinema and use cinema's *techne* to provide a criticism of the very means that allow them to perform the critique in the first place.

Cinema is an explicitly industrial, technological and urban art form. It grew up in the aftershocks of industrial revolutions and amidst urban factory production, technological innovations of speed and sensory extrapolation and elaboration. In a nearly allegorical gesture, some of the first footage shot by the Lumière Brothers is of their factory workers leaving the plant; labour, industry and mechanical light (given the brothers' name) merge in the now-grainy images of the earliest moving pictures. Also simultaneous with the emergence of cinema and these other larger social–cultural–technical phenomena are two important works of theorisation on comedy, one by Henri Bergson and one by Sigmund Freud. This chapter uses the comparative and contrastive case study of Chaplin and Keaton as metonymic for and illustrative of a number of other films but mostly of a range of issues, including Bergson's and Freud's theoretical writings on comedy and their fundamentally different relationship to visual technology, through the extensions of the photographic experimentation of movement by Etienne-Jules Marey and Eadweard Muybridge, and their links to Taylorism; and the advent of sound and the threat posed by this specific technological innovation to the careers of both comedians. As noted in the previous chapter, US comedic film often explicitly addressed technological innovations, including those that created the conditions for the emergence of cinema itself as technological product, art form and business, and thus becomes, almost from the outset, self-reflexively if not solipsistically engaged in its own influence within visual culture's emergence, as well as its larger contextual frames.

Bergson and Freud are writing about comedy at the time that cinema first appears on the scene: Bergson in a work that appears in 1899, *Laughter: An Essay on the Meaning of the Comic*, and Freud in his seminal *Jokes and Their Relation to the Unconscious*, which he wrote between 1905 and 1916. Both are interested in the ways comedy portrays something formal under attack by something informal, something organised and controlled as being assaulted by something vital and energetic. For Freud, comedic outbursts often result from aggressive drives, whereas for Bergson, comedy is the release of a spontaneous, vital life force that is being curtailed or repressed. In both theories, comedy's capacity to attack, overturn or expose dominant structures as the constructs that they are stage and query rules blindly or mechanistically followed by social contract and decorum. These concerns prove integral to early cinematic comedy through its offering an anarchic release of virtually all drives and actions that society and morals/mores keep under wraps. Bergson in particular is interested in how comedy addresses the mechanisation or the automatic that resides within the organic entity: mechanical arrangement and the illusion of life, if not life itself. For his cultural–historical moment, this would clearly invoke labour and factories. Thus the kind of illusory life found in mechanical operations provided for Bergson a kind of social release valve of humour found in the dehumanisation of humanity in the factory. Bergson revelled in comedy that revealed humans as automatons, all of which had influence and effect on René Clair, whose 1931 *A nous la liberté* in turn influenced Chaplin's *Modern Times* deeply.

For the early film comedians, objects and machines are often (but not always) things against which the protagonist must struggle. Keaton, Laurel and Hardy, and of course Chaplin have films that feature electrical houses with almost an electrically willed capacity to go haywire, pianos that, like water, find gravity's pull instantaneously, and demonic hideaway beds of superhuman mechanical athleticism – these are just some very famous examples of hundreds of possibilities, as these early film comics often found themselves acting mechanically in response to automated objects, or objects that appeared animated if not animate. Bergson and these early film comics remind us that the animate is not always alive, as the animation of photographic images by the cinema projector reveals; they merely appear alive. The automated image is therefore animate and animated, although it is not necessarily alive either; it is simultaneously dead and animate. And cinema's capacity to engage the increasingly thin line between animate and inanimate entities, between the organic and the mechanical / electric, was rendered even thinner by the technologies that altered labour and vision.

The numerous connections between the machine of the factory and the vision machine of the cinema factory/industry system reveal the many roles of visual technology within the cultural politics of the first few decades of cinema, leading to a self-reflexive examination of the status of the image, and cinema's engagement and thematising of its own power. Although operating within very different socio–economic moments, both Chaplin's *Modern Times* (1936) and Keaton's *Sherlock Jr.* (1924) present meta-cinematic reflections on the mechanisation of vision found in film. Chaplin's film allegorises his relationship to the industry he helped establish as a global hegemonic power and the imperilment of his career via the advent of sound, while Keaton's parodies the manipulations of editing and the mechanistically deterministic nature of Hollywood's narrative and genre demands. Keaton's film, replete with visual puns, endeared him to the European Surrealists and the avant-garde (e.g. Luis Buñuel and Salvador Dalí), while Chaplin's audience took in the same experimental crowd, along with the majority of the international cinema audience. Both films speak explicitly to many social conditions apparent in their specific moments and which continued to exert influence on US society, while more fully working through the routinisation of sight and vision by cinema formulae that rendered problematic the many manifestations and uses of mechanical vision. In addition to discussing these two films, this chapter also examines Chaplin's *City Lights*, and looks briefly at the short films of Laurel and Hardy in so far as they exemplify a rigid logic of momentum indicative of technicity itself, which is the unavoidable object of derision and assault in these films. The chapter ends with a short reading of the recent animated film *Wall-e* to address industrialised robotic labour, consumer culture, and the culmination of social and technological trajectories found in these earlier films and projected into the not-too-distant future.

Factory Visions: *Modern Times*, Movement and Labour

The passage of time
Is flicking dimly upon the screen.
I can't see the lines
I used to think I could read between . . .
Who would believe what a poor set of eyes can show you . . .
Putting grapes back on the vine.

Brian Eno, 'Golden Hours'

The mass movement in the US from rural areas to urban ones in the first decades of the twentieth century saw an extension of the allure, liberation, danger, risk and alienation of city life intimated as early as Edgar Allan Poe's 'The Man in the Crowd', an example of urban writing that influenced Modernists such as Charles Baudelaire, and is in dialogue with the social satirical critiques offered by Charles Dickens. Urban sites rapidly grew in size and influence as industrial production flourished under laissez-faire capitalism in the US. Prior to the Industrial Revolution, people worked from dawn to dusk, varying between 8 and 14 hours; with the establishment of the urban factory system in the late eighteenth and early nineteenth centuries, the working day began to average 14 to 15 hours, especially with the aid of various forms of artificial lighting.

Although mechanised assembly or labour has its roots in antiquity, found more solid shape in the Renaissance, and experienced a boom in the eighteenth century (especially with agro-business such as food processing and grain milling), it was not until the introduction of electrical conveyance techniques that the problem of moving workers around within a factory could be solved (Giedion 77–9). With conveyors and pulleys powered by electrical motors, the worker became increasingly stationary and static, while the inanimate object being produced became dynamic and mobile, eventually evolving into a standardised object: a mechanical ballet of the kind that captured the fancy of artists in the early part of the twentieth century. The electrical mechanised line-assembly factory production created a new class of labourers who sold their time and minimal body movement as abstract commodities and were thus wage-dependent for their livelihood. This kind of Fordist production also made workers the last standardised, replaceable part in assembly-line production. Anybody could stand at the spot and perform the simple act. It did not matter who was there: anybody – and any body – would do. Thus a deskilled labour force with minimal leverage on ownership (being deskilled, after all) was assembled alongside massive amounts of consumer goods rolling off the same assembly lines. During the so-called boom era of the Jazz Age 1920s, Chaplin consistently populates his films with characters at the dire end of the economic continuum, the working poor in urban sites who also, as it happens, constituted the majority of the cinema-viewing audience.

The prosperity and freedoms supposedly wrought from this first moment of mass media, urban production, rampant consumerism and humming factories come to a very rapid halt with the 1929 stock market crash that signals the onset of the Great Depression. The wealth of the Twenties had not been evenly distributed throughout the economy, especially for unskilled workers and farmers, thus resulting in their inability to consume what was produced (a situation Ford explicitly sought to avoid with his own workers). Consumption and consumerism, essential to neo-liberal economies, had failed within the US to buy up what was being produced. The workers could not afford to buy their own products or those of others, or at least not in the quantities required to keep the machinery moving. Many stocks were over-valued and inflated, including those related to radio and the burgeoning broadcast industry as it was set to merge with cinema. As a result, sound film, after a fashion, is a media event that emerges out of economic crisis while simultaneously helping to perpetuate that crisis. Tariffs and war debt policies imposed by the successive Harding–Coolidge–Hoover administrations into the 1920s reduced the efficacy of foreign markets for US-produced goods (the ostensible reason for US imperial activity beginning in the late 1890s). These policies especially hurt Europe and damaged the German economy during the Weimar Republic, helping set the stage for Fascists to pose an alternative to US-directed capitalism or Soviet-generated Communism. By 1933, 16 million people in the US are unemployed, constituting one-third of the entire labour force. The New Deal helps alleviate some of the labour problems but it is not until World War II and the military-driven war build-up that the Depression fully ends.

An embedded and important set of related issues in this thumbnail sketch of the socio–economic conditions of the period leading up to Chaplin's *Modern Times* can be found in the connections between the motion studies of Etienne-Jules Marey and Eadweard Muybridge in the latter part of the nineteenth century and the emergence of Taylorism, with its time and motion studies. Marey and Muybridge capture motion in sequential still images. These exemplify the formula that 'to understand speed, you have to slow it down' (Bishop and Phillips 58). Their photographic studies of movement in nature visually converted time into space and allowed for the analysis of motion in nature invisible to the unaided eye, with the aid here being some of the sequential photographic technologies that helped the development of what became cinematography. With these technologies came the ability to study motion by seeing the mechanics of movement. As Marey and Muybridge constructed sequentially photographed images, or chronophotography, of the wings of birds in flight or the gait of horses in the 1870s and 1880s, and conducted their experiments in time arrest, Fredrick Winslow Taylor, at roughly the same moment, set out many of his ideas for increasing efficiency in labour through scientific management principles and the empirical study of labour in its work context, often deploying the most up-to-date technologies to measure and refine movement in order to minimise waste and maximise efficiency. Sequential photography, and later cinema cameras themselves, proved productive for these studies to increase industrial production. Taking Marey and Muybridge's innovations explicitly toward Taylor's interests, Frank and Lillian Gilbreth conducted their investigations of human motion and time–space studies in the 1910s using the latest visual technologies, including their own invention: the cyclograph. The cyclograph was a 'motion recorder' that traced and stored the absolute path of movement through a long exposure shot and an illuminated source, thus leading to abstractions of motion that found their way into the art works of Paul Klee, Joan Miró, Paul Eluard and many others (Giedion 100–13). The images produced by the cyclograph showed the continuous line of motion, not its individual moments, and thus continued but varied the kind of studies performed by Marey and Muybridge. Taylorist innovations in industry found both useful.

Time and motion studies provided a means of controlling and managing labour in unprecedented fashion using the justification of empirical and practical scientific methods, and at the same time helped establish the building blocks that would become the metaphysics of film. Through the breaking down of continuous action into isolated and 'unseeable' parts that could then be used for physics inquiry, these visual technologies laid the groundwork of a visual mimesis capable of an unprecedented imitative capacity (though a thoroughly constructed aesthetics of mimesis), while at the same time allowing for Surrealist and/or comic subversion as well. That is, the camera's visual verity in its early days of documenting movement could be manipulated such that physical acts impossible in nature could be seen as having occurred and documented by the unblinking empirical eye of the cinema camera – for example, having events run backward (putting grapes back on the vine, to borrow Brian Eno's image found in this section's epigraph) – the metaphysics of film.

Technologically aided means of seeing that which had not previously been seen with regard to movement, speed and mechanics affected not only scientific management studies and the visual technologies themselves (in an endless intensification of increasing sophistication) but also emerged with experiments in art, painting and sculpture, e.g. Cubism, Futurism, Dynamism and Photodynamism. The influential writings by Anton Giulio Bragaglia on photodynamics as part of the Futurist manifestos envision a machine capable of taking further the photographic studies of Marey, Muybridge and even Ernst Mach, who photographed a bullet travelling at the speed of sound. Extending Marey's atomistic tendencies, Bragaglia imagined a machine able to freeze and visualise the 'almost infinitesimal calculation of movement' by rendering the invisible visible and the evanescent concrete (Giedion 43). The Futurists' desires proved realisable and helped guide visual technology in the decades following the statement of their dreams. Similarly, the dynamic temporal flow that Duchamp brought to Cubism clearly emerged from long–exposure photographic techniques developed by Marey to capture individual moments of movement in the walking motion of a person. Borrowing a descriptive title from a set of chronophotographic images Muybridge had made some twenty-five years earlier, Duchamp's own *Nude Descending a Staircase* (1912) refashioned a standard visual trope within painting, 'the female nude', not only to fit the age of mechanical reproduction, but also to place it in the age of mechanical *pro*duction. In so doing, he put cinema into the art gallery and captured it within a single, framed canvas while also pushing Cubism's experiments toward an engagement with temporal, as well as visual and spatial, complexity by allowing several different temporal moments and visual perspectives to occupy the same canvas simultaneously. All of this was made possible through decades of innovation within visual technologies and the possibilities of new visions they offered.

The complex interactions between urban, line-assembly production and its effects on labour, time and motion investigations for the study and application of scientific management principles, the machinic image and studies of movement in nature, innovations in art that reflected and critically engaged visual technologies previously outside its purview, and the emergent but soon quite dominant art/factory form known as cinema become important contextual parameters for understanding the density of the factory visions found in Chaplin's depression era *Modern Times*.

Modern Times: Consuming Machines / Eating Machines / Machines that Eat People

In order to extract from bodies the maximum time and force, the use of those overall methods known as timetables, collective training, exercises, total and detailed surveillance ensued.

Michel Foucault, *Discipline and Punish* (220)

A technological rationale is the rationale of domination itself. It is the coercive nature of society alienated from itself. Automobiles, bombs, and movies keep the whole thing together until their leveling element shows its strength in the very wrong it furthered. It has made the technology of the culture industry no more than the achievement of standardization and mass production, sacrificing whatever involved a distinction between the logic of the work and that of the social system.

Adorno and Horkheimer, 'The Culture Industry' (121)

The epigraph above from Foucault addresses issues related to the *techne* of discipline and punishment, but it was the same organisational and managerial – if not the same bureaucratic, institutional and control – priorities and methods for realising them that provided support and rationale for assembly-line factories in urban sites. That the prison and the factory should be related institutions functioning in similar ways caught not only Foucault's attention, but Chaplin's as well, for *Modern Times* places the two (as well as the insane asylum, another Foucauldian site of investigation) in comparison with one another, with the penal facility coming out better than the so-called 'free' world of the factory. (At least one had a place to sleep and food to eat in a prison during the Depression.) Given that Chaplin's Tramp operated as a symbol of hope, compassion and ingenuity, and thus made him perhaps the single most recognisable figure in the world, what did it mean for Chaplin to make this film at this time? With the autonomy afforded him by setting up the United Artists studio with D. W. Griffith, Douglas Fairbanks and Mary Pickford, he had unprecedented artistic control over his projects and over distribution. So his signature sat heavily on the film, so heavily that it caught the attention of the Federal Bureau of Investigation (FBI), who waited for nearly a decade to find a chance to deport him. The direct targets of his critique are relatively self-evident, the indirect ones only a little less so, but regardless, the film provides a stunning and sustained meditation on technologies of production and reproduction, including those of cinema and Hollywood, as well as on the larger impacts of mechanisation and automation, and the status of the human subject *as* human and subject.

For Chaplin as a boy in late Victorian England, consumption meant something rather different than it did to the filmmaker as auteur in Jazz Age America, though perhaps the air of an abstracted illness hovered over the latter. Chaplin grew interested in the systems of production, labour, economics and the techniques to enhance them that made the boom of the 1920s also go bust at the end of the decade. The US inability to consume what its humming factories churned out helped precipitate the 1929 crash, which led to worse conditions that put millions out of work while the Dream Factory of Hollywood became more productive and prosperous than ever. Hollywood, in fact, entered the eras of sound film and the Depression poised to take advantage of its leverage and become more successful than ever; it entered what many historians of cinema consider its Golden Age.

Outside of the Hollywood studios, the age was far from golden. The opening inter-title of Chaplin's film addresses just this point in irony-laced prose. The placard reads: 'A story of industry, of individual enterprise – humanity crusading in the pursuit of happiness.' The statement that 'industry' provides the means to pursue happiness highlights the multiple meanings of the term 'industry', including those relating to individual endeavour, as well as the large-scale mechanised production that was discursively formulated as the future of labour and economic practice and would supposedly lead to the betterment of all. The implication is that the former meaning of the term, in the US, could be attained only through the latter. Further, 'the pursuit of happiness', by echoing the Declaration of Independence, foregrounds a condition removed from wage-earning labourers dependent on factory owners' whims and profit margins.

The opening shots of the film establish Chaplin's direct target: the effect on labour wrought by mechanised urban assembly-line production. The first shot is of sheep entering a pen, likely headed for processing themselves, and fades into a shot of men spilling out of the underground to be herded through the factory gates. The commentary provided by this provocative fade is multi-layered and takes a few forms. One is the obvious connection of lambs to the slaughter, but less evident is the way in which the idiomatic phrase invokes the earliest moving assembly line, which was actually and more accurately a disassembly line: the slaughterhouse. With a slaughterhouse, the product comes in whole and is broken down into its constituent parts as it moves through the factory, with the labourers grounded firmly in place. The large-scale slaughterhouses in Chicago in the 1870s included trolleys and means for suspending and moving carcasses. At the same time that motion and stasis were being deployed to disassemble animals in a mode of factory production, Muybridge and Marey were disassembling the flow of animal movement by means of photodynamism. The assembly line in Ford's massively intensified model of assembly-line production merely provided the inverse of the charnel house: the product enters the building in its constituent (and standardised parts) and is assembled as it moves through the factory. The opening fade thus encapsulates in mere seconds the relatively brief transformation of factory production from its pre-rationalised form to the wholly automated version that had so rapidly taken over and thoroughly controlled production in the consumer society of the US, perhaps even contributing to the over-production that precipitated the Depression. The assembly line, in the two quick opening shots, functions for Chaplin as a disassembly of something else (namely, humanity, society, labour, economies).

In this and in other ways, Chaplin's critique not only is about the past or the present but addresses futural concerns too. A standard strategy of satire, of course, is to take current conditions at the time of the production of the work and push them to their (il)logical conclusions to comment on the underlying assumptions driving these processes, as well as their potential unintended consequences. One of the more striking extensions of extant visual technology within the film is the anticipation of the ubiquity of screens and the potential of broadcast technologies for surveillance. Chaplin's factory owner keeps his eyes on all parts of the factory at all times by means of a pervasive televisual panopticon, allowing him to tell his foreman to increase production and to chase assembly-line workers out of the toilets if they linger to have a smoke. Although television and the broadcast of moving images would not emerge in any large-scale form for almost a decade after Chaplin's film, the basics of television technology and experiments with it had been around since at least the 1890s and in use to a limited extent in the 1930s, so Chaplin's audience would have been familiar enough with the concepts to understand this fictive display and application of them.

The real innovation, though, is the use they are put to in the film: their role in management and surveillance, as well as the unidirectional nature of broadcasting. The conceptual application of maximum control of the factory's labour force through visual domination of all spaces at all times anticipates a range of later applications of these technologies, such as security camera systems, urban policing, and the satellite global surveillance in 'real time' necessary for the US military to apply the Truman Doctrine during the Cold War. Chaplin's insight about the televisual panopticon of the factory floor addressed the fact that the means for closing gaps of perception and overcoming time–space constraints through prosthetic extensions of sensory capacity could be converted into the power to regulate space-at-a-distance mechanistically and electronically, as well as to control what transpires within that space.

At the most obvious levels, *Modern Times* critiques the conditions that give rise to the 1929 crash and the Depression, as well as the lack of social welfare systems to aid the urban poor created by unregulated factory production. The class system in the US, the power of the factory owners over those who laboured for them, also comes in for obvious critical engagement at the diegetic level. Less evident are the criticisms of the technologies and technicities of the mind, or enframing (*Gestell*), as Martin Heidegger describes it, that led to the emergence of the very mechanical and technological art form that allows Chaplin to create his film in the first place, as well its deep interconnections with management systems deployed for maximised efficiency in the factories. Prior to the critique of the culture industry posited by Theodor Adorno and Max Horkheimer just a few years later in *The Dialectic of Enlightenment*, Chaplin takes to task the factory systems that exist in parallel to Hollywood, as well as the factory system that resides in and is Hollywood, for their inextricable interdependence. He was by no means alone in the art world for his stand, though he stood in marked contrast to many in Europe who followed his lead and paid homage to him. With Chaplin, as with Bergson, the mechanical within and that *is* the human is a source of both humour and concern.

As is readily apparent from the most cursory engagement with modernism, the relationship between humans and machines provides one of the key themes in the arts during the 1910s and 1920s. When the Tramp goes insane from the tedium and pressures of assembly-line work and enters the mechanics that drive the line, he creates a mechanical ballet that alludes to a tribute to himself, in a kind of self-referential tribute to a tribute (a film about a film) but one that has an altogether different agenda regarding the mechanised art of cinema: Léger and Murphy's 1924 Dadaist experiment, *Ballet mécanique*. In addition to its directors, the film was stocked with avant-garde practitioners, for it was shot by the artist/photographer Man Ray and was to be accompanied in screening by music composed by George Antheil. The score not only is longer than the film itself and thus exploits the isomorphic routinisation of sound and image, but also includes a siren as an instrument. The film's full title is *Charlot présente le ballet mécanique* and opens with a homage to Chaplin – Charlot being the French name of Chaplin's Tramp. The cutout figure of Charlot is but one inanimate object to gain animation in this film, thus drawing attention to cinema's primary illusion. Léger and Murphy use the camera to film pendulum-like swinging movements and then to film itself in explicitly self-reflexive ways in order to exploit its capacity for repetition and exact mechanical imitative mimesis, with the same clips being repeated time and again. The film articulates the cinema camera's capacity for analogical representation, endless repetition, and the capacity to animate the inanimate – the human in the object and the machinic, and vice versa, with an endless bouncing back and forth between an organic original (often a body part) that can be realistically realised by the camera and its prosthetic extension – for example, a human leg and that of a mannequin – both rendered animate only through the mechanical representation, or dance, of the medium (Bishop and Phillips 41–3). The inanimate objects that are animated by filmic processes and techniques, as well as the organic ones that move not under their own power but through the same visual technological power, create a dream-like replication of the mechanical ballet found on the factory floor of the more 'advanced' industries at the time.

Despite the explicit homage to Chaplin, and his return of the favour a few years later, the filmmakers are seeking different analytical and critical goals from their ostensible and fêted colleague. Chaplin is concerned with the fate of the human under the knout of mechanisation, while Léger and Murphy evoke a human long lost to *techne* and only understood otherwise with the advent of humanism of a certain stripe. The avant-garde view argues for no human originary but rather for the human as possible only through the capacities of *techne*, both of the imaginary and of the material (a point central to the works of Bernard Stiegler, especially his *Technics and Time* series). The ballet of the film is mechanical because it would have always been thus, though manifested differently at different times due to the technological regimes of the moment. The insight posited by Léger and Murphy is one also taken up by their comedic hero, Chaplin: that the cinema camera is as much to do with the technological regime that made this specific type of mechanical ballet as the motorised assembly line, as both cinema and factory production operate under the same agendas of *techne*. Therefore, the intentions and mode of critique found in *Ballet mécanique* and *Modern Times* differ significantly but the target remains the same: the camera and all of its attendant apparatus that make their art works possible, screenable, viewable and repeatable.

Buster Keaton's *Sherlock Jr.*: the Subject Becomes Film

> Here they feel as though they were in exile. In exile, not only from the stage, but also in a sense from themselves. Because their action, the *live* action of their *live* bodies, there, on the screen of the cinematograph, no longer exists: it is *their image* alone, caught in a moment, in a gesture, an expression, that flickers and disappears.
>
> They are confusedly aware, with a maddening, indefinable sense of emptiness, that their bodies are so to speak subtracted, suppressed, deprived of their reality, of breath, of voice, of the sound that they make in moving about, to become only a dumb image which quivers for a moment on the screen and disappears, in silence, in an instant, like an unsubstantial phantom, the play of illusion upon a dingy sheet of cloth.
>
> Luigi Pirandello, *Shoot!* (68)

Deeply attuned and predisposed to the sensibilities of the avant-garde in Europe, Buster Keaton actively explored the formal experimentations afforded by manipulation of the visual technologies that produce cinema. Almost a vaudevillian cross between Dziga Vertov and Luis Buñuel, Keaton's silent comedic outings bespoke and exploited the manipulation of vision and thought produced by cinematography and editing, a new way of seeing that might in turn lead to new ways of perceiving and thinking. The whimsical engagement of the medium that Keaton frequently displayed found form in his deep affection for the visual pun and for the possibilities of positioning the human subject in the nexus of film text and context. As did many in the European avant-garde, Keaton sought, examined and ruefully revealed the ineluctably technical in the human. His interplay of fantasy, reality and perception revelled in the same manipulation of the imitative mimetic veracity produced by analogue photography that struck the fancy of the Surrealists. Buñuel and Dalí assumed they had found a kindred spirit in Keaton, and thus cast Pierre Batcheff, an actor who resembled Keaton, as the lead in their masterpiece of cinematic Surrealism, *Un Chien andalou*, and instructed him to copy 'the great stone face's' affectless expression. Keaton's influence extends to the characters in Samuel Beckett's work, a debt the latter repaid by writing *Film* for an under-employed Keaton in the 1960s (though Beckett sets it in 1929, the year Buñuel and Dalí made their cinematic homage).

Beckett's film, crafted specifically for Keaton, works the very terrain that Keaton traversed some forty years earlier in numerous silent films. He writes that Keaton's character is 'in search of non-being, in flight from extraneous perception breaking down in the inescapability of self-perception' (163). This persona's search provides a considered response to Bishop Berkeley's assertion that 'to be is to be perceived,' which Beckett intended to have read out prior to all screenings of the film. The quotation reverberates with ambiguity and added layers of possibility in a twentieth century of increased and increasing mechanical and opto-electric technologies of perception – including machine-only perception – such as those encountered by Chaplin and Keaton, and later Beckett. Keaton studiously explored the effects of cinema on individual subjectivity, positing an extended Lockean *tabula rasa* inscribable by a host of *techne* of the self. In his deservedly famous and influential *Sherlock Jr.*, Keaton provides us with the subject as film, and thus anticipates by several decades Virilio's analysis that people no longer want to be in a film but rather they want to be film (Live 181). Beckett's *Film* takes up Keaton's position that self-perception not only is inescapable but that it too is formed by modes of external perception in a kind of cybernetic feedback system. There is no outside to the system of perception, and thus no true auto-perception is possible. The camera and the edits that cut the organic eye like the razor in *Un Chien andalou* also operate in Keaton's earlier work.

In *Sherlock Jr.*, Keaton plays a rather hapless projectionist who wishes to be a detective. Vying for the affections of the female lead are Keaton and an unsavory womaniser known as 'the sheik'. After being set up by the sheik for the theft of a watch (owned by the girl's father, no less, and played by Keaton's own father), the projectionist is jettisoned from the house but not from her heart, though he is unaware of this last point. Disappointed at losing the girl and failing to solve the crime, the feckless Keaton falls asleep at work and, in the film's most famous sequence, leaves his corporeal body to take on a spectral cinematic one. The doubling effect of film that allows a doppelganger to inhabit the frame with its other is, according to Kittler, 'the film trick of all film tricks' and thus emblematic of film as a medium (Literature 96). The cinematic dream Keaton enters is the screen world of the film he is projecting. The diegetic world of the projectionist and the various people he interacts with find a new diegetic in the melodrama transformed into a mystery, in which Keaton is Sherlock Jr. Film not only has shaped the projectionist's unconscious and dream world, but has done so to the extent that it offers a meditation of the mediation brought about by cinema techniques and the standardised plots of genre films, with all the narrative clichés firmly in place. Keaton's interest here resides in the material and immaterial *techne* of film vision and its effects on the viewing subject, now no longer separable from the films s/he views. The parallel worlds of diegetic (the projectionist outside the melodrama) and non-diegetic (Sherlock Jr. inside the crime mystery) gesture toward a meta-diegetic scripted by mass media and consumer culture.

Henry Jenkins has argued persuasively that Keaton's film wages a battle at the level of performance between Keaton's vaudeville virtuosity and the increasingly delimited possibilities provided by Hollywood cinematic conventions, already ossified by the 1920s. The non-linear and disruptive elements of *Sherlock Jr.* go back to the vaudeville tradition in which Keaton grew up. Jenkins claims, and the film reveals, that a tension exists between the chaotic, inter-subjective and performance-centric nature of vaudeville and the smooth, seamless (almost mechanistic) nature of Classic Hollywood Narrative, where character and plot determine all. The constant breaking of the narrative flow by virtuosic gags draws attention to the performances *as* performance (hence, Keaton's often static camera). Thus the virtuoso performance and spectator desire for narrative coherence struggle with one another, and Keaton works this tension through two sets of tricks: one, his own mastery (where the camera merely records), and the other, self-reflexive cinema manipulation in which filmic technique is foregrounded rather than hidden from view. When Keaton's character enters the screen and the film world of the cinematic mystery genre, he immediately becomes the plaything of the editor, being shifted through the metaphysics of film from one spatio-temporal moment to another in rapid succession. Jenkins argues that this is a direct comment on Keaton's position as a performer shifting from the freedom of vaudeville to the constraints of the film industry. On the stage as a young boy, Keaton would stop the act cold with his flamboyant entrance (being tossed headlong on to the stage). In cinema's relentless, mechanistic grind toward narrative and forward propulsion of plot, Keaton's character is completely at the whim of the medium. He can only capitulate to the logic and power of the form (much as the character capitulates to the detective genre and self-help books in his non-film diegetic existence). Such a view is borne out in the final chase sequence, in which cross-cutting, continuity editing and cause–effect relations are taken to absurd lengths in a dream–world parody of 'the last-minute rescue': the staple of certain cinematic genres, as established in the first decades of the twentieth century by D. W. Griffith.

However, to supplement Jenkins, we should note that Keaton also fully engaged the medium to understand what it was doing to the viewing subject and to manipulate its possibilities. In his short film, *The Playhouse* (1921), Keaton's character, dreaming again, plays every member of the audience as well as every performer in a vaudeville show. One of the audience member looks at the programme to find that all of the acts are performed by 'Buster Keaton' and comments, 'This fellow Keaton seems to be the whole show.' Without recourse to laboratory-based superimposition, mechanical manipulation of the camera allows Keaton to play on screen all the members of a several-piece orchestra, a minstrel act, a dance duo and the audience. Although the cinema constrained his performative skills in specific ways, it allowed his imagination ways of performing that took advantage of the metaphysics provided by film and to examine its effect on the collective psyche of the cinema audience. Also, one should consider the fact that many vaudeville acts, in true Bergsonian fashion, performed the same sketch in unyieldingly mechanistic fashion for years on end, as played up in Neil Simon's *The Sunshine Boys* (1972), which puts a bit of a crimp in the bifurcation central to Jenkins's elegant argument.

Thus it might be that the industry and the performative restrictions are not the only targets of Keaton's critique; indeed, he might be going after the bigger game of visual technologies writ large, in which cinema played a specific but important role. Perception in Keaton's film no longer (if ever) has recourse to an originary, unmediated state, but is always mediated at the outset by various media that shape how we perceive and engage ourselves, others and perception (the sensorium). If 'to be is to be perceived,' then, at least from the late nineteenth century on, we are already viewed by cinema and cast as viewers who might wish to be characters in a film, if not film itself, as Beckett implies. The self-perception that persists, rather like the auto-cognitive dimensions of the Cartesian *cogito*, is not and never could be 'auto', for perception will have been formed by material and immaterial *techne* that make the subject indiscernible from the mediations of its perceptions.

Keaton's character in *Sherlock Jr*, just as much as his character O in Beckett's *Film*, provides a thoroughly mediated apprehension of self and perception. When we first see him, he is reading a 'How to' book on sleuthing. The extended Lockean *tabula rasa* appears in the form and visage of the affectless projectionist. That other media have shaped him is nowhere more apparent than in the initial sequence in the section of the film-within-the-film (when Keaton enters the melodrama-turned-mystery and runs full into the power of editing techniques). This sequence has been heavily analysed and the import for us here is the extent to which it is self-reflexive of cinema as *techne* of the mind, as most beautifully articulated in the visual puns that so entranced the Surrealists. Keaton as the projectionist is cinematically transformed into the character Sherlock Jr., transformed by narrative and genre conventions, but also and equally by the editing conventions that allow the manipulation of time and space so central to cinematic mimesis but which took a few decades for audiences to internalise. That opening set of shots provides an unprecedented engagement with the medium and technology of cinema, *and* narrative ramifications, occurring as it does just after the female love interest has banished him from her life. The sequence provides a dream-world engagement with the language of romantic relationships and does so through visual puns, in which figurative language becomes literal visualisation, as occasionally happens in dreams.

The concretisation of editing's transformation of metaphysics in the material world into cinematic metaphysics found in this montage sequence is not a random set of editing tricks but a concrete, dream version of clichés about the loss of romantic love: he has been 'swept off his feet', 'kicked out in the street', 'left high and dry', 'thrown to the lions'. He is 'in a rut, at sea, all wet and out in the cold'. He is 'run out of town on rails', with his romance 'washed up and gone cold'. Hence Keaton's 'extra-cinematic' self, having suffered the pain of romantic love gone awry, places his cinematic self in contact with lions, snow, the sea, a train, a street, railway tracks, and so on. Much as clichéd phrases shape discursive engagements with the self and the world, so the narrative and technological demands of cinematic convention shape, both consciously and unconsciously, the self-perception we can never flee, and in fact, the two can often work with profound reinforcing complementarity.

The closing sequence of the film takes place after the projectionist awakens and serves to reinforce the internalisation of cinematic convention in the lives of viewers. The romantic interest proves to be the actual Sherlock Jr., who solves the crime Keaton has been accused of and then asks his forgiveness. Confronted by what he has sought – the availability of the woman in a romantic relationship – the blank projectionist is at a loss as to how to express his affection until he catches a glimpse of the melodrama on the screen, where a similar scenario of romantic reconciliation is unfolding. Keaton's character takes instruction well and meets with success, as it all goes to stock-narrative plan with a pat on the hand, a ring slipped on a finger, and a kiss (an out-of-character leer followed by a chaste peck on the cheek). Everything goes to plan, that is, until the fadeout. The introduction of editing's ability to leap many months, more than nine in this instance, in a matter of a few seconds of black screen time finds the happy couple with bouncing twins, which leaves the projectionist scratching his head in confusion and perhaps worry.

The humour of the projectionist following in machinic fashion the dictates of 'the happy ending' until the logical conclusion of romance appears on the screen could mean that he is unsure of what happens during the fadeout and is thus left to his own inadequate or even non-existent devices, in which case procreation is literally out of the picture. Or, it could be a commentary on the institutional state apparatus of the family, to invoke Althusser, and the equally mechanised trajectory of human existence within the social mores and expectations of bourgeois culture.

Keaton's projectionist could be reeling from the ill-considered ramifications of following the techniques of 'how to' manuals and other media, with the happy screen ending conflating far too neatly with heteronormative modes of family formation and reproduction. The self-perception he cannot elude resides in the fadeout and its single shot follow-through, a glimpse of a prescribed future for the entire audience.

The *techne* that Keaton pursues in the final sequence brings him a bit closer in touch with Chaplin, for it is the immaterial as well as material *techne* found in economics, organisation, medicine, genetics – as discussed by Jacques Ellul's *The Technological System* (1964) and that Foucault also read in the form of institutions and practices – that occupy their concerns: the internalisation of *techne* as deterministic engagements with the world. However Keaton differs from Chaplin in so far as he would be in accord with Stiegler's understanding of *techne* as rooted in the human, though we fear it and disdain its influences (at certain moments). We do so despite the fact that the tools for the critique of *techne* are indeed kinds of *techne* themselves, rather as Enlightenment critique is made possible because of the critique offered by the Enlightenment itself. The many technics that made up cinema bring these two great silent (or not) comedians in touch with each other in important ways, though the fundamental engagements operate from different *a priori* as they pertain to the constitution of the human subject.

Charlie Chaplin and Buster Keaton: the Feeding Machine and Feeding the Machine

Much has been said about technique in films like *Metropolis* and *Napoleon*. No one ever talks about technique in *College* [Keaton's 1927 film] and that's because the technical achievements are so indissolubly mixed with other elements that we aren't even aware of them, just as we don't give thought to the strength ratings of the building materials of a house we are living in. The super-films serve as a lesson to technicians; Keaton's films give lessons to reality itself with or without the techniques of reality.

Luis Buñuel, *Cahiers d'art*, 1927 [reprinted in *An Unspeakable Betrayal*, p. 111]

More than machinery, we need humanity.

Charlie Chaplin, in *The Great Dictator*

Cinema, photography and gramophone embody how art in the age of mechanical reproduction changes the status of the object. Sound in film, for example, has less to do with sound as we experience it than with the history and manipulation of recorded sound (Chion 3–34). Mechanical, electrical and electronic media mediate our relationship to objects and therefore to ourselves as subjects, as Keaton's *Sherlock Jr.* reveals (and as theorists from Walter Benjamin to Jean Baudrillard have examined). The same is true for other technologies and art forms, including print and the novel, in which 'natural' dialogue bears virtually no relationship to the activity of daily quotidian conversing (Bishop 58–78). The meditations and explorations of form, content, medium and technology offered by Chaplin and Keaton captured the imaginations of the Surrealists. Following Freud and psychological inquiry, the work of the Surrealist movement displayed an explicit awareness of form, expression, subjective (individual/collective) categories of experience, and symbolic behaviour, especially as modes of thought are produced and altered by rapid changes in material culture, including the role of technology in these. The Surrealists explored form and play, as well as the play with form, helping initiate continual experimentation with form that became the watchword of art in the early part of the twentieth century. Though primarily considered by Hollywood as a commodity, cinema was right in the midst of early twentieth-century experimentation in the arts, shaping larger philosophical/artistic schools and being shaped by them (which seems not to have been the case for some time now).

Deleuze suggests that Keaton differs from Chaplin in that Keaton is interested in machines while Chaplin is interested in tools because they can be used *against* the machine (175). This difference, in turn, relates to two separate 'socialist' visions: one 'communist–humanist in Chaplin, the other anarchistic–machinic in Keaton' (176). The oppositions and differences offered by Deleuze, of course, relate to the larger arguments he makes in the text but provide a provocation to think the role of the machine, both material and immaterial, in the work of these two directors, especially in as much as the machine finds an analogy to the 'machine' of the Repressive State Apparatus, as Althusser has termed it (177). That is, the immateriality of the socio-cultural order finds reification in the machines that allow citizens to envision themselves as subjects operating within that order and, to a certain extent, determine the ways in which they perceive themselves. The machine-as-object (the cinema camera/ projector and the entire cinema apparatus) projects audience relations to social power and vice versa. The material and immaterial domains feed one another.

Such interdependence and reciprocal connectivity is clearly articulated in the scenes from *Modern Times* that involve first the feeding machine, and second the machine being fed. In the first scene, a machine intended to perpetuate Taylorist logics by supplementing the human element in the larger machine that is the factory is demonstrated using the Tramp as the guinea pig. The supplemental machine feeds the worker on the assembly line, thus eliminating the lunch break and converting it to work time. The metaphor of being force-fed machinic solutions and desires is somewhat undermined by the feeding machine's flamboyant failure, in robust glitch fashion, though the factory owner dismisses it solely because he did not see its use value. The second scene is the one discussed in the opening paragraph of this chapter, in which the Tramp's romp of insanity lands him on the assembly line itself and he is fed into the gears of the machine that drives the conveyor belt. Chaplin's body winds about the spokes like film through a camera or projector, the sprockets of industry and mechanised labour conveying him along and projecting their power through his filmic body. Although Keaton's character feeds himself into the machinery and apparatus of cinematic narrative and editing, Chaplin's Tramp, as subject of the state at that particular time–space moment, is fed into the machine and feeds it, just as he does when standing still at his assembly post. The difference resides in being the agent or the recipient of the action in relation to the machine, though both Keaton and Chaplin make problematic the division between active and passive grammatical voice when it comes to cinematic *techne*. The sequences in all three instances reveal complementary technicities that articulate subject–audience positioning. The possibility of agency disappears into their operation, or at least it is reduced to the conditions of its possibility for articulation.

The feeding machine alludes to the long-standing and oft-used gag of the sausage machine in cinema, a joke machine that dates back to earlier modes of performance and entertainment including circus and vaudeville, according to Tom Gunning, in which an animal is fed into a box-like machine that, when activated, immediately produces sausages out of the other end (98). Chaplin's feeding machine plays on the shared reference with the audience and the foregrounding of the apparatus. In the Lumière Brothers' *La Charcuterie mécanique* (1895), the hand-cranked stoppage of the film produces the immediate effect in which a worker places a pig inside the eponymous machine and immediately another removes from the opposite end a string of sausages, as well as other pork products. The visual and mechanical correspondences between the hand-cranked mincing machine and the hand-cranked film camera appear at the end of a newsreel in the animated *Bosko's Picture Show* (1933), which offers a send-up of an afternoon at the cinema. More pertinent to Chaplin and his opening shot is an early Edison film that visualised Ford's insight years ahead of the great mobiliser of the US populace by also flipping around the charnel house with a 1904 gag film entitled *The Dog Factory*, in which sausages are fed into an apparatus that spits out puppies (98). The densely layered allusion to feeding/sausage machines and their references to the content and apparatus of filmmaking helps Chaplin's humour operate within a long-standing set of allusive jokes while providing variations of them that offer cultural critical engagement along with the humour.

Although Keaton appears more at ease with machines than Chaplin does, this might not necessarily be the case. Both understand the emergent cyborg implications of motorised industrialisation, and each simultaneously embraces and is repelled by them in different ways. With Chaplin, machines in and of themselves appear to be the problem because humans lose something essential through their interactions with the tainted technology. The irony, of course, is that the camera and cinema technology allow *him* the perfect venue for *his* art and enable him to articulate this concern – all on an unprecedented scale. Michael North productively links this point to the film generally as a restatement of Chaplin's earlier career as the comedian recycles and repeats sketches from his filmic past, caught in the machinery of cinema and that is cinema (188). Thus the film becomes a vehicle for examining Chaplin's relationship to the film industry as industry and to his own important role in establishing and perpetuating it.

Deleuze argues that Chaplin advances by tools and is opposed to machines, which provides an interesting and useful distinction. With Keaton, he says, machines become his ally, especially the ones of his own invention (173). Although I do not find this concise articulation of difference completely convincing, it does indicate a different engagement with technicity by the two directors, in that Chaplin still finds the tool (and perhaps even the machine) neutral in and of itself and wholly detached from the human, except as inert potentiality for good or ill, while Keaton understands machines as extensions of the human from the outset. The technicity of the mind is what Keaton finds most compelling, confusing and worrying. His engagement with technology reiterates a Heideggerian engagement with technology's delimitations to instrumental causality while also gesturing toward other latent potentials in its enaction. Similarly, as with Heidegger, the interest in technology concerns its emplacement of thought, the routinisation rather than the liberation of imagination articulated in the pithy formulation that 'the essence of technology is nothing technological.' In *Sherlock Jr.*, for example, the technology of cinematic narrative that limits the medium comes under scrutiny, as Tom Gunning and Lisa Trahair have usefully examined. Yet with a bifocal vision on the irritating matter of cinematic enframing or emplacement (*Gestell*), Keaton acknowledges that the actual, material technology of cinematic production and reproduction provides the means for subverting this narrative linearity and mechanised mode of making art. His scrutiny extends to the mechanics of editing, the displacement of time and space, and auto-educational media generally. For Keaton, the technicity of cinema is rather like ideology for Althusser: each is deterministic while simultaneously providing the possibility for action, thought and critique – but, in so doing, also limits the options for such action. The process of enabling is also always the process of disabling.

The Senses and Cinema: Screening the Human

In other words, technical media are models of the so-called human precisely because they were developed strategically to override the senses. These are actually completely physiological equivalents for the methods of image production employed by film and television, but these equivalents themselves cannot be consciously controlled.

Friedrich Kittler, *Optical Media* (36)

Sound Thoughts

In 1928, a film event is brought to the screen that changes the landscape of cinema for good: *The Jazz Singer* (Alan Crosland), the most important and sustained attempt at synchronised sound film until that moment. It signalled the death of the silent era and the birth of the talkies, as well as a major shift in Hollywood power arrangements. Dialogue and language suddenly become important, and novelists as well as playwrights find themselves in demand in a town that largely ignored the power or beauty of the written word. The shift to dramatists and novelists indicates, too, the delimited sense of what a sound would be: dialogue to further plot and music to cue emotion. For our purposes, the story is one of modifying the image through sound and altering a several-decade trajectory of the moving and silent image to accommodate not sound per se but the electric reproduction of voice, music and sound effects primarily for the purpose of advancing plot.

A most useful insight into this situation arrives courtesy of Sean Cubitt when he writes: 'If, as Tynianov argues, "social life enters into correlation with literature through its verbal aspect" (1965: 131), then it enters into the moving image under a triple aspect: the visual, the aural, and the written' (162). One might wish that Cubitt and Tynianov before him had perhaps considered even more aspects under which the moving image enters social life, including that of the technological and the mimetic. But rather than being churlish, let us allow Cubitt to continue because the next step in his argument leads us directly where we wish to go. He continues:

Films enact rather than depict social change, especially the swift evolution of media and communications technologies. By the time sync-sound film arrived in the late 1920s, it had to mark its position not simply in relation to silent film, nor to a by now nostalgically reconstructed 'natural' hearing, but to recorded sound, telephony, and radio. Indeed the social history of sound in the cinema can be charted primarily not by its relationship to a unified and hypostatized sense of hearing, but by its relationships to other aural media. (161–2)

In other words, technologies of reproduction and representation refer primarily to themselves, their productions and histories, and less so to the external world they supposedly reproduce. The aural world made accessible by sound cinema is not the quotidian world of noise and speech directly profound in its empiricism but a construct as a highly stylised work of art. This is so because sound cinema needed to address its own productions to the range of other aural productions that had been around in various forms since the middle part of the nineteenth century. This insight is also one made by Derrida regarding writing and Baudrillard regarding electronic media generally. Different systems of production and reproduction do not necessarily operate with external references accessible without the systems of production and reproduction, at least not in a transparent and universal manner.

Sound cinema, in the classical, mature US system, is the result of combining two industries – electronic and photomechanical (the aural line on a strip of celluloid) – and with their combination, the capacity to reproduce somewhat accurately what has transpired aurally before the lens at the same time as the visual material is recorded. The photomechanical strip at the side of the film allowed not only for synchronising of image and sound but also for the manipulation of the sound that accompanies the image, such that the sounds can be allowed to supplement and alter the viewers' relationship to the image in transparent or obvious ways. Even with sound film, the sound of bustling about in front of the camera, for instance, is not necessarily heard. The 'sound' in sound film is just as artificial as the silence of silent film.

Though clearly a leading resistance figure in the inexorable movement toward the incorporation of sound into film, Chaplin had numerous allies, including the art critic Rudolf Arnheim. Arnheim asserted, according to Elsaesser and Hagener in their book on cinematic theory and the senses, that sound pushes cinema more towards a more direct and unsophisticated mimesis by converting a two-dimensional moving image that never claimed authenticity into a three-dimensional 'realistic' representation of the actual: from a two-dimensional abstraction of light and movement into a three-dimensional medium of representational realism. The advent of sound and its rapid codification within the industry and the box office meant a stronger push toward a crass, naïve copying of the empirical world (135). This interpretation of sound's invasion is echoed by Artaud's writings on cinema, in which he claims that sound killed cinema, a technological shift that Virilio asserts pushed Artaud out of cinema and into the theatre (Accident 38).

Chaplin as an artist and as a filmmaker had no choice but to embrace artifice, for there is no art without it, but this one – sound film for character development and plot progression – was a bridge too far for him. Or so it seems at the time, and he spends the years between the advent of sound film and his final nose-thumb at sound (called *Modern Times*) inventing gags in two major filmic statements meant to underscore the sound myopia (a useful synaesthetic metaphor) that had gripped the cinema industry in Hollywood. Perhaps it is more accurate to say that electrically reproduced sound was not a bridge too far for Chaplin, as his later films reveal, but one too far for the Tramp. Calling sound cinema 'a ventriloquist's act', Virilio, in conversation with Sylvère Lotringer, argues that sound in conjunction with movement is what has led to upheavals in our understanding of the image (37–41). Once the image could speak, the audience became mute and any dialogue with the cinematic image ended.

Chaplin knew the Tramp could not speak, that speech would kill him as a character, for his global appeal was predicated on a somewhat vague cultural agenda. Chaplin starts *City Lights* in 1928 with the knowledge of the sea change fully upon him and takes almost three years to make the movie. In spite of being an endangered species, the Tramp ekes out two more films and, as mentioned, allows Chaplin broad engagement with various technological innovations in cinema that were making his slice of United Artists less appealing than it had initially been, and ironically just as he had solidified his massive influence and power in and through the Tramp. The opening title sequence, in fact, refers to the film as a comedy and a romance written 'in pantomime' to underscore its silence, or rather its oblique relationship to sound film.

The opening sequence of the film fires the first salvo and does so straight away. In a prototypically Chaplinesque, swift kick in the pants of social smugness, the scene opens with a group of politicians, socialites and other high-ranking and quite obviously well-fed members of the bourgeoisie dedicating a statue to the city. The statue is entitled 'Peace and prosperity', two qualities of life largely missing in most urban sites at the time of production, especially for the lower classes. During the ceremony, Chaplin has the city's élite 'speak' to the cinematic audience through the use of synchronised electric sound, but their language is

gibberish produced by speaking through a kazoo. The fact that it is gibberish merely reinforces what most people think of politicians' speech, not
to mention ceremonies that celebrate the betterment of the community.
Once the statue is unveiled, we find the Tramp encamped asleep under
the awning and in uncomfortable repose on the statues. An affront to the
very civic virtues extolled by the kazoo-speakers, the Tramp attempts
to remove himself politely from the situation, constantly tipping his
hat in acknowledgement of those bellowing at him, and in the process
he manages to position his facial profile such that the large hand of the
statue provides the entire civic gathering with a nose-thumb, and later he
positions his buttocks on different body parts of the statue. William Paul
makes much of this anal play and makes a worthy argument about it, but
for our immediate concerns, attractively ribald though this may be, the
main object of lampoon is Hollywood and its fascination with sound film,
blatantly scandalised by kazoo-ed voices.

Chaplin takes his taunting further by using a silent 'sound' as the linch-
pin for the plot of mistaken identity at the heart of the film. The blind girl,
who cannot see the alluring eponymous city lights, mistakenly believes the
Tramp to be wealthy because he has cut through a traffic jam by clamber-
ing over and through cars, the final one being a limousine, the door slam of
which signals to the blind flower seller that a potential client has alighted
on the pavement. The device is clever within the diegetic but even more so
within the technological context, for Chaplin perversely makes the sound
silent, as in a silent film. For a film that has already deployed music and
sounds, gibberished speech and other synchronised sounds, a statement
is being made when the all-important clue to the mistaken identity that
confuses the Tramp with a gentleman of means is the sound of a limousine
door being closed – presented on screen as utterly silent. Chaplin shouts
out the capacity of silent film to use sound: showing it need not be so
blatantly literal as to require the sound itself, that the audience can fill it
in themselves and in so doing perhaps engage with the film at a different
level. The silent sound of the car door opens the theme of blindness that
is central to the film, a theme that operates in both literal and figurative
ways. The flower girl is blind to the Tramp's true identity, a ruse he per-
petuates in many ways, just as the then-current fashion for sound films is
blind to the possibilities of silent film as still having a future.

If the die was cast with regard to sound and the fate of cinema when
City Lights finally emerged, then the die had been tossed out as utterly
redundant when *Modern Times* rolled off Chaplin's personal assembly line
some five years later. While *City Lights* tweaked the technological noses
of Hollywood for their uncritical embrace of sound film, *Modern Times*

provides a full-blown assault on technology and *techne*, on the ways in which societies and economies had given themselves over to the power of the machine and suffered terribly as result (as discussed above). Chaplin, though, fully understands the implicit difficulties (if not hypocrisy) of critiquing technological society, much less cinema, through an artistic medium thoroughly dependent for its very existence on the self-same technologies brought into question in the film.

In this kind of critical cinematic statement, then, it makes sense that Chaplin's assault on Hollywood and sound would be intensified. With his second critical engagement with sound film, a kind of *surenchère* occurs – a repetition of events or engagements but with an increasing of the stakes built into each subsequent occurrence. The modernity on display in *Modern Times* is overtly technological, and as such, almost every voice heard in the film comes from machines within the diegetic, reinforcing mechanisation and dehumanisation as humanist themes for Chaplin. When the boss surveys the plant via his futuristic televisual panopticon, he can and does speak to his workers through a 'real-time' audio system, and like cinema, it is a monological, unidirectional broadcast system. When the feeding machine arrives for its less than successful demonstration, its virtues are lauded by the self-identified 'electronic salesman' (a gramophone record). The radio provides a commentary on gastrointestinal discomfort that proves especially pertinent for the prison chaplain's wife, who is seated next to the Tramp in the warden's office. Human voices in the film emerge directly through means of mechanical reproduction or broadcast, as they do in sound films, providing Chaplin with a very sly set of comments on the verity of representation that synchronised sound supposedly provides. All of the voices appear mechanically, all save one specific voice.

Of course, the exception would be the Tramp's. Intentionally devised as the Tramp's last appearance on film, as Chaplin bowed to the ineluctable trajectory of sound film, Chaplin plays the Tramp to the bitter end, landing as many blows against power as he can while he goes down swinging; hence the many sound gags embedded in the film and the mechanisation of voices that populate it. To add insult to injury, though very happy for the work, the Tramp takes a job as a singing waiter in the same restaurant in which the gamin dances. Worried that stage fright will steal the words of his song from his memory, the Tramp writes the lyrics down on his cuff, which immediately sails off his wrist as he dances to the introduction of the song. So now, as always, the Tramp must think (or sing) on his feet and improvise quite literally off the cuff. Forced to make up the song, the Tramp sings nonsense lyrics, a song in an improvised language of non-words that still manages to convey the meaning (via his mime and performance) quite well. The Tramp's singing gag combines the kazoo-gibberish of the *City Lights* opening sequence and the silent door slam that tricks the blind girl; the tramp finally has a voice and his is the only voice in the film unmediated by machinery (or at least diegetically so). Yet when the voice emerges it is irrelevant, and he uses the 'direct access' to the Tramp's voice to manifest and underscore its explicit irrelevance. The whole thing could have been done as mime just as effectively, if not more so, which is Chaplin's cheeky point to begin with.

As the last film Chaplin planned for the Tramp character, he included an appropriately different ending for the film. In almost every other Tramp vehicle, certainly the feature-length ones, the film closes with the Tramp alone on the road, heading off to an uncertain future, penniless and alone but with pluck, inventiveness and a decent heart to guide him. Alone on the road, he becomes as emblematic of the basic human existential position as Beckett's own tramps or Giacometti's thinly striding figures. The outline of his costume heading toward the unknown became emblematic of the art form of cinema itself. With *Modern Times*, the Tramp is joined by a despondent gamin, who receives a pep talk for facing existence with no apparent material backing, and thus the two venture off together. The moment seems to indicate Chaplin talking to himself about his own future in cinema, one without his well-honed vehicle: the Tramp.

Blind Spots and Haptic Cinema: the Body and Subversion

Returning to *City Lights* and its use of sound and the senses generally, we find that blindness provides an operational echo of silence in the film. It works literally in the form of the blind flower girl the Tramp befriends and eventually provides sight for by paying for an operation to restore her vision. Blindness also figures in the schizophrenic eccentric millionaire the Tramp saves from suicide on several occasions. The millionaire, whose drunken generosity allows the Tramp to perpetuate the case of mistaken identity on the part of the blind flower girl by permitting him to buy her entire lot of flowers or to take her home in his limo, also is blind in literal and figurative ways. When 'blind drunk', he recognises the Tramp as a dear friend who has helped him many times, but when sober and hung over, the millionaire becomes blind to the Tramp's friendship, has his servant turn him out of doors, and denies the Tramp's very existence. As with Tiresias and Oedipus in Greek myth and drama, the millionaire can only 'see' when he is 'blind' (drunk). With faculties fully in place and operative, the millionaire becomes metonymic of our blindness to various situations and conditions that prevail. At the level of analogy for the sound film, when Hollywood gains sound, it becomes blind to the possibilities of silent film, the medium that had given Hollywood its global clout and sway. The appropriation of the senses by various reproduction technologies are on full display in this film, and it even ventures into that most proximate of senses, one badly undervalued by cinema: touch – though Laura Marks's excellent work makes a strong case for the haptic in the cinematic.

Largely considered the closest sense to sight that we possess, touch is a complex and foundational sense, one distributed over the entire body (Goh and Bishop). Many of our terms in English for either sight or touch can be metaphorically mapped on to the other. Touch plays a central role in silent and early sound film by drawing attention to the visual and tactile nature of the object on the screen, a commodity object and a fetishised object. The concreteness of the 'reality' created visually by cinema depended significantly on the capacity of film to project the heft and tug of the materiality it screened, to offer the depth of three-dimensionality on a clearly flat screen of shadow and light, and touch proved necessary to give objects the illusion of actuality within the *mise-en-scène* of the cinematic image.

Vivian Sobchack argues a common sensory experience akin to touch that occurs in the cinema audience due to 'a carnal modality' that allows the weight and texture of cinematic images to touch us and to be touched by us (64–9). Her constitution of a carnal modality problematises the static categories of viewing subject and viewed object through the medium's mediation; that is, film alters our relation to our senses and our sensory experience – an argument Kittler makes in the epigraph to this section and elaborated wonderfully by Elsaesser and Hagener. As such, 'the cineaesthetic subject' (a lovely portmanteau term that also puns on 'synaesthetic') operates in a manner that confuses standard conceptual categories of subject/object, perceiver/perceived, sense/sensible, here/there, figurative/literal; this cinematically rendered subject functions in a liminal space between action and reception, rather in the ways Keaton and Chaplin articulated in their constitution of the material and immaterial *techne* in cinema. Sobchack's arguments come readily to mind as we watch the flower girl navigate her business duties through her fingertips. The Tramp surreptitiously observes her thus, only to be rewarded for his affectionate voyeurism with a face full of water as she washes out her pots and thinks she is discarding it into the bushes. In this moment, Chaplin allows the flower girl's blindness to cause laughter but at the expense of the Tramp.

The film's heart-rending ending includes the use of touch to make its ambiguous narrative conclusion. Having secured the operation for the flower girl, and having spent time in jail as a result, the Tramp emerges into society a more pathetic character than ever. Their paths cross when the flower girl sees him from the window of the store she now runs and which finds her hoping that each dashing millionaire whose car door she hears (silently) signals potential reunification with her visual benefactor. When she spies the Tramp on the sidewalk, he scuttles off in crustacean fear of being discovered for who he is, embarrassed by his hopelessly ragged state. As with the millionaire, once the blind girl can see, she is blind to the tramp's true identity. It is only when she touches him that she sees. Offering him a rosebud for his lapel, the flower girl's fingertips feel the textures of his jacket and the truth of who he is slowly dawns on her, with her dreams of wealthy rescue fading into the reality of a kindness born of sacrifice so that she could see. The scene is deeply moving due to touch, and the audience's response provides just the flow and ambiguity of synaesthetic experience that Sobchack articulates. The viewing subject enters the screen (much as Keaton's projectionist did) through the visual articulation of touch, linking us back to the media that our senses are, prosthetically projected and receiving at all times, and altered by their engagements with information and stimuli.

The tactile, though, operates in other ways in *City Lights*, primarily through the sheer presence of the Tramp, who manifests all that society wishes to repress as untouchable. Or at least he outwardly manifests it. He is the abject character who has washed up in urban centres of industrialised production. Yet, despite his outcast state and rude treatment by most in the social formations he must engage, he is fastidious, polite, generous and kind (often) beyond the capitalist norms of Spencerian 'social Darwinism' and laissez-faire economics. In spite of this, the Tramp is not above using his body in multiple ways to send up social decorum in order to make a larger point. The body itself, in its sheer materiality and in the expression of its appetites, often overturns what is proper and staid because they are repressed in the name of civility. Comedy operating as cultural critique often works against larger social forces by foregrounding the repressed body and allowing its less decorous attributes to escape containment. The body is the trickster that wins out in the end: the marker of our downfall as not being pure mind (à la Descartes) and consistent reminder of our own mortality. The opening sequence of *City Lights* operates on several levels at once: as critique of sound film but also as critique of a society smug in its values and its conflation of upper-class opportunities and daily lives with that of all dwelling within the city. The Tramp is the secret hiding beneath the cloak of civility and somewhat unwittingly gives society's monumentalising of itself a heavy dose of fairly crude humour. Chaplin's two final Tramp films project the fluctuating status of the body and the senses under the industrial mechanisation of culture and media to make a last stand for the humanist resiliency that was disappearing under the onslaught of the forces that made his films possible. The Tramp in the factory and on the streets performed his own cinematic ghost dance.

Laurel and Hardy: Perpetual Wreckage, or When Children Enact Machinic Logic

Laurel and Hardy's stunningly long career spanned the silent and sound eras too, but they successfully leapt the sound gap and proved to be even more successful when they could speak than when they could not. An enduring tribute (or resistance) to the emergent field of psychoanalysis in the early decades of the twentieth century and its propensity to find the child lurking inside the adult, Laurel and Hardy's film personae made the insights of the field virtually redundant. Always playing the same characters, Laurel and Hardy's personae exemplified the Id, barely contained beneath the surface at all times and which would come spilling out whenever a task of any order needed to be performed. If industrialisation led to a kind of infantilisation of individuals in the then-contemporary social moment and its relationship to labour in the paid rewards for deskilling, then Laurel and Hardy's films address this perpetual infantilisation with perpetual wreckage. Their shared emotional attribute is childish spite and is found in all of the character variations on the theme of 'Stan Laurel' and 'Oliver Hardy'. In a political economy predicated on the accumulation of material goods and capital, their films provided an all-out attack on the material world, wreaking revenge on the objects hauntingly evoked through tactility in silent film. As with *Modern Times*, many of Laurel and Hardy's roles cast them as labourers, allowing the work site to become the focus of humour and chaos.

According to Gerald Mast, Laurel and Hardy films have a cumulative logic operative in humour as classified by Bergson: that of the momentum of the snowball rolling downhill to a valley. Their films operate with one single problem taken to its absolute disastrous conclusion (the one measured to infinity) and thus a kind of perverse, ironclad logic of fate-like inevitability prevails. This is also the machinic logic of children: the machinery of nihilistic wreckage. To use Mast's examples from different Laurel and Hardy films, if a car gets dented in the beginning, every car on the motorway will be stripped by the end; if a Christmas tree salesman gets a branch caught in a door at the start of the film, the tree, the house, the salesman's car must be totally destroyed by the end. The material world, for all its concrete power, ends in rubble and chaos that no amount of technology or agency can stave off.

Their 1928 short film 'The Finishing Touch' exemplifies this logic perfectly. One can note the wit in the title because the ambiguity of the phrase 'house finishers' becomes the source of inter-title humour common to silent films, providing a foreshadowing not only of the specific down-wardly accelerating snowball in this particular film but also of the building structure's fate; once they encounter a house, it is finished. Offered a large sum of money by a property developer if they can provide the finishes to a house within forty-eight hours, the boys go about their work with maximal noise (they are near a hospital) and destruction (especially to the clothing, body and psychological well-being of a policeman, played by the long-suffering Edgar Kennedy – occasionally a target of the Marx Brothers too). Taking aim at get-rich schemers scamming around the Southern California property boom in the 1920s, the film climaxes with three inter-related events: the alighting of a bird, a chase and fight over money, and the obliteration of the house they have finished in every sense of the term.

When the developer arrives and finds the house, to all outward appear-ances and in spite of the boys' efforts, perfectly appointed and ready to go immediately on to the rapidly moving housing market, he gladly hands the quick money for quick work over to the boys. As he does so, a bird alights on the chimney, causing a chain reaction of Rube Goldberg machine-like connectedness but with no predetermined outcome – simply sheer destruction. The chimney starts to collapse, followed by slates sliding off the roof, windows falling out and the porch shattering. The house almost literally flies apart as the bird flies away. The scheme of the developer crashes about his ears, forcing him to attempt to take his money back. This attempt segues into a fight in the form of an American football match and eventually a long-range, stone-throwing battle between the boys and the developer. It ends when Stan removes the rock serving as a brake for their work truck so that he can hurl it at the developer. Before he can do so, the truck has plummeted downhill to finish off the house truly. The driverless machine blindly hurtling to destruction provides an exquisite analogy for Laurel and Hardy in their films.

This short film works on the undeviating logic that Bergson via Mast identifies, and does so at multiple levels. The shift from the chaos of house finishing and the wreckage accomplished there to the fight over the money extends the mechanistic logic of collapse and chaos to that of economics as well. The materialism of the house and its acquisition is negated by the boys' luxuriantly ineffective efforts, which in turn negate and reflect the shabby work the developer wishes to palm off on unsuspecting buyers. Everyone is out for a quick buck, and no one gets it due to the Ancient Greek-like quality of processes and events set in inexorable motion. The gears of Fate or Destiny grind away like the gears of a machine, of a child-like fixation on one-upmanship at any and all costs and without regard for a future (but minutes away) that is being fulfilled by their heedless acts. For Laurel and Hardy's personae, the machinery of industry is the thoughtlessness of childhood coupled with a mechanistic universe of cause and effect, consistently placing all placid valley villages in the path of their own unique, ever-accelerating, ever-growing snowball. Unbeknownst to the audience, especially the US audience, the target for that snowball has been drawn on them: the infantilised labourers and beware-buyers of get-rich-quick, anything-for-a-buck materialistic culture.

Chaplin in Dystopia: *Wall-e* and Twenty-first-century Robotic Labour – a Coda

The first decade of the twenty-first century provided a strong string of 'children's' animated films that offer sophisticated cultural critique to go alongside entertainment for the kids. Animated shorts have long worked on split levels of audience address to keep parents as amused as children. The films in the Noughts did so with stunning success. An excellent example of these is *Monsters Inc.* (Peter Docter, David Silverman and Lee Unkrich), in which a futuristic world of monsters is literally powered by the screams of human children, and the large corporation that figures at the centre of the film resembles a rapacious oil company in the present, haunting children's lives in oil-producing countries by keeping the local populations impoverished and indebted to the very companies that have created the conditions of their immiseration.

The same writing and directorial team of Andrew Stanton and Pete Docter, who were behind *Monsters Inc.*, brought out the 2008 animated film, *Wall-e*, which places Chaplin's mechanistic labouring automata of the Tramp in *Modern Times* into the future, and literalises the metaphor of human labour as robotic labour by making the worker a robot. The initial portion of the film follows Chaplin's conceit of silent film with sound, or a pantomime with sound effects, and in so doing uses animated film as a site for performing cultural critique. Some of their satirical targets are foreshadowed by the use of the 'bureaucracy' music from Terry Gilliam's *Brazil* in the film's trailer. Like Gilliam's 1980s vehicle, *Wall-e* is interested in unchecked trajectories of the present and their deadening mechanistic qualities, whether as labour or as the labour of leisure, as the world becomes increasingly automated, polluted and uninhabitable. The future that Wall-e occupies and must help clean up is an earth overflowing with rubbish from a consumer society unchecked, unaware and unconcerned, only producing more and more goods for profit and mindless consumption without a consideration of the goods' own afterlife. It is a world where 'the revenge of the object', as Baudrillard might term it, pertains.

Wall-e is a robot designed to compact all this rubbish, which he forms into blocks that become the basic building unit of structures for future habitation. He is the entire planet's waste management specialist, programmed to restore the earth to the point where it could potentially sustain human life again. The human population, for its part, carries on in the same robotic but viscerally corporeal consumption in a large space ship. They have become obese, gelatinous, non-stop eaters and pleasure-seekers: the couch potato life made extraterrestrial and manifest everywhere on the ship's deck. Wall-e, in contrast, embodies a set of cinematic allusions and qualities, from something resembling a metallic version of the beloved alien E. T. to a head composed of stereoscopic cameras locked together, presumably to give him parallax vision but which also hark back to the stereopticon 3-D images so ubiquitous in late nineteenth-century American parlours. That Pixar's computer-generated imagery (CGI) and characterisation have the same tug and heft as objects in silent film furthers the medial genealogies brought into the future that the film depicts. Alone on the earth, at night, Wall-e entertains himself by watching *Hello Dolly* on an old video recorder, an outmoded filmic reproduction technology now consigned to the dustbin (that is, to the world writ large), thus implicating the film industry and its many outmoded delivery systems in this garbage-determined eschatology.

The film veers away from its bleak condemnation of current Id-driven cultural trajectories of robotic consumption of food, images, goods and energy, and ends on a hopeful note of technological redemption of the natural world that the self-same technology has almost obliterated when tethered to industrial and post-industrial production within markets driven by global capital. Wall-e finds and cultivates a plant, and through him – in his guise as an avatar of cinema – visual technology and the culture it has wrought provide enough heart, even if not enough nous, to save humanity from itself. The vision at the end of the film differs widely from that proffered by Chaplin or Keaton due to these closing moments, thus blunting the beautifully crafted and somewhat savage critique established earlier.

Much as Keaton submitted himself to the *techne* of Hollywood narrative when he enters the dream screen in his mind, so Stanton and Docter capitulate to the redemptive (if not happy) ending of romantic promise and hope for a future that seems all but impossibly closed. And the mechanical labourer who not only updates Chaplin's robotic assembly-line worker but also serves as a metonym for cinema itself brings all of it to us. Elsaesser and Hagener read the film as returning audiences to object-centric philosophical positions, including those of a certain phenomenological strain, starting with Husserl and ending at Merleau-Ponty (180–1). Their excellent, though brief, reading of the Pixar films proves to be provocative, especially within a larger mediascape of digital production and hand-held devices, but their reading of *Wall-e* seems to end before the film itself does, for the critique that they assert leads us to a meditation on the status of objects in the world actually returns us to an uncritical engagement of cinema's thematising of itself. The self-reflexivity operative in this film is one of cinema's power, yet again, but not necessarily of its influence on its audience's perception of themselves as subjects nor on its role in creating their object-like status of robotic consumption, including that of products such as films. Rather, the power of cinema here finds form in the power to exact change for the good, not only for a few but also (hyperbolically) for the fate of the earth. The thematising of cinema's relation to its audience has rarely been presented in so unproblematic and unproblematised a fashion. The internalised electronic panopticon of *Modern Times*'s factory has transmogrified into an internalised delivery system of more happy endings that it manufactures and delivers in the realisation of a hopeful vision to come, the old story of technology solving problems resultant from unforeseen consequences of its own enacting through the application of yet more technology. The technicity that Heidegger ascribes to technoscience is made manifest by the propulsion of the material and immaterial dimensions of cinema. This is cinema's perpetual song of itself – its usual ode of its performance and status – and not an extended commentary on it, though it starts that way. That is the role of the para-ode, or parody, that constitutes the focus of a later chapter.

Works Cited

Adorno, Theodor and Max Horkheimer. *The Dialectic of Enlightenment*. London: Verso, 1979.

Althusser, Louis. *Lenin and Philosophy and Other Essays*, Ben Brewster (trans.). London: New Left, 1971.

Apollonio, Umbro (ed.). *Futurist Manifestos*. Boston: MFA, 2001.

Armitage, John (ed.). *Virilio Live*. London: Sage, 2001.

Baudrillard, Jean. *Fatal Strategies*, Philippe Beitchman (trans.). New York and Los Angeles: Semiotext(e), 2008.

Beckett, Samuel. *Collected Shorter Plays*. New York: Faber & Faber, 1984.

Bishop, Ryan. 'There's Nothing Natural about Natural Conversation: A Look at Dialogue in Fiction and Drama', *Oral Tradition*, 6:1, 1991, pp. 58–78.

Bishop, Ryan and John Phillips. *Modernist Avant-Garde Aesthetics and Contemporary Military Technology: Technicities of Perception*. Edinburgh: Edinburgh University Press, 2010.

Buñuel, Luis. *An Unspeakable Betrayal*, Jean-Claude Carrière and Garrett White (trans.). Berkeley: University of California Press, 2000.

Chion, Michel. *Audio-Vision: Sound on Screen*, Claudia Gorbman (trans.). New York: Columbia University Press, 1994.

Cubitt, Sean. *The Cinema Effect*. Cambridge and London: MIT Press, 2004.

Deleuze, Gilles. *Cinema 1: The Movement-Image*, Hugh Tomlinson and Barbara Habberjam (trans.). Minneapolis and London: University of Minnesota Press, 1986.

Ellul, Jacques. *The Technological System*, Jochaim Neugroschel (trans.). New York: Continuum, 1980.

Elsaesser, Thomas and Malte Hagener. *Film Theory: An Introduction Through the Senses*. New York and London: Routledge, 2010.

Foucault, Michel. *Discipline and Punish: The Birth of the Prison*, Alan Sheridan (trans.). New York: Vintage, 1977.

Giedion, Sigfried. *Mechanization Takes Command: A Contribution to Anonymous History*. New York: W. W. Norton, 1969.

Goh, Irving and Ryan Bishop (eds). 'Plus d'un toucher: Touching Worlds', a special issue of *SubStance*, 40:3, 2011.

Gunning, Tom. 'Crazy Machines in the Garden of Forking Paths: Mischief Gags and the Origins of American Film Comedy', in *Classical Hollywood Comedy*, Kristine Brunovska Karnick and Henry Jenkins (eds). New York and London: Routledge / AFI, 1995, pp. 87–105.

Jenkins, Henry. '"This Fellow Keaton Seems to be the Whole Show": Buster Keaton, Interrupted Performance, and the Vaudeville Aesthetic', in *Buster Keaton's Sherlock Jr.*, Andrew Horton (ed.). Cambridge and New York: Cambridge University Press, 1997, pp. 29–66.

Kittler, Friedrich. *Literature: Media: Information Systems*, John Johnston (ed.). Amsterdam: OPA, 1997.

Kittler, Friedrich. *Optical Media*, Anthony Enns (trans.). Cambridge: Polity, 2010.

Marks, Laura. *The Skin of the Film: Intercultural Cinema, Embodiment and the Senses*. Durham, NC, and London: Duke University Press, 2000.

Marks, Laura. *Touch: Film and Multisensory Theory*. Minneapolis: University of Minnesota Press, 2002.

Mast, Gerald. *A Short History of the Movies*, 2nd edn. Indianapolis: Bobbs-Merrill, 1976.

North, Michael. *Machine-Age Comedy*. New York and Oxford: Oxford University Press, 2009.

Paul, William. 'Charles Chaplin and the Annals of Anality', in *Comedy / Cinema / Theory*, Andrew Horton (ed.). Berkeley and London: University of California Press, 1991, pp. 109–30.

Pirandello, Luigi. *Shoot!* C. K. Scott Moncrieff (trans.). Chicago: University of Chicago Press, 2005.

Poe, Edgar Allan. 'The Man in the Crowd', in *Thirty-two Stories*, Stuart Levine and Susan F. Levine (eds). Indianapolis: Hackett, 2000, pp. 120–9.

Sobchack, Vivian. *Carnal Thoughts: Embodiment and Moving Image*. Berkeley: University of California Press, 2004.

Stiegler, Bernard. *Technics and Time 2: Disorientation*, Stephen Barker (trans.). Stanford and London: Stanford University Press, 2009.

Trahair, Lisa. 'The Narrative Machine: Buster Keaton's Cinematic Comedy, Deleuze's Recursion, and Operational Aesthetic', *Senses of Cinema*, 28 October 2004. http://sensesofcinema.com/2004/33/keaton_deleuze/#b55.

Virilio, Paul and Sylvère Lotringer. *The Accident of Art*, Michael Taormina (trans.). New York and Los Angeles: Semiotext(e), 2005.

CHAPTER 3

The Constitution of the Real: Documentary, Mockumentary and the Status of the Image

There's something about the nature of the tape, the grain of the image, the sputter black-and-white tones, the starkness – you think this is more real, truer-to-life than anything around you. The things around you have a rehearsed and layered and cosmetic look. The tape is superreal, or maybe underreal is the way you want to put it. It is what lies at the scraped bottom of all the layers you have added . . . The tape has searing realness.

Don DeLillo, *Underworld* (157)

The 'eyes' made available by modern technological sciences shatter the possibility of passive vision; these prosthetic devices show us that all eyes, including our own organic ones, are active perceptual systems building in specific translations and *ways* of seeing, that is, ways of life. There is no unmediated photograph or passive camera obscura in scientific accounts of bodies and machines; there are only highly specific visual possibilities, each with a wonderfully detailed, active, partial way of organizing worlds.

Donna Haraway, 'The Persistence of Vision' (679)

In its present endeavors cinema increasingly approaches, with ever increasing per-fection, absolute reality: in its banality, in its veracity, in its starkness, in its tedium, and at the same time its pretentiousness, in its pretention to be the real, the immedi-ate, the unsignified, which is the maddest of enterprises . . .

Jean Baudrillard, *The Evil Demon of Images* (30–1)

The Pan-American Exposition in 1901 intended to promote commerce between the Americas in a more profound manner than the nineteenth century had accorded and with an agenda suggesting that the US clearly would lead the technological way to a better and brighter future. Thus the exposition provided an extended advertisement for one of the US's leading technological lights, literally. The many inventions by the Wizard of Menlo Park, including Edison's kinetoscope camera and electric light bulb, contributed to the self-representation and presentation of the event as it became a site of motion pictures, phonograph recordings and elec-trical illumination. Vice-President Teddy Roosevelt attended and even named a child born to an indigenous Amazonian woman on display there as examples of anthropological diversity on the continents. President McKinley visited too in what proved to be a fateful event. Edison decided to have his cameras rolling outside the Temple of Music, from which the President was slated to emerge and address the crowd. However, the speech never took place because McKinley was permanently detained inside, being assassinated by the Serbian anarchist Leon Czolgosz, and all Edison managed to capture was the chaotic and angry response to the news of the President's death, in a short now entitled 'The Mob Outside the Temple of Music'. Edison later filmed the extended and multi-sited funeral of the slain President, as well as the trial of Czolgosz. However, Edison's cameras were allowed no further than the outside walls of the prison where the assassin was hanged. So Edison staged it. In 1901, he spliced together all of these reels in sequence, thus combining history, news and entertainment in the form of historical reconstruction, if not history itself, turning it all into a commercial product that deeply troubles the truthfulness of the documentational dimensions of cinema technology. The portmanteau film Edison produced neatly reveals the problematic ontological status of the cinematic image and what it depicts.

Edison, however, was merely participating in a form of cinematic trickery evident essentially at the outset of its emergence as an art form, technology, and medium of representation. 'Actualities', as they became known, often combined actual footage and acting, documentary-like clips and staged re-enactments, and began as early as 1891. William Uricchio argues that actualities provided a peculiar access both to temporality (the current) and to the actual, and thus to presence in metaphysical and historical senses (125). The combination of temporal and physical access provided the actuality, as a precursor to the documentary, a kind of genre-based gravitas that eluded other early cinematic forms, even those that simply documented daily occurrence, for these were momentous events being committed to film by the camera's lens as they actually unfolded, or were actually re-enacted. Prior to the events surrounding McKinley's assassination, Edison and Edwin Porter had created actualities related to the Boer War (filmed in Brighton) and the attacks leading up to the Spanish–American War, thus stirring imperialistic fervour in visual documents that could complement those in print manufactured by William Randolph Hearst. The slippery nature of representation and its relation to the actual became fully evident in these visual and print/photographic media that helped drive the country to a war virtually generated by representations and repetitions of them, setting a pattern of jingoistic sabre-rattling, representations and formulations of the enemy, and military deployment that remains popular to the present day.

A particularly compelling set of cinematic restagings within documentary filmic presentations can be found in the 1917 and 1918 productions, 'War Neuroses'. The films were meant to show the psychological traumas inflicted by World War I on soldiers who had seen battle, especially those traumas that manifested themselves physically in some fashion, along with the successful outcomes of the treatments provided to the afflicted in military hospitals. The set of films ends with a rather shocking re-enactment of the specifics and details of trench warfare, staged by the shell-shocked patients as further evidence of their cure – indeed, as *part* of the treatment that supposedly led to their cure. In this way, the use of the simulation to address war-caused traumas anticipates the use of virtual reality and digital immersive environments by the military in the present both to train soldiers for battle *and* to help with post-traumatic stress disorders and other forms of negative psychological effects of war engagement.

Elizabeth Cowie, in her excellent article 'The Spectacle of Actuality', discusses the realistic nature of the battle scenes in the film and speculates as to the extent to which conventions for battle scene representation in cinema had already been codified by the 1910s through films such as *The Battle of the Somme* (a documentary with propagandistic aspirations, 1916) and D. W. Griffith's epic, *Birth of a Nation* (a fiction film that also had propagandistic aspirations, 1915). With regard to actualities and a kind of visual intertextuality, it is worth noting that Griffith borrowed heavily from and made direct reference to the impressive store of visual representations from the US Civil War, including Matthew Brady's battle photographs and prints by Currier and Ives that adorned many walls throughout Reconstruction America, as well as the piles of stereoscopic photos that delivered the war in 3-D; this allowed Griffith's film to resonate on several levels of visual authenticity for the audience, as well as to incorporate the larger, widely distributed visual culture objects for a collective optic memory of the war. The US Civil War is often called the first modern military conflict because of its advanced mechanised weaponry, but it should also be considered such because of the advanced mechanised technologies of seeing, documenting and remembering used during and after the war.

With the World War I battle scenes performed by patients of the military hospital in 'War Neuroses', the dynamic combination of immaterial *techne* and documentary imaging as it pertains to the 'real' is simultaneously pictured and elided. The 'real' of the battle traumas that the veterans suffered is absent from direct visual representation but is figured in their cure as pictured in the re-enactment (Cowie 40). Similarly, the re-enactment of the war-as-staged becomes figured as war-as-cure, thus displacing the 'real' of the war-as-cause of their trauma. Through the lens of re-enactment, as well as cinematic and medical technologies, the war shifts its status from impediment to boon. Taking a Lacanian tack, Cowie argues that 'War Neuroses' function at the level of 'the real' that upset stable psychiatric definitions of mental trauma, as well as documentary filmic modes of representing the actual. Cowie writes, 'just as "War Neuroses" documented a reorganization of conceptual categories within psychiatry following World War I', so the psychic state of the spectator shifted toward a desire for that which lies beyond 'symbolic and social discourse' to include the 'domain of a compulsive repetition of trauma that comes to be figured in this documentary' (22). Cowrie's use of Lacan in this context reminds us of the extent to which the latter's work is influenced by Marshall McLuhan, in so far as the materiality of the medium provides the vehicle and figure for suggesting and manifesting psychological and perceptual desire on the part of the viewers: the Real made manifest on the cinematic screens of theatres and of the mind. The staged-for-film traumas of trench warfare represented as means to a cure, as found in the mechanical repetition of cinematic screenings, further reinforces the role of repeatability in the constitution of the Real, but more importantly signals a deep connection between technological wounds (from the military) and technological healing (cinema): guns and cameras, again. The prosthesis of the mechanical eye went hand in glove with the prostheses of mechanical arms and supplemented psyches abundant after the war.

There is a kind of large-scale black comedy found in the 'War Neuroses' films, one that from an historical distance reveals an absurd audacity operating in the linkages between early psychological care, warfare, and technologies of cure and representation. Shifting toward a slightly less bleak but equally audacious comedic trajectory of 'actualities', we can turn to the decades-old examples of living museums that deploy re-enactments as an integral part of their educational mission. The justifiably foundational Colonial Williamsburg in Virginia includes historical characters wandering about or strategically placed within the premises. The attraction's website, under the 'history' tab followed by the 'people' links, lands one at a list of historical personages pictured either with portraits of these figures from the times in which they lived or photographs of the actors playing them today: each occupying the same representational and historical weight. The lines between actuality and acting blur in various performative modalities as they tend toward proliferation, with Edison and other purveyors of actualities (including the doctors supervising the

mock battlefield filming in 'Medical Neuroses') leading the way for contemporary cutting-edge theme parks masquerading as museums and sites
for knowledge dissemination. (With such phenomena, Baudrillard seems
more of an amanuensis of trends than philosopher or analyst.)

In its earliest guise, cinema's apparently – though logically impossible
– unmediated access to the world of objects, its analogical representational power, coincided with numerous other inventions and discoveries
about the visible and invisible domains of nature, thus foregrounding the
problem of the Real in ways that simultaneously rendered it inherently
unstable and manifestly obvious. Within its own domain, cinema's verisimilitude – its ability to document that which appears before the lens –
provided the source for early non-fiction film experimentation and opened
the door for unadulterated propaganda and misinformation. The work of
Jean Baudrillard, Martin Heidegger, Walter Benjamin, Paul Virilio and
others questions, directly and through extrapolation, the changing status
of the image, cinema's self-reflexive (and often naïve) engagement with
this status, and the possibility for fomenting and/or quelling cultural criticism. Such inquiry leads to exploring the aesthetics of the documentary as
a genre in the creation of that oxymoronic phenomenon of media that can
be called 'unmediated representation'. The aesthetic and stylistic strategies
include: hand-held camera, incorporation of extant footage (into which
film dips while also adding to the archive of film itself), voice-over, and
interviews with experts and/or participants (authoritative commentary
and the metaphysics of presence). Along with these aesthetic qualities,
documentary gains its unique filmic status by partaking of the historical
authority of the newsreel and its presentational format, a kind of visual
store of collected moving image memory and historical events that is ampli-
fied exponentially with the coming of television, and later the internet and
online streaming, as well as platform-to-platform media sharing.

This chapter reads a somewhat 'straight' or traditional documentary (Michael Moore's *Bowling for Columbine*) alongside an important
example of mockumentary: Woody Allen's *Zelig*, which parodies many
Hollywood genres, including the documentary, but also offers a parody
of visual culture and mass media generally. The main topic of inquiry in
Allen's film is the status of the photographic image, including cinema as
embedded within the entire network of distribution and publicity. The
film shows how a cooperative or simply parasitic combination of artistry,
technology and economics can work together to create a new environment
of mediated reality for the individual and the mass audience. Because of
the richness of the film's sustained engagement with visual and screen
culture as it pertains to individual and mass politics, Allen's *Zelig* receives

a sustained interpretation in this chapter and does so alongside and in conversation with readings of two Orson Welles films, *Citizen Kane* and *F for Fake*, revealing a productive and unexpected elasticity of US film comedy and cultural critique.

The Changing Status of the Image or the Question Concerning Sight

The world picture does not change from an earlier medieval one to a modern one, but rather the fact that the world becomes picture at all is what distinguishes the essence of the modern age.

Martin Heidegger, 'The Age of the World Picture' (130)

The photograph stands at once as the triumph and the grave of the eye.

Jean-Luc Comolli, 'Machines of the Visible' (123)

The 'actualities', as found in the Edison–Porter portmanteau film related to the McKinley assassination and its aftermath, exemplify how cinema has added exponentially to the knotty problematic known as mimesis that resides at the heart of Western notions of representation, mimicry, knowledge and presentation. Mimesis provides profound, if murky, relations between art and science, aesthetics and knowledge, and philosophy and culture. Plato's rather heated dismissal of mimesis relates to both elements of the mimetic process that prove worrisome (and he disapproved of both). These qualities are that mimesis is primarily predicated upon imitation and results in production. Mimesis is thus parasitic on the object or action being imitated while, at the same time, unavoidably adding something to the object being represented through the act of representation – a blind productivity that mechanistically alters the object. The cinematic image, frozen in its frame but imitative of movement and its micro-temporalities, takes mimetic problematics further than photography did and further than any technology of representation had hitherto performed, leading the way, as it does, to the digital image, virtual reality and the massive collusion of realer-than-real technologies that Baudrillard calls 'integral reality'. Fortuitously and perhaps inevitably, these two strands of mimetic capacity and concern – that is, imitation and production – can be found in some of cinema's earliest pioneers: namely, the Lumière Brothers and Georges Méliès. Through these twinned dimensions of mimesis, we can avoid what Gunning has identified as the pernicious 'Manichean division' that often occurs around film studies discussions of these earliest of filmmakers, for they but manifest the unavoidable elements of mimetic production (96).

The first films by the Lumière Brothers provide the most naïve form of representation offered in film, for the content of the films took a back seat to the novelty of mechanical reproduction of moving objects and phenomena. The Lumière Brothers showed movement and temporality, bodies in motion and duration, while showing off the technology of the film apparatus. What they filmed initially – workers leaving the brothers' own factory, trains pulling into stations – hardly mattered. That they could be filmed and reproduced at all was the point. The probably apocryphal stories that these earliest films seemed so real as to cause uninitiated audiences to believe that what they were seeing was actually happening at the moment of the viewing reveals, at some level, the mimetic power of their machine. It was imitation mechanically incarnate. In contrast and by playing with film's elastic capacities of what it represented, at the same time as such similarly experimental pioneers of early cinema as Robert Paul, Cecil Hepworth, Edwin Porter, Wladislaw Starewicz and Ferdinand Zecca, Méliès worked the other side of mimesis: the productive one that added to the object being depicted. As a magician, Méliès immediately saw the value of a tool capable of altering time and space and of arranging objects within it in impossible ways, prefiguring the Surrealist engagement with the medium, but with only the desire to heighten a realistic illusion as his goal. Thus objects disappeared from the screen simply by switching off the camera and removing them from in front of the lens, or replacing them with other objects, in the blink of the audience's eye: the easiest magic trick in the world, and very effective too. Méliès realised the production resident in reproduction, and exploited it making a metaphysical shell game of the powerfully realistic capacities of the newly animated photography.

The tensions operative within representation can be articulated in the prefix 're-'. Jean-Luc Nancy, writing in *The Ground of the Image*, claims 'The *re-* of the word *representation* is not repetitive but intensive (to be more precise, the initially iterative value of the prefix *re-* in Latinate languages is transformed into an intensive, or as one says, 'frequentive' value)' (35). Nancy is correct, of course, but only partially so, for the prefix's value is not either repetition or intensification, but rather an intensification resultant from repetition, a both/and situation. The 're-' of the troublesome mimetic act of representation is both repetitive and intensive, qualitative and quantitative, imitative and innovative. Thus the history of reproduction actually also provides the history of production (the two sides of mimesis are the same), and we judge the verity of the image by its relation to the *memorio* of visual history as much as, if not more than, to any external referent. In Baudrillard's three stages of simulation, these points are made with the realisation that the first and the third stages are the same: that is, the real simulation and the hyper-real simulation. The result is an end to aesthetic illusion that is driving representational and reproductive technologies, as well as the aesthetic mode of realism.

The imitative powers of cinema, its mimicry, seem singular but should actually be understood as operating in a continuum from perspectival painting to *trompe l'œil* to photography to digital technologies. The pivotal technology in the trajectory likely belongs to photography and the illusion of unmediated access to the original with analogue photography. Roland Barthes famously argues that the illusion of unmediated access can be found in what he calls 'the denotated image'. The illusion reiterates the utopian character of denotation in language: that is, the meaning of a given term is obvious in and of itself and resides *in* the term, as it were, clearly and equally accessible to all who speak the language to which the term belongs. The denotated image achieves the ideal of transparent representation through the photograph, in which the relationship between signifier and signified is one of 'recording' or 'documenting' without any mediation created by the medium of photography. 'The denoted image naturalizes the symbolic message,' functioning as a kind of 'being there' of objects (Image 45). The medium of photography, so the analogical story goes, necessitates an actual object's actual presence at the moment of representation. Analogical representation therefore equals two simultaneous temporal moments: *here–now* and *there–then*, which is the power of all representation: to re-present what was present (or pre-sent, or given). All representation necessitates illusion, a trick of presence, without which representation would not be required. So image technology 'helps mask the constructed meaning under the appearance of the given meaning' (46), providing photography (as well as cinema, digital representation, simulations) with an easily generated message that conflates with the image.

Yet, all of this, as Derrida and many others have noted, depends ineluctably on absence, which makes the presence of representation possible and indeed necessary. Without absence, we would not have representation. Through the *techne* of the medium, the absent object emerges as if present, incapable of existence other than through the act and medium of representation. The history of representation in all of its guises and manifestations, therefore, is 'thus traversed by the fissure of absence, which, in effect, divides it into the absence *of* the thing (problematic of its *re*production) and the *absence within* the thing (the problematic of its [re] presentation)' (Nancy 37, emphases in original). The status of the represented object becomes attenuated by the media of representation, as well as by representation itself. Thus the hoped-for purity of representation of the real becomes but a dream, and yet the logic of the analogue image and its reliance on presence, as well as the verity of its likeness, keeps the dream alive. The mere documentation of the world by the cold objectivity of the Lumière Brothers' lens remains not only possible, but indeed unavoidable, for many audiences. The concentration on just the one side of mimesis – the strictly imitative – results in the elision of its ineluctably productive side. The power and truth of the image emerge from covering one mimetic eye, and they gain momentum in the trajectory that runs from the analogue photographic image through cinema to the digital image and simulation. The kind of precision thought possible with such prosthetic extensions of the biological eye has ramifications for two important yet related concerns about vision, verity and representation: one is 'realism' as an aesthetic mode of expression and its relation to the Real, and the other is the apparently irrefutable yet wobbly empirical ground charted by vision machines that render the invisible visible, such as black light and the X-ray.

The emergence of realism as an important aesthetic device has specific historical and intellectual parameters, not the least being its relation to the sovereign subject of the Western intellectual tradition. Realism's somewhat Platonic approach posits that universals or abstractions exist independently of the mind and are thus capable of appearing and being represented in an unproblematic fashion to anyone, anywhere, at any time and thus resulting in the recognisability of the object as itself. The ubiquity of images and visual culture has not only helped perpetuate the power of realism as a means of artistic representation but also helped secure its 'common-sense' linkage between realism and the Real. Realism would be the mode of representation that adds nothing to the object being represented, but merely documents an external reality in an apparently unaltered manner. Yet, realism is no less mannered or artificial than any other mode of representation, though its predominance in Western cinema, television and fiction as the default choice of narrative and visual organisation helps many to think it achieves just this transparency. Such confusion in the common-sense sphere clearly has antecedents in the emergence of perspectival painting and depth-of-field illusions created by parallax vision, antecedents that find formulation in Baudrillard's three orders of simulation in which the final stage collapses any difference between representation and reality to create what is constituted as the Real. This is our current moment of pixelled digital imagery. The confusion, then, between realism as a stylised mode of aesthetic expression and the objects / ideas it represents disappears into the invisible operation of its technics. In this confusion, the whole of reality or form of life is available to us and understood as a universal that cuts across time, space and culture, not as a medium mediating the world but merely presenting it via representation and media.

This naïve sense of the cinema camera merely documenting the real took a rather hard knock when it came to pass that the real contained invisible phenomena that could be rendered visible through the intervention of yet further-reaching and different visualising machines. The concept known as 'black light' emerged to explain the visual range that lay beyond the organic eye's capacities. Atomic light, or the X-ray, exemplified technology's ability to outfit prosthetically and enhance our biological vision while simultaneously placing in question the power and efficacy of empirical knowledge. An invisible yet accessible real lay beyond the unaided eye, and this insight proves important in the development of a specific mental *techne* for understanding the relationship between the human senses and the natural world, a mindset that understands technology as capable of accessing a deeper, truer real, as well as a demand for its increasingly intensified use for exploring the previously inaccessible real. The vision machine we wish to highlight here differs somewhat from Virilio's in that it is the technology itself, as well as the effects rendered in the immaterial domain of epistemology and even ontology resultant from the developments in material technology: the vision machine as cause and effect of noetic formations.

With the emergence of scopic instruments that pierce invisibility and reconfigure it as visible (machinic vision, as it were) also comes an uncertainty about vision and its veracity, thus exposing the problematic that resides at the heart of empirical inquiry. Empiricism might overturn dogma with the drop of an apple or the kick of a stone, but we also know full well how easily duped are our senses. With the arrival of vision machines of all kinds throughout the nineteenth century, from photography to chronophotography to X-rays, 'light becomes less obvious, sets itself as a problem and challenge to sight' (Comolli 123). Rather than destabilising a positivist sense of the real, the shifting understandings of light and the discoveries made by wresting the visible from the dark domains of invisibility only served to reinforce the idea that reality does indeed exist 'out there' in a way that is understandable in the same manner by anyone, and that we can get at it through technological means that prosthetically aid the organic operation of salvageable but ultimately flawed biological senses. Sight and access to the real become a matter of technology, not empiricism or epistemology. The desire to pursue the real through technological means becomes manifest in the materiality of the technologies and in the immateriality of the desire, with each reinforcing the other in a closed feedback system. Clearly, this is a Heideggerian point but is one worth repeating in order to explore the supposed oppositions generated by mimesis and examinations of the real that become essential to understanding documentary as a genre.

Aesthetics and Poetics of Documentary

Cinema is at the risk of disappearing at the hands of reality.

Jean Baudrillard, *Intelligence of Evil* (125)

I think you still want to be open to just the power of an image. The sheer act of *photographing* something has an inherent power.

Filmmaker Errol Morris (http://www.documentary.org/content/
career-achievement-award-cinematic-investigations-errol-morris/)

The kind of looking, recording and witnessing that a single photograph occasions is always bearing witness for the technical medium *tout court*; that is, a photograph, for all its singularity, cannot but evoke in more or less subterranean ways, its relationship to photography as such.

Gerhard Richter, *Copy, Archive, Signature* (xxv)

James Moran extends Roland Barthes's insight that 'the same century invented History and Photography' (Camera Lucida 92) to include documentary, whose credibility depends on 'the authenticity of the former and the objectivity of the latter' (257). Moran continues his argument to claim that documentary is a kind of historiography designed to elude the evanescent vicissitudes of human memory, while also trafficking in the metaphysics of presence: the cinematographer had to have been there, or at least in the presence of others who were. Clearly, this insight holds concerns similar to those of the analogue 'punctum' that Barthes discusses in relation to photography. However, it also echoes strongly Heidegger's concerns about representation generally moving from the wonder of presence and the uncertainty of 'presencing' toward the calculation, securing and fixing of presence operative in representation. Heidegger writes, 'Representing is no longer a self-unconcealing for . . . but is a laying hold and grasping of . . .' (149, ellipses in original). Representation joins the larger enframing and emplacing process of the techno-scientific setting and securing of the Real, of calculating and setting in place. Heidegger's concern with representation finds resonance with the violence done not by the image but to the image, as argued by Baudrillard. Baudrillard claims that, whereas the image once had the capacity to surprise, to undermine assumption, to challenge our understandings of the world (to aid the process found in truth as unfolding, fluid, 'unconcealing for'), it now has fallen prey to the project of integral reality in which the entire trajectory of all processes is to avoid surprise at all costs, to destroy secrecy and mystery, and to render all of the world and existence visible (and therefore controllable). Certain modes of documentary neatly fall within this project of integral reality, as do most visual technologies and their products. But it is from comedy and parody that the possibility for uncertainty, incalculability and fluidity perhaps re-emerges as they turn their sights on the stable, the certain, the Real in order to destabilise and unsettle them. 'Humor', as Freud writes in a 1927 essay with that title, 'is not resigned, it is scornful' (563). Comedy is the aesthetics of displacement and destabilisation, of breakage and disruption.

To enact this aesthetics, comedic parodists of documentary in cinema use its audience's shared knowledge of visual history, technologies and products, as well as their overall faith in truthfulness complete with their assumptions of being in the presence of the real. All of these are used against the audience. Our knowledge and the assumptions it is predicated upon are used against us for critical ends. The aesthetics and formal elements of the genre become the point of self-reflexive engagement of the *techne* operative within them – to lay hold of the ways documentary frames the real and render its invisible operation visible. As with Classic Hollywood Cinema, documentary largely operates with the technique of no technique, but does so for different ends. As opposed to creating realist narratives the audience can lose itself in, documentary is meant to create the illusion of objectivity, simply documenting what is front of the camera in an unmediated manner. If documentary shows 'things the way they are', then Classic Hollywood Cinema shows 'things the way they are for others and could be for you' – all of which connects to Adorno and Horkheimer in their still-prescient critique of the culture industry, for fictional film entertainment provides its own Real and set of audience expectations about the life that exists outside the frame of the screen, while collapsing the space between existence and its double.

Even though documentary has and makes certain claims on the real and its relation to it, the default documentary aesthetic is fairly recent, despite drawing upon a long history of supposedly objective and universalist representational modes. The caveat here, with respect to our current common-sense documentary aesthetic, is that it comes out of a very different way of understanding non-fiction film from that offered up by Robert Flaherty or John Grierson, in which documenting and entertainment were not held as antithetical impulses in so far as they pertain to the real and cinema's relation to it. The current aesthetic and stylistic strategies include: hand-held camera, incorporation of extant footage (in which film extracts from while adding to the archive of film itself), voice-over, interviews with experts and / or participants (authoritative commentary and the authority derived from metaphysics of presence), long takes, few close-ups (mostly medium and long shots to highlight the unfolding of events in a specific chronotope), and an allergic reaction to the staged event or to performance generally, which stands in marked contrast to Flaherty's massively influential and successful 1922 documentary, *Nanook of the North*. The explicitly Romantic dimensions of the documentary or non-fiction film that we find in Flaherty thrived until the 1930s, including work by F. W. Murnau in this domain, and later into the 1940s with Orson Welles's unfinished Brazilian odyssey, *It's All True*. These non-fiction films do not lay claim to truth or reality per se but embody the double negative of the term non-fiction: if fiction is 'not real' then non-fiction is 'not not real'. These more romantically inflected documentaries also take their cue from the heroic filming of famous expeditions that began in the first years of the twentieth century, including a Theodore Roosevelt safari and Robert Falcon Scott's Antarctic venture captured by Herbert Ponting, as well as the long history of travel writing, the myth of exploration and boys' adventure stories.

As with Classic Hollywood Cinema, the documentary aesthetic that emerges in the late 1940s and 1950s and which has become the standard today, editing is hidden as editing, unless it is used to reinforce the seemingly artless 'unaesthetic aesthetic/style' that articulates the real as simply and inelegantly documented (as in photojournalism). The preference for long takes, deep focus, and firmly established spatial relations within the *mise-en-scène* reinforces an aesthetic that attempts to keep time and space together with regard to the events being documented. As Trinh Minh-Ha puts it, 'The more, the larger – as if wider framing is less a framing than tighter shots' (80). The filmic techniques only draw attention to themselves to serve the larger rhetorical purpose of minimal manipulation by the medium. To this end, the grainy image, hand-held camera work, artless and inelegant editing and framing lend a curious handmade quality to the documentary that returns us to the naïve position of mere documentation. In fact, a simple equation is operative in which the worse the image, the less slick the presentation, the higher the verity. This aesthetic–truth ratio operates up to the present with the rapid increase in hand-held video devices that allow for citizen journalism and other such visual interventions into the stronghold of dominant media. Nothing perhaps articulates the power of this ratio as forcefully as the image generated by security cameras and CCTV. The ghostly, grainy image of CCTV constitutes that which is watching always (machinic watching), but only ever watched by humans with any care *after* the fact of an event. It is truthfulness itself, the slurry grey figures barely recognisable in the self-erasing, evanescent video loop, that speak with a haunting power to current audiences. This is what DeLillo, in his epigraph for this chapter, calls the 'underreal' – which oddly complements and completes Baudrillard's hyper-real. These images are constitutive of the Real in a way that emerges from and feeds back into the aesthetics of documentary film.

This aesthetic relates to a specific moment and specific technological innovations: the increased use of portable cinema cameras in the 1940s and early 1950s, and later the consolidation of film camera and sync sound in one portable machine. The innovations for portable cinema photography were largely developed by Allied and Axis forces during World War II for documentary and propaganda purposes. As with so many scopic innovations, the military leads the way. The Eyemo and the Arriflex weighed about 12 pounds and saw and recorded much action during battle. Immediately after the war, Arriflex upgraded its machine and Eclair of France brought out the Cameflex in 1947. Trinh Minh-Ha comments that the independence of the hand-held camera comes from its being freed from 'the fixed observation post' of the tripod, and hence its apparent capacity to be 'mobile and invisible' (80). The real advance came with the Eclair NPR, the first portable 16-mm sync-sound film camera, launching a generation of independent filmmakers roaming the globe.

The NPR became a standard in all genres of filmmaking by 1960, but most especially documentary, playing a pivotal role in the 1960s boom of *cinéma vérité*. Its portability helped establish the quality of presence – of spontaneously capturing events as they unfolded – so essential to documentary film. But the influence of this machinery was not limited to documentary filmmaking, shaping French New Wave and Italian neo-realism amongst other important stylistic movements. Drawing on an earlier tradition that linked ethnography, photography and Surrealism, practised in the 1920s by Georges Bataille, Marcel Mauss and others (as documented by James Clifford and Denis Hollier), the aesthetic that emerged in the 1940s, 1950s and 1960s documentary boom worked with the power of objects and cultural variations of aesthetics. Again, early decades of cinematic intervention skirted surrealistic critique of mainstream culture in documentary as much as in straightforward comedy. The documentary directors Michel Brault and Jean Rouch helped re-establish and modify this aesthetic, as also practised in fictional works, in their semi-politicised, semi-ethnographic, semi-postcolonial films.

The mobility of the camera, paradoxically enough, led to a more focused locationality of the image, a more circumscribed point of view: that of the director/camera operator as author of the film. The director becomes, ironically, the tripod or 'the fixed observation post', though a mobile one.

The aesthetic that emerges with and through this new portable technology actually underscores the presence and agency of the filmmaker involved in a corporeal and spontaneous manner with the events being documented. The resultant aesthetic banks on our faith in the technology of analogue photography, that the light we see captured on the film was light reflected off the object on to the emulsion of the film and held there; we see *that* light, that reflection, and thus that object (as Barthes, among others, has argued). In a slightly contradictory manner, documentary partakes of this power of analogue presence as reinforced by the authority of the newsreel and its presentational format: that is, through the visual archive of historical material generated and stored in the twentieth century. The collective visual historical memory of that century finds its roots in the visual news at the cinema with the newsreel prior to the advent of television and televised news, which in turn greatly perpetuated and reinforced these ways of seeing and understanding historical events. The documentary genre similarly contributes to this visual archive while simultaneously exploiting its claims to unmediated witness.

With this insight, we return to the verity of the analogue image as unmediated by the very medium that delivers it, removing absence and basking in the presence that the representation provides. To reinforce this presence, the documentary aesthetic plays with temporal disjunctures through eyewitness or participant accounts. The events to which we gain direct access, as if in the real time of their spontaneous unfolding, become grounded in a past more distant than that of the eyewitness account. Yet through these simultaneous temporal displacements and anchors resultant from the eyewitness/participant interview, the documentary partakes of 'I was there–I saw' and converts it through the magical media manipulation of time and space to 'You are there–you see,' repeating the temporal formula of *here–now* and *there–then* found in analogue images. Such rhetorical moves convince viewers of the account's authenticity through their participation in the representation. With this common-sense documentary aesthetic, entertainment takes a back seat to 'Truth' and a securing of the Real that the genre maintains as a dividing line between it and fiction film. Documentary film has long relied on indexicality (as offered by Barthes on photography), the profound relationship between the object portrayed and the medium of its portrayal (the unquestioned ontology of that which is pictured, even when digital technology is deployed), and a connection to scientific, medical, objective visualisation of the world. It is thus that documentary and the Real remain deeply intertwined, in spite of the genre's long and complex past, one that makes its separation from fiction film very difficult to discern.

It All Started With a Gun (and a Screen): *Bowling for Columbine* (2002)

But the movie [the Zapruder film] in fact was powerfully open, it was glary and artless and completely steeped in being what it was, in being film. It carried a kind of inner life, something unconnected to the things that we call phenomena. The footage seemed to advance some argument about the nature of film itself. The progress of the car down Elm Street, the movement of the film through the camera body, some sharable darkness – this was a death that seemed to rise from the streamy debris of the deep mind . . . there was some trick of film emulsion that showed the ghost of consciousness. Or so she thought to wonder. She thought to wonder if this home movie was some crude living likeness of the mind's own technology, the sort of death plot that runs in the mind, because it can seem so familiar, the footage did – it seemed a thing we might see, not see but know, a model of the nights when we are intimate with our own dying.

Don DeLillo, Underworld (495–6)

For the problem of the flight of birds, I have dreamed of a kind of photographic gun.
Etienne-Jules Marey in a letter to Eadweard Muybridge, December 1878
(quoted in Dagognet 95)

The history of the movie camera thus coincides with the history of automatic weapons. The transport of pictures only repeats the transport of bullets.
Friedrich Kittler, Gramophone, Film, Typewriter (124)

Travelling as it does from the amateurish grain of the moving image to the fine folds of the viewer's brain or reframed mind, the quotation above from Don DeLillo's novel *Underworld* continues the author's sustained engagement with visual culture in the twentieth century, with his interpretation being that visual culture *is* the twentieth century. The excerpt addresses that pivotal mid-century event in US political history: the assassination of John F. Kennedy in Dallas, Texas, in November 1962. More specifically for us, though, it addresses the role of the Zapruder film in our collective memory of this very public, though heavily veiled event. Our primary visual access to this seminal US historical event is the film segment caught unintentionally by a suburban dentist on a Super 8–mm hand-held camera, a moment in which the home movie becomes historical evidence and shadowy tragedy, capturing on film further proof of a violent heart beating at the centre of the American polity. The unintentional filming or documenting of a shooting (the inadvertent documentary) becomes an icon of this latent violence while displaying the power that blocks of colour and movement of blurry film images can wield for decades.

The Zapruder film is also a representational precursor for the events at Columbine High School, similarly documented by an array of security cameras intended to record misbehaviour and crime but not necessarily of the type that these specific cameras eventually videoed; none the less, an inadvertent quality remains. There is little inadvertent in Michael Moore's carefully crafted and manipulated comic documentary on the Columbine High School shooting, *Bowling for Columbine*. This blatantly constructed documentary uses comedy to focus attention on its very artifice and this comedy, in fact, arises from the constructedness. Although comedy is the mode or register of Moore's films, which Amber Day has called 'Satiric Documentary', his work also might be dubbed didactic documentary. Comedy is also, counter-intuitively, the mode through which he delivers an examination of guns, and the role of the powerful National Rifle Association in American public discourse, US history and geopolitics, as well as the media and screen ubiquity of guns generally as contextualisations for, though not explanations of, the shootings at Columbine. In the process, Moore turns his camera on visual and screen culture more than he attempts to unveil the acts of violence at the high school, and it is through the comic juxtapositions of absurd societal views within the various contextual frames he examines that the director provides the gallows humour central to the critique, one that in essence questions the very nature of his own project.

Video games and guns took centre-stage in the public analysis of potential causes for what occurred with the shootings. Moore's film glides over the computer-gaming dimension of their action, though he does give it some attention. In so doing, he offers yet another avatar of media and information technology as capable of blurring reality and fantasy, as we saw with Keaton's *Sherlock Jr.* in the last chapter. However, this blurring has taken a step even further; just a few years after the event, the Columbine shooting itself became a video game that one can play in the role of first-person shooter. The game is the work of new media artist Danny Ledone and comments indirectly on the critiques levelled at gaming in relation to the violence committed by the two assailants. The game's graphics are anything but state of the art. Rather like the hand-held, artless aesthetics of documentary verity, the game deploys crude, simplistic figures and eschews any of the drive toward the hyper-real operative in numerous ultraviolent video games, including those used as recruiting tools by the US military. The game is available free of charge at http://www.columbinegame.com/ and offers self-reflexive statements and forums from the artist that explain its own critical interventions and venues for users to comment. Because media, especially gaming, took so much of the blame in public discourse (that is, within the media itself) for the perpetrators' actions at Columbine, and with the event now also a game, we have another example of the Möbius strip, as Baudrillard frequently has called it: that is, the mash-up of media and the actual in which no discernible inside or outside of media exists. Paul Virilio states provocatively that, in the past, people used to want to be on film, but now (ever since Jenny Cam and the advent of online real-time streaming of private cameras documenting daily lives), they desire to become film (Live 181). In the case of this shooting, the desire seems to have shifted yet again, as if the shooters wished to become a computer game, or to be CCTV film / video. If so, they succeeded wildly.

The self-description of games that uses the perspective of the player(s) invokes the rhetorical voice and the grammar/semantics of transitivity, commenting indirectly not only on the subjectivity and agency of the player(s) but also on the individual within ever-increasingly mediated sites. Those games in which the images appear to be seen from the player's perspective – say, staring over the barrel of a gun glimpsed at the bottom of the screen or guiding the player's vision – are called 'first-person shooters'. These differ from the games in which the player manipulates a figure on the screen that becomes the virtual proxy of the human competitor by placing the viewer in the middle of the action. The industry's designation of these games as 'first-person' works against the common net-rhetoric of communal connectivity and alternative social relations by reinscribing the player grammatically and semantically as manipulator of all s/he surveys (the vaunted sovereign subject of Western thought). The origins of such games are well known: 'first-person shooters' were initially developed and are still used by the US military to develop hand–eye coordination, as well as to desensitise soldiers to the violence of urban warfare. In the process, the very information tele-technologies that claim to overcome time and space (here and there), subject and object, self and other, merely serve to reinforce the difference and the distance between agent and recipient (or the shooter and the shot), to underscore the transitive grammar of a subject dominating and controlling objects in the world.

The metaphysics of presence that the media, computer technology, telecommunications and documentary (as a genre) bank on – 'you are there' – subsumes the 'here' that is 'there', and renders it a noplace 't/here'. The tantalising promise of overcoming the constraints of the self cooperating with a world of others, of infinite linkage, seemingly dangled by telecommunicative possibilities as well as other high-tech prosthetics, only partially manifests itself. The subject (viewer) and the object (viewed) are indeed implicated in, and undergo change through, the verb / medium that links them, but only to be differentiated by the process the verb signifies while the mediation provided by the media between subject and object further serves this differentiation. Just as the collapse of 'here' and 'there' into 't/here' by electronic media only apparently overcomes the distance of time and space, so too the subject (viewer) and object (viewed) are further separated by the very process (electronic media) that brings them together, and the process reifies their difference and distance. The gaze remains unidirectional, as the screen becomes a mirror and the mirror a screen, with the self caught in its chiasmus of solipsistic infinite regress.

Moore's virtuosic editing of previously existing footage from a vast array of visual archives drives home the fully mediated subjectivity of the two Columbine shooters, but more importantly that of his audience to show that they occupy the same interpellated positions. They are similarly bedazzled by his filmic barrage that draws attention to its constructedness, its re-editing and recontextualising of salvaged clips from TV, security cameras, educational films, computers, propaganda, news footage. These moving images have been played out over decades on multiple screens, and here these many screens are reduced and enframed (in a Heideggerian sense) by the one screen of Moore's film, creating what Doug Kellner calls 'exploratory documentary montage' (Cinema Wars 140). This explicit focus reveals the screen as the necessary, though invisible, ground for the appearance of any moving image. The tain of the moving image self-reflexively reminds viewers of the conditions that make their viewing possible, though hidden in the seemingly naturalness of its appearance. Moore's indexing of screen mediation leads us to issues of screen culture and the ubiquity of screen culture, especially in the post-World War II era, with an exponentially increasing proliferation of visual delivery systems and portals for viewing: from cinema screens to TV to computers to hand-held devices to architectural facades. *Bowling* offers its viewers a palimpsest of screens constructing and reconstructing a specific event and its myriad contexts: a visual storehouse of the Real that acknowledges simultaneously its own problematic position within the entrapments of screen culture and a supposedly critical engagement with it.

Screen culture distinguishes itself from visual culture in a few important ways, one of which being the attributes of temporality and animation (time and movement) that build upon the earlier use of still photography (itself the provenance of visual culture). As a result, screen culture considers a range of delivery systems for screens to broadcast while also addressing the increased mimetic capacity of visual technologies found with the imitation of movement and animation. This repetition of elements from still photography is actually intimated in some of the earliest experiments with motion studies conducted by the 'biologist–mechanician' Etienne-Jules Marey (Dagognet 44). Marey's deep resistance to Vitalist explanations of time and movement (such as those proposed by Bergson) led to his concerted attempts to measure, graphically represent, and extrapolate from movement and time observable, documentable and abstractable knowledge of the mechanics of animal and aerial movement. These studies, as we noted in the previous chapter, led directly to the movement and animation of photography, but not simply in a bland pre-cinema fashion, in so far as his interests resided in the discrete analysis of phenomena unobservable without some manner of visual prosthesis or mechanical seeing. Thus Marey is not interested in the cinematic persistence of vision that mimics movement, as found the Lumière Brothers' work, but rather in a fundamentally different way of seeing movement. He wishes to see movement in its isolatable micro-moments, a way of seeing that can be considered a precursor to digital media (Mamber 83–92), though clearly not evident in the digital video games of 'first-person shooters' that are more cinematic in their formal qualities.

His experiments lay as much with the machines of documentation and graphic representation as with the phenomena he explored, whether the circulation of blood in the body and the attendant arterial movements, the wings of birds in flight, the gait of a horse or the leap of a human. The graphic dimension pertains to the abstraction of analysis that so fascinated him: the capacity to extract, store, reproduce and apply to other forms of movement or simply movement as abstract entity in and of itself, but not in its elusive fluidity. Rather, pushing an atomist logic, Marey concentrated on movement in its micro-positions. His interests led to the deep design connections between motion-capturing photographic equipment and weapons – for example, his most famous machine, the 'photoscopic gun'. The photoscopic gun allows for chronophotographic capacity to reside in one machine (whereas Muybridge, for example, often used multiple machines to capture movement and time), and in this, his consolidation is reminiscent of the innovations leading to hand-held cameras that are integral to the documentary aesthetic. The linkage found in Marey's inventions between photographic equipment and weapons, when combined with screen culture, forms a central nexus residing, perhaps unknowingly, at the heart of Moore's documentary: camera, gun, screen, viewer, psyche as deeply implicated in one another – rather as we find them in the DeLillo riff on the Zapruder film, in the film experiments 'War Neuroses', and the theoretical work of Kittler and Virilio, who consistently remind us that the delivery systems of rapid-fire images and ammunition emerged simultaneously and in contact with one another.

One of Moore's primary institutional targets for critical engagement is the National Rifle Association. Established in 1871, the association's goal was 'to promote and encourage rifle shooting on a scientific basis' (NRA website), a goal that perpetuated the strong influences between scientific exploration into the operation of the senses and technological innovations emergent from this investigation, including increased development in optics and manipulation of the optical sphere for commercial, medical, entertainment and military applications. The emergence of a specific strand of visual culture dominant in the twentieth century and the early twenty-first finds important formations in the latter half of the nineteenth century, especially in the post-Civil War moment, with an increasing suspicion about the capacities of the organic eye coupled with a belief in the accuracy of science. The NRA was thick in this mix, helping to develop a scientific and technological basis for research and development in firearm targeting accuracy as part of a much larger movement of sensory prosthetics for the greater good and advancement of society as a whole. In fact, Marey's experiments at this time fit neatly into this same general ethos, as his writings, graphic representations and instruments attest.

A villain in Moore's uncharacteristically non-accusatory film is the then-contemporary president of the NRA, Charlton Heston. Serving in that very public capacity from 1998 to 2003, Heston is mobilised by Moore for his own rhetorical aims in much the same way as Heston mobilised the NRA faithful and their beliefs in the sanctity of freedom, as found in the form of specific readings of the Second Amendment of the US constitution, as well as in the iconicity of the gun during a time of national trauma. At the most basic level of Moore's film, the casting of Heston as villain plays against type: a heroic Hollywood leading man type indeed typified by Heston, who had the chutzpah to play Moses in Cecil B. DeMille's *The Ten Commandments* (1956; someone had to, of course), as well as leading parts in *Spartacus*, *Ben Hur*, *Planet of the Apes* and the excellent Orson Welles vehicle *A Touch of Evil* (1958; a film made possible by Heston, to give him his due, at a time when Welles was a Hollywood pariah). Heston used his star power as purchase for a set of specific conservative political goals represented by the NRA, but also, and here the villainy emerges for Moore, to allow the NRA to stage high-profile rallies in various cities or towns in which tragic school shootings had occurred recently, often within days of the violence. Without Heston's Hollywood status, such rallies would have been impossible to pull off, even with the vast resources and power of the NRA. The sequence and image that Moore repeats is one with Heston onstage before a large, supportive crowd of gun rights advocates who fear greater federal control of weapons, standing in a spotlight and holding aloft in one hand a replica of a US Revolutionary War era musket, as he intones with the voice of God (or at least Moses), 'From my cold dead hands!', to the appreciative roars of the audience.

Not the most subtle political moment on Heston's part, but one guaranteed to stir up public opinion on all sides of the gun control issue in the US. At best an insensitive act, at worst a provocation by a certain segment of the American public parading as besieged freedom lovers who see the gun as a metonym for US liberty, this defiant gesture and Moore's repetition of it speak to the film's audience on equally unsubtle levels. But within the screen culture that Moore enframes in the film, the moment speaks in many ways and at many levels. Heston as an icon of Hollywood and as a potent trope of screen culture brings the full brunt of cinema's construction of Americana into the politicised scene of gun control discussions. Though he would only have had a certain resonance with a specific age group at the time, and certainly *not* with the Columbine students who suffered the violence, Heston functions with the NRA and in Moore's film as a fully mediated celebrity operating as an icon of the power of media and screen culture themselves, a metonym of Hollywood and its power to shape individual and collective imaginaries. Further, Heston trots out the frontier ethos of Henry Nash Smith and evokes the sense of rugged individualism as found in the somewhat dormant genre of the Western and the long-standing iconicity of the gun in Hollywood cinema, standing as it does for maleness, freedom, action and lone justice. (All of these points will be taken up in the next chapter in reference to Mel Brooks's *Blazing Saddles*.) As Doug Kellner concisely circumscribes in his book on school shootings in the US, the male subject has long been cast as the site of autonomous action and individual agency, especially when coupled with the technology of the gun – all of these converge in an image of the subject gaining control over his environment and others that is accessed through screen culture, including on a grand scale in video games. The nexus of the camera, gun, screen, viewer as deeply implicated in one another comes to the fore with the Heston sequence and his deployment by Moore. The first-person shooter of video games is the image that both Heston and Moore mobilise for different socio-political and cultural ends, though both do so through the mediating power and dense intertextuality of screen culture.

Politics with a capital 'P', such as that addressed in many of Moore's films (for example, health-care policy, gun control and regulation, corporate responsibility, US geopolitical policy in relation to oil and terrorist acts, financial crises), and politics with a lower-case 'p' (including labour, technology, media, identity, desire, and the construction of status quo values) work both in tandem and in conflict with one another in this film, with cinema (visual culture/screen culture) mediating between the two. The comedy of juxtaposition operative in the display of competing discursive positions is generated by Moore's attempt to contain within one film the massively proliferating screens projecting these and other positions. Moore's film cannot enframe the multitude of frames he wishes to address, but the editing flamboyance and skill highlight this spillage, the excess of images and information, as well as our embeddedness within them. Rather like Derrida's famous dictum 'there is no outside the text,' for the audience watching this documentary and its exponentially bur- geoning number of screens and enframings, there is no outside the screen. Moore's film does not say that there is any singular cause for the actions of the killers at Columbine High School but rather that it represents a clas- sically overdetermined site of such multi-causalities, and that his barrage of a film is but one of many ways in which it could have been addressed. No matter how the events would be discussed or explained, however, they would have always been implicated in the ways in which the gun and the screen, and the camera and the viewer, influence and indeed generate one another.

Cinema's Sleight of Hand and the American Image Empire: Woody Allen's *Zelig* (1983) and Orson Welles's *Citizen Kane* (1941) and *F for Fake* (1972)

> Zelig's own existence is a non-existence. Devoid of personality, his human qualities long since lost in the shuffle of life, he sits alone quietly staring into space, a cipher, a non-person, a performing freak. He who wanted only to fit in – to belong, to go unseen by his enemies and be loved – neither fits in nor belongs, is supervised by enemies, and remains uncared for.
>
> Narrator's voice-over, in *Zelig*

> On this overpopulated and mechanized planet, it is not so easy to remain oneself.
>
> Orson Welles as narrator, in *F for Fake*

Any two of the three films for examination in this section make sense together, with threads linking the two being easily found. Yet for some reason, the three together, especially in a book on film comedy, seems to make less sense, at least on first appearance. And since all three are interested in appearance, perhaps this is as good a place as any to start. The cinematic image and the deceptiveness of appearance prove central to these films. The banal observation that things might not be as they seem – despite the medium's verisimilitude – yields to an inquiry into how we arrive at false understandings to begin with, how the mistaken ontology results from unavoidable elements of epistemology, perceptual genealogies and the medium's interaction with other media in a larger ecology of communicative technologies. Thus, one obvious link between the mockumentary *Zelig*, the documentary-inflected *Citizen Kane* and the documentary-essay film *F for Fake* is their thorough working through of cinema's capacity to operate as if telling the truth, even when we know it is not and the film itself is telling us so. What cinema has done to the status of the image and vice versa receive full airings in these films. 'I am lying,' these films say about the image (and themselves), each in its myriad ways, and in so saying, paradoxically, tell us truths. The films return us to that hoary performative and poststructuralist chestnut in which the content of the utterance or image is put asunder by its articulation or appearance. To say 'I am lying' is to tell the truth about not telling the truth and thus is both true and untrue, simultaneously returning us to the most fundamental problems resident at the heart of representation and its claims for verity that opened this chapter. Further, the statement highlights, again, the level of the address with which cinema engages us.

The three films work the cinematic grammar of narrative, especially that of the standard documentary film, against itself, to turn the medium self-reflexively against its conventions in ways that are humorously unsettling and which leave the means by which the messages have been delivered in a tatty and subverted state, but perhaps still potent in their productiveness, as if the three films had never been made or viewed or commented upon. In Woody Allen's *Zelig*, for example, he examines critically the technology of media in much the same way that Chaplin critically examines assembly-line industrialism. In both, the thrust of the technological and mechanical forces of conformity and cultural reproduction are deployed against the individual to manipulate, subvert and domesticate him / her. Allen, however, asks us, his contemporary audience, to consider the interactions of art, popular culture, consumer culture and propaganda, along with psychoanalysis, sociology and intellectual introspection. The same can also be said for the two films made by Welles. Catherine Benamou argues that one finds in Welles's *F for Fake* a combination of Baudrillardian concerns about the effects of the simulacrum coupled with an Adorno–Horkheimer critique of the ways in which the culture industries position the individual in relation to society (152). Hers is just as apt an observation for *Zelig* and for *Citizen Kane* as it is for *Fake*. Thematising the power of the media, as we have seen, is one of US cinema's favourite tropes, and Bemanou alludes to this. However, as with Keaton's *Sherlock Jr.*, the critique found in these films is not a crude version of Adorno and Horkheimer but rather a more nuanced one, as found in those authors' work itself, if less so in that of some of their commentators; this critique relates inextricably the materiality of the technology that delivers ideological content to the immateriality that so positions the individual (126–7). The films deliver the argument that there is no other means for becoming an individual than through the collectivity, no other way to arrive at truth than through falsity, no other way to arrive at content than through a medium and various media. The films explore the extent to which we are the effects or products of various media *techne* and materiality that generate communication, its nodes, and those who participate in them (pace Heidegger, McLuhan, Baudrillard, Kittler, Stiegler and others).

To this end, we can say that, ultimately, the topic of inquiry for *Zelig*, and to a certain extent the two Welles films, is the status of the photographic image, including cinema and the entire network of distribution and publicity, as well as the creation of celebrity. The fact that Allen places Zelig at William Randolph Hearst's home, San Simeon, complete with a gaggle of early Hollywood celebrities, brings this inquiry to the fore (and furthers the allusions to *Citizen Kane*). If mass electronic media created celebrity, then Hearst created mass electronic media through interlocking complementary forms of broadcast delivery: newspapers, radio, cinema. Allen wants to examine the role of media technology in shaping personal identity, as well as manipulating needs and desires. The film shows how a skilful combination of artistry, technology and economics can create a new environment of mediated reality for the individual and the mass audience – all of this with nods to Jean Baudrillard. In fact, the path for achieving individuality winds through the mass audience. The individual becomes an individual when immersed in the comfort of mass entertainment and consumerism. In consumer-based culture, the acquisition of the commodity, so we are told, makes us more uniquely ourselves. The irony, of course, is that the goods in question are mass-produced, mass-marketed and mass-consumed. This irony pulsates throughout the film.

Further tipping our hat to Baudrillard, we should note Allen's use of multiple cinematic genres, each of which is the latter's fictional invention and all of which are evocative of how cinema works to represent and create the Real. The primary genres included in the film are the documentary (complete with 'actual' US, indeed New York, intellectuals as expert commentators on the Zelig phenomenon), the newsreel (à la Welles) and the Hollywood biopic *The Changing Man*. Allen cuts fluidly between these, establishing a close unity between a fake documentation of historical reality and Hollywood's version of the same set of events – not unlike the 'actualities' of the early part of the twentieth century. Using interviews with participants in the event to comment on specifics of the narrative,

Allen pokes fun at this stock documentary technique and at Hollywood when one of the mock interviewees says, 'It was nothing like it was shown in the movies.' In each instance, Allen forces us to consider the suspension of disbelief that is important to art and which is equally important to the non-fiction of documentary film. The intervention of the interviewee's comment on the veracity of the Hollywood biopic serves to differentiate the diegetic of the documentary from the machinations of Classic Hollywood Narrative, but within the presentation of the mockumentary it serves to underscore further the mediation operative in both fiction and non-fiction film. The baroque layering of artifice of this Hollywood product (*Zelig*, that is) complements similar operations found in *F for Fake*, with the latter perhaps manifesting less of the realist aesthetic essential to mainstream film than either *Kane* or *Zelig*, despite its ostensibly being a documentary that attempts to present reality.

In both *Citizen Kane* and *Zelig*, the directors used the newsreel to their advantage. In Welles's film, the newsreel provides audiences with a brief, chronological overview of Kane's life, thus allowing Welles to piece together an impressionistic narrative that relies more on patterns of association than chronology. In this way, the film's main narrative operates in a less linear fashion and rather more in the manner of consciousness and memory than realist narrative normally allows. For Allen, the newsreel is not used to steer notions of narrative away from realist modes, but rather to query the mediation of experience in general. In *Zelig*, the newsreel footage explores how history has been documented in the mechanical age: that is, through the movie camera lens, as Edison's films surrounding the McKinley assassination embody and bespeak. One of the primary differences between the twentieth century and previous ones is the capability of having moving images as a record of historical events, and many of our collective memories of this recent history are comprised of the flickering images of shadow and light that played on screens throughout the world. Allen's film offers us yet another examination of an artistic topic as old as representation itself: the thin line between fantasy and reality, with the two integrated in a film that pretends to be a documentary. Orson Welles's *F for Fake* works the same terrain but with little pretence to explicitly fictional material or recourse to the attributes of narrative film.

Naremore argues that *Fake* as a whole (if it is indeed a whole, coherent film) operates as a 'collage' (a term used very loosely in this instance) in the same manner as the newsreel segment of *Kane*, which Welles then parodies by constructing a similar mock newsreel about the Kane-like figure of Howard Hughes (246–7). The use of the newsreel collage in *Fake*, though, goes in related but different directions from what it does in *Kane*. With

Welles as narrator perched at his editing Moviola, he provides an onscreen version of the post-production powers of the editor as the ultimate manipulator of images and clips that we see performed in the famous Keaton sequence in *Sherlock Jr*. He renders visible the invisible machinations of filmmaking and places it within the screen image as he navigates footage that he has manipulated and will continue to manipulate. Welles's larger-than-life presence at the editing machine foregrounds an explicitly self-reflexive engagement with cinematic form, authority, narrative/narrator. Further, he inserts himself as narrator/editor as and when he wishes, even stopping the temporal flow of the film through freeze-frames to modify, supplement or refute any claim made by another 'dramatis persona' in the role of expert or documentary subject.

Because his subject matter is forgery and duplicity, the status of the 'characters' remains in question, for we know their truthfulness when they discuss their abilities at deception. However, with forgery, as the film continually argues, the game of authenticity upon which the high art world depends – from galleries to museums to auction houses – is fulfilled, justified and validated through the fake. Thus, in spite of the apparently subversive play that Welles relishes in the film with his borrowed film clips of the forger Elmyr d'Hory, along with his own puckish retellings of the 'War of the Worlds' hoax and Clifford Irving's forged autobiography of Howard Hughes, each ultimately ends up fulfilling its role of vindicating the authority of the logos of the art work as authentic masterpiece, or actual radio newscast, or authentic autobiography. The parodic engagement, rather like Eco's reading of Bakhtin's theorisation of carnival, merely reinscribes the power structure it seeks to overturn or simply take advantage of. None the less we believe d'Hory when he tells us roguishly that he is lying. We believe his artifice, his performance as real. The provenance of his art productions might prove suspect but not his character, for it is manifestly and forthrightly false, and therefore true.

In an odd manner, the character of Zelig performs a similar ironic paradox in that he is most identifiable as himself when he has no discernible self: that is, when he is the Chameleon Man. He achieves fame and becomes a pop culture personality when he has no personality, or at least, no singular personality. In his pursuit of anonymity, Zelig has achieved celebrity. He has ended up at the other extreme of the continuum. As such, the individual is celebrated for his capacity to mimic the taxonomic singularities of specific elements of the collective; he is all the others in society and not anything himself and is thus fêted for it. Yet another paradox emerges when we note that, even though Zelig supposedly fits into various social groups through a transformation that allows for physiognomic and performative mimicry, he is always recognisable as Zelig; he still stands out. The documentary technique of using physical evidence – in this case photographs, it should be noted – provides audiences with a way to identify Zelig as Zelig when he is supposedly hiding in the anonymity of the somatic traits of a given social or ethnic group. So, although he is famous for being a human void, he can always be identified as Zelig in any photograph. His metamorphosis is external and performative, never internal or actual. But the film could be asking, and this may be the more salient point, whether is there any difference between the external and the performative and the internal and the actual. Just as the moment of insight or truth found through a hermeneutics of overcoming opacity merely shows how far we are from understanding fully a situation or an event, the desire to realise a unified self is proportionate to its impossibility, leaving us only the mediation that allows the inquiry to be undertaken and even initially conceived.

One important theme in Allen's film, then, is self-transformation, which is played out most extravagantly in Zelig's capacity for metamorphosis. Self-transformation is integral to both the Enlightenment project and to psychoanalysis. In fact, the latter can be seen as a scientific model for the historical phenomenon found in the former. The drive to change oneself, society, culture and world is emblematic of the modern world-view, but it is important to note that 'change' is understood in this context as being synonymous with progress and improvement. Zelig's own profligate capacities for change, however, do not exhibit this specific goal-oriented view of self-transformation. It, in fact, reveals the opposite: unreflexive, directionless conformity. Allen, therefore, exposes the insidious subtext of the therapeutic elements of self-transformation. A fictional intellectual in the film – the author of the equally fictional book *Interpreting Zelig* – explains that the American public found in Zelig 'a symbol of possibility, of self-improvement, of self-fulfillment'. In other words, they found in him a blank screen on to which they could project their desire for transformation: the Enlightenment subject as crafted in US ideology and mythos. They fell in love with an image of Zelig created and mass-marketed by the media; they fell in love with their own projected desires. And when he seemed to be other than what they made him out to be, their disappointment turned to moral outrage, as it often does in America. In the film, a self-proclaimed defender of America's ethics and values makes a radio address denouncing Zelig. She says, 'America is a moral country; it's a God-fearing country. We don't condone scandals, scandals of fraud and polygamy. In keeping with a pure society, I say lynch the little Hebe.' Underlying the rhetoric of individuality and self-realisation is the reality of control and containment often achieved through prejudice and violence. The quest for individual freedom that the US personifies is curtailed by strong pressures to conform to a whole battery of behavioural and value-laden constraints. Personal freedom thus is best exercised by not exercising it at all; you can best be yourself by being like the neighbours.

The drive for self-realisation that provides a central strand in the supposedly unique American character, of course, opens up the other pole of tension that Allen explores in the film: conformity. To what extent, Allen asks, does self-transformation really become conformity? When does the desire to be part of the crowd translate into being lost in the crowd? Allen, in an interview, claimed the film was not a 'pleasant fantasy of metamorphosis but about the kind of personality that leads to fascism' (James). The Nobel-winning author, Saul Bellow, who is used as onscreen talking-head expert discussing the Zelig phenomenon, analyses it in terms of the desire for anonymity. Bellow says that 'Fascism offered Zelig [an] opportunity [to] make something anonymous of himself by belonging to this vast movement,' even a mass movement predicated upon destruction, including one's own. So, Zelig's yearning for acceptance finds its logical conclusion in Fascism. Similar ideas about Fascism are taken up in fiction by Don DeLillo's *White Noise*, and in a more sustained fashion in philosophy in the work of Frankfurt School thinkers such as Herbert Marcuse and Erich Fromm. Tellingly, two other Frankfurt School exiles in the US, Horkheimer and Adorno, find the same drive for conformity operative in the cult of celebrity that is integral to popular culture and the culture industry. The technologies and industries – both material and immaterial – that produce cars and bombs uncritically also produce films and popular music, consumer goods, celebrity, all of which render the individual subject a cipher. Charles Foster Kane and Zelig might well represent different ends of the broadcast media regime, from robotic producer to consumer/product, but they inhabit this continuum in an equally mechanistic way, incapable of living outside the screen of the world it produces.

The blank screen that is Zelig resides at the heart of the Zelig phenomenon that is central to the film's exploration of celebrity and media/mediated culture. The centre of the phenomenon is a *tabula rasa* of the likes that Locke only ascribed to children but which the comedic critique here ascribes to mediated culture. If one lesson of *Citizen Kane* is that the inner self remains inviolate, as the 'No Trespassing' sign warns viewers at the film's beginning and end, then a lesson of *Zelig* is that there may be no inner self to violate in the first place, no place on which to trespass. That self has been emptied out, or rather filled in and made flat, by a host of various technologies of communication, by popular culture, information technologies and consumer culture – by technological reproduction at all levels. Rather as Baudrillard argues in 'The Ecstasy of Communication', the situation articulated in these three films is one in which we have lost the scene of subject–object relations and are left with the obscene of screen-network relations. Subjects and objects, according to this Baudrillardian take, are replaced by screens for the transmission and reception of ideas, images and information, and networks for the delivery of them, yielding individuals as nodal points broadcasting what has been delivered via the host of technologies and technicities that constitute and articulate contemporary conditions. The individual, then, gives way to the screen as the subject similarly disappears into the network. Subjects and objects, Baudrillard writes, have been 'screened out', along with a number of paired phenomena reliant upon distance to determine difference, pairs such as the real and simulation, the written text and the virtual (Screened Out 176–80). The distance necessary to maintain these distinctions – say, for the subject to observe, engage, manipulate and differentiate itself from objects – has been erased by tele-technologies, including screen culture (such as cinema), whose entire existence depends solely on the erasure of the gap of perception. Dropped into that disappearing gap is the individual, the self, the subject that plays an integral role through its evanescence in *Kane* and *Zelig*.

The process of screening out the subject–object relationship as pertaining to specific historical trajectories is taken up in these two films, as noted as well in the reflections of Adorno and Horkheimer on the decades of the 1920s and 1930s and their influence on the moment of their contemporary writings on the culture industry. Allen, writing on the media at the same time as Baudrillard, understands fully the complexities of mediated culture and its historicity. The Twenties brought the full force of the mechanical age's ability to create celebrity quickly (and just as quickly destroy it). Radio, phonograph and cinema all come to large-scale, mass fruition in this decade, marking the ascendancy of electronic mass media and popular culture. When these are wedded to the entrepreneurial spirit and consumer culture of the US, we see the full-bore effect of product linkages that we still witness today: for example, with blockbuster children's films and the marketing linkages of action figures, toys, clothes, fast-food restaurant links and promotions. *Zelig* parodies these phenomena while reminding us that they are not altogether new, but were present at the initiation of mass media and popular culture into the collective psyche of the American imagination. For the film, Dick Hyman wrote original songs in the style of the Twenties about the Zelig mass-market phenomenon, including 'Leonard the Lizard', 'Doin' the Chameleon', 'You May Be Six People, But I Love You' and 'The Changing Man Concerto'. Zelig memorabilia included a Zelig doll, Zelig clocks, the Chameleon game, a Zelig ashtray, a Zelig wristwatch, Zelig pens, Zelig aprons, a chameleon-shaped meat thermometer with a Leonard Zelig head, Leonard Zelig-approved chameleons, Leonard Zelig-endorsed Camel cigarettes and Leonard Zelig-endorsed Pendleton underwear. All the flotsam of shysterism and jetsam of commercialism washes up in this detail-laden film to document not just that moment but also the moment of the production of Allen's film, a moment in which these earlier phenomena had been allowed several decades of repetition, intensification and modification.

The 1920s are also important for the US and its role on the international stage. One reason that American popular culture began to dominate international popular culture had to do with the infectious rhythms of jazz. Another was bound up with the technological innovations in broadcast media – both radio and cinema – that helped deliver these rhythms and of which American artists took full advantage. Yet another related to the combination of cultural production and marketing already discussed. But, perhaps most importantly, the US began to dominate international pop culture because it had begun to dominate the international geopolitical, military, manufacturing and technological stages. With the end of World War I, the US emerged as a superpower. Although it embodied the dynamism of modernity, it was still struggling with the growing pains involved in moving from second-rate imperial power and backwater nation status to major world player. As such, concerns about and debates over national identity formation came to the fore. The country may have been plunging headlong into a century it would come to dominate, but many concerns about what the nation was, what it stood for and how it could account for the various social and economic inequities still manifest within it plagued many citizens. Add to this situation the massive influx of immigration, particularly from parts of Southern Europe, Ireland and Asia that had no tradition of immigration to the US, and there were many questions being asked about the shape and face of the country. Isolationism struggled with internationalism. 'Melting pot' assimilation wrestled with multicultural acceptance. Extreme wealth resided next to and profited from tenement poverty.

Thus many reasons explain why both Welles and Allen set their films in this pivotal decade, especially as those films dealt with a struggle for individual identity formation that mirrored a struggle for national identity formation. Kane and Zelig, therefore, become metonyms for the nation in the early part of the century: one larger than life and empty at his core, the other smaller than life and also empty at his core. Both characters are prototypically American. Both *Citizen Kane* and *Zelig* view the struggle for identity, whether at the individual or national level, through the lenses of broadcast media and *as* broadcast media. They examine the role these technologies, especially those constituting the media, including cinema, play in shaping or manufacturing identity and history, as well as recording them. They are the mediated beings of a kind of Baudrillardian or Virillian present; they have become cinema. Like Welles at the helm of his editing machine in *Fake*, navigating a future filled with sleights of hand, the persistence of vision and evanescence of images, these three films exemplify the mediation of the world and self through a kind of technological determinism without agency or clearly articulated ideology other than the perpetuation of itself that results in a fascination with the continuous and swelling stream of images, text, sounds, films, language produced by the machine's seemingly endless functioning.

Coda: The Garden of Forking Mistakes

The Borgesian title for this subsection draws attention to the ineluctable intertextuality of all interpretation and knowledge production, while also acknowledging the fragility of the same. Indeed, each layer of intervention, by layperson and expert alike, only adds to the palimpsest of misunderstanding. Such proliferation of misreadings, falsehoods and cinematic chimera becomes an aside in Jerome Rosenbaum's brief engagement with Deleuze's *Cinema* books, and more specifically their English translations. In a discussion of *F for Fake*, Rosenbaum cites the many non-existent films found in the index and discussed in the body of Deleuze's books, the products of translators, proofreaders and even Deleuze himself. Revelling in the vertiginous barrage of copies and fakes generated by the texts, Rosenbaum cannot help but draw attention to the inadvertent problems of Deleuze's work as exemplifying perfectly Welles's very themes. Quite tellingly, a truly inspired example comes in Deleuze's discussion of Welles's films with a beautifully evocative but absolutely false conflation of the aptly titled lost work *It's All True* and the fully realised *F for Fake*, generating a confusion of the two films as the same (141–2). One can almost hear Welles's tympanic laughter at the mangled title and the confusion of his two semi-documentary mediations that, in their missteps, merge true and fake.

Just as most of experience eludes our finite memory and resides in our near-infinite 'forgettory', as Salman Rushdie calls it, so too falsity proliferates with vegetable abandon while truth barely puts up a hand.

Lest this sound like a fairly conservative economy of scarcity argument when it comes to truth, the chapter is not trying to argue that we should clear the ground of falsity so that the light of truth can cause more reality to grow. Rather, it is to say that the situation cannot be otherwise. The drive to reduce the noise, to ensure the verity of the representation and to eliminate misinformation is admirable but ultimately quixotic. Our language, our images, our celluloid, our pixels just will not allow it. They are, as Plato well knew, simply too fecund, too generative for there to be efficiency in getting at the truth, but they are splendid in mediating the world and thus producing the Real.

The films discussed in this chapter address critically the technology, machinery and industry of media in much the same way that Chaplin and Keaton critically examine assembly-line industrialism (either as factory or studio production), as discussed in the previous chapter. In each of these films, the thrust of the technological and mechanical forces of conformity and cultural reproduction (including those of genre and the culture industry-qua-industry) is deployed against the individual to manipulate, subvert, domesticate – even empty out – him/her. While Allen asks his contemporary audience to consider medial relations with regard to art and propaganda, *Fake* and *Bowling for Columbine* do something else, something closer to Keaton in that they explicitly address the cinematic construction of the Real without any pretence of aiming for reality.

The topic of inquiry in all of these films concentrates on the (cinema) photographic image and the grammar of cinematic technique, as well as the entire network of distribution and publicity that can also lead to the creation of celebrity. Conversely, celebrity reflects back on the mass audience and its composition of individual subjects. The films discussed in this chapter and the previous one directly and obliquely question the vaunted notion of the individual as constructed in consumer culture. With the advent of mass marketing operating in tandem with visual and screen culture and coupled with consumerism, the individual emerges as a thoroughly mediated entity and technological byproduct – as does the Real, truth and representation's attempts to capture them all in ways that allow the *techne* of representation to disappear, or so we believe, into its content. The films in this chapter constitute an extended engagement with the indivisible nature of individual, society, culture, economic system, technology and media, with the films manifesting as enunciative and performative moments/statements of this indivisibility and mutuality. And the comic mode provides a critical distance to identify the operations of these vision machines functioning as operations, a meta-view of the conditions that allow us to view, if not see.

Works Cited

Armitage, John (ed.). *Virilio Live: Selected Interviews*. London: Sage, 2001.

Barthes, Roland. *Image – Music – Text*, Stephen Heath (trans.). London: Fontana–Collins, 1977.

Barthes, Roland. *Camera Lucida: Reflections on Photography*, Richard Howard (trans.). New York: Hill & Wang, 1981.

Baudrillard, Jean. *The Evil Demon of Images*, Paul Patton (trans.). Sydney: Power Institute of Fine Arts, 1986.

Baudrillard, Jean. *The Ecstasy of Communication*, Bernard Schutze and Caroline Schutze (trans.). New York: Semiotext(e), 1988.

Baudrillard, Jean. *Simulacra and Simulation*, Sheila Faria Glaser (trans.). Ann Arbor: University of Michigan Press, 1994.

Baudrillard, Jean. *Screened Out*, Chris Turner (trans.). London: Verso, 2002.

Baudrillard, Jean. *Intelligence of Evil*, Chris Turner (trans.). Oxford and New York: Berg, 2005.

Benamou, Catherine. *It's All True: Orson Welles's Pan-American Odyssey*. Berkeley and London: University of California Press, 2007.

Cixous, Hélène. *Insister of Jacques Derrida*, Peggy Kamuf (trans.). Stanford: Stanford University Press, 2007.

Clifford, James. *The Predicament of Culture: Twentieth-Century Ethnography, Literature and Art*. Cambridge, MA: Harvard University Press, 1988.

Comolli, Jean-Louis. 'Machines of the Visible', in *The Cinematic Apparatus*, Teresa de Lauretis and Stephen Heath (eds). New York: Macmillan, 1980, pp. 121–43.

Cowie, Elizabeth. 'The Spectacle of Actuality', in *Collecting Visible Evidence*, Jane M. Gaines and Michael Renov (eds). Minneapolis: University of Minnesota Press, 1999, pp. 19–45.

Dagognet, François. *Etienne-Jules Marey: A Passion for the Trace*, Robert Galeta with Jeanine Herman (trans.). New York: Zone, 1992.

Day, Amber. *Satire and Dissent: Interventions in Contemporary Political Debate*. Indianapolis: Indiana University Press, 2011.

Derrida, Jacques. *Copy, Archive, Signature: A Conversation on Photography*, Gerhard Richter (trans.). Stanford: Stanford University Press, 2010.

Eco, Umberto. *Carnival!*, Monica Rector (trans.). Berlin and New York: Mouton, 1984.

Freud, Sigmund. 'Humor', in *The Penguin Freud Reader*, Adam Phillips (ed.). London: Penguin, 2006, pp. 561–6.

Gaines, Jane M. and Michael Renov (eds). *Collecting Visible Evidence*. Minneapolis: University of Minnesota Press, 1999.

Gunning, Tom. '"Primitive" Cinema', in *Early Cinema: Space, Frame, Narrative*, Thomas Elsaesser (ed.). London: BFI, 1990, pp. 95–103.

Haraway, Donna. 'The Persistence of Vision', in *The Visual Culture Reader*, Nicholas Mirzoeff (ed.). London and New York: Routledge, 2002, pp. 677–84.

Heidegger, Martin. 'The Age of the World Picture', in *The Question Concerning Technology and Other Essays*, William Lovitt (trans.). New York: Harper, 1977, pp. 115–54.

Hollier, Denis (ed.). *The College of Sociology, 1937–1939*. Minneapolis: University of Minnesota Press, 1988.

Horkheimer, Max and Theodor W. Adorno. *Dialectic of Enlightenment*, John Cumming (trans.). New York: Continuum, 1997.

James, Caryn. 'Auteur! Auteur! The Creative Mind of Woody Allen', *New York Times Magazine*, 19 January 1986.

Juhasz, Alexandra and Jesse Lerner (eds). *F is for Phony: Fake Documentary and Truth's Undoing*. Minneapolis: University of Minnesota Press, 2006.

Kellner, Doug. *Guys and Guns Amok: Domestic Terrorism and School Shootings from the Oklahoma Bombing to the Virginia Tech Massacre*. Boulder, CO: Paradigm, 2008.

Kellner, Doug. *Cinema Wars: Hollywood Film and Politics in the Bush–Cheney Era*. Boston: Wiley–Blackwell, 2009.

Kittler, Friedrich. *Gramophone, Film, Typewriter*, Geoffrey Winthrop-Young and Michael Wutz (trans.). Stanford and London: Stanford University Press, 1999.

Mamber, Stephen. 'Marey, the Analytic and the Digital', in *Allegories of Communication*, John Fullerton and Jan Olsson (eds). Rome: John Libbey, 2004, pp. 83–92.

Minh-Ha, Trinh T. 'The Totalizing Quest of Meaning', in *Theorizing Documentary*, Michael Renov (ed.). New York and London: Routledge, 1993.

Moran, James. 'A Bone of Contention', in Jane M. Gaines and Michael Renov (eds) *Collecting Visible Evidence*. Minneapolis: University of Minnesota Press, 1999, pp. 255–73.

Nancy, Jean-Luc. *The Ground of the Image*, Jeff Fort (trans.). New York: Fordham University Press, 2005.

Naremore, James. *The Magic World of Orson Welles*. Oxford: Oxford University Press, 1978.

Renov, Michael (ed.). *Theorizing Documentary*. New York and London: Routledge, 1993.

Rosenbaum, Jerome. *Discovering Orson Welles*. Berkeley: University of California Press, 2007.

Segrest, Taylor. Interview with Errol Morris (http://www.documentary.org/content/career-achievement-award-cinematic-investigations-errol-morris/).

Uricchio, William. 'Storage, Simultaneity and the Media Technologies of Modernity', in *Allegories of Communication*, John Fullerton and Jan Olsson (eds). Rome: John Libbey, 2004, pp. 123–38.

Virilio, Paul. *Live*, John Armitage (ed.). London: Sage, 2001.

CHAPTER 4

Parody: Targeting Cinema's Narrative Technics

Wherever one things stands, another stands beside it.

Chinua Achebe, *No Longer at Ease* (145)

Aristotle's thoughts on comedy are limited to a pile of fragments, now duly and very usefully gathered and annotated (see Richard Janko's excellent work on this). As fragments go, these are very fragmented indeed, and we glean not a great deal more than what is on offer in *The Poetics*, in which Aristotle's general disregard for the form is apparent. In this work, though, he does mention Hegemon of Thasos as the founder of parody, a mode of address, Aristotle claims – as with comedy generally – that makes men out to be worse than they are. Tragedy, on the other hand, presents men as better than they are. In both instances, representation does too little and too much at the same time, imitating life in a less than sufficient manner, but being productive as well, as the earlier discussion of mimesis examines. Hegemon of Thasos, though, makes an important mark on the Attican dramatic scene with his *Battle of the Giants*, which parodies a war that is under way in Sicily. The story about it runs as follows: news of a horrible defeat reached the citizens' ears during his performance, but the audience did not leave the theatre to mourn. Rather, they stayed to laugh and weep at the same time. Thus, one can hear an almost heroic rumbling in the reception of Hegemon of Thasos, despite Aristotle's dismissal of him, for here is the stuff of cultural critique through the comedic intent of performance withstanding the horror of events beyond the audience's control, to which they are none the less subject. Despite tragedy's elevation in *The Poetics*, the parody as a counter-song to the main song of drama – or even historical events or society – emerges as an almost unavoidable result of the main song, a means of revealing or highlighting the ode *as ode* – as representation, construction and performance – while maintaining a kind of critical distance or necessary perspective on it.

Film and parody share a relationship almost as old as the medium itself

– but then again, the same can also be said for the novel. as Cervantes's *Don Quixote* illustrates. The emergence and success of almost any new form or genre inspire an almost simultaneous parodic engagement with it. None the less, cinema arrives at a moment of profound self-reflexivity and dissatisfaction in Europe and the US with all tenable structures in the arts generally. The ubiquity of parody in twentieth-century art (music, literature, painting and so on), as charted by literary theorist Linda Hutcheon in her well-known book *A Theory of Parody*, in some ways reflects a particular type of ethos and critique that emerge from the industrialisation and intensification of mechanisation operative in the second half of the nineteenth century. The ability to reproduce art and other objects mechanically results in wider circulation and greater general familiarity with the art work and thus in critical engagements with production, authorship, originality and value, which of necessity emerge from the tradition. Walter Benjamin's seminal 1936 essay on the effects of this mode of production famously includes several views of cinema's uniquely technological nature and role in shifting engagements with and understandings of the art object and its place within socio–economic value systems, especially as an intensive technological step beyond the medium of photography. As an art medium for which there is no original (other than a negative) and only multiple copies, cinema provides a catalyst not only for analysing the status, value and even 'aura' of the unique art object but also for examining the results of intensifying conditions at play for other art forms and media.

Because of its place within these various trajectories, cinema seems to have had no choice but to be both parasitic (as parody is) and self-reflexive (as parody is) from the outset. We need only consider the Edison comedic short, 'Uncle Josh at the Moving Picture Show' (1902), or his earlier 'The Countryman and the Cinematograph' (1901), which made fun of early cinema audiences, or Keaton's many parodies of various genres, as well as of D. W. Griffith and other important directors, to get an initial indication of the centrality of parody to cinema and its history. Writing about the early work at the Keystone Studios by Mack Sennett, Simon Joyce argues that, if the Keystone films have a signature, it is one forged from extant styles and tropes developed by Griffith (from whom Sennett learned the cinematic craft). The house style at Keystone at this early and pivotal stage of Hollywood's development, Joyce writes, comes out of cinema and is constructed by 'a mediated reprocessing of formal elements and narra- tive traits associated with melodrama, the western, or the historical drama, each of which Sennett sought to neutralize' (50). If narrative and narrative types provided a means for cinema to become more than a display of the apparatus's operation or a visual effect in the years after its invention, then parody helped to codify and challenge those narrative types, as well as audience engagement with them. So prevalent has parody been in cinema from its beginnings that Dan Harries has argued persuasively for considering parodic film as being an anti-canonical canon (3–11): that is, as a *de facto* canon constructed from works that largely parody the mainstream canon of cinematic production.

Hutcheon claims that one formulation of parody is as '*repetition with critical distance*, which marks difference rather than similarity' (6, emphasis added). When one considers what this gap, this critical distance, allows and demands, then the ramifications of the gap, or distance, indicate parody's capacity to operate within a social and critical field. If the assertion that parody is one of the most pervasive enunciative modalities of art in the twentieth century proves viable, then the role of parody for cultural, self-reflexive critique provides a key to comedic film's efficacy, or not, for engaging cultural relations. Such would be the case especially as it pertains to cinema's own role within the generation and constitution of the cultural as it relates to technology, the senses, the Real, and the status of the art / visual object. Parody is inherently self-reflective, aware of its status as cultural production, product, medium and mode. Parody, though, depends on shared knowledge and shared codes, primarily of other texts (literary tradition, cinematic history, artistic tradition and so on): of media and texts that mediate experience. It is, therefore, essentially and unavoidably divided and doubled.

Parody might be even more splintered than its inherently divided nature indicates. If we extend Umberto Eco's critique of Bakhtin's carnivalesque to the modality of parody, then parody, like the carnivalesque, might well become a site of sanctioned transgression: simultaneously anarchic and conservative, transgressive and contained – Harries's 'anticanon-as-canon'. It is, therefore, worth considering whether or not parody overturns the power and authority of the logos (of the Law), or if it merely reinscribes this authority by drawing attention to the centrality of the main text (or ode) that the parody (para- and ode combined) addresses. These are central concerns to the comedic film tradition in relation to cultural critique. In this chapter, a few of the films discussed earlier are taken up again in light of their parodic operations, but I also provide a special focus on and extended readings of Mel Brooks's *Blazing Saddles* and Trey Parker and Matt Stone's *Team America*, as filmic parodies deeply concerned with cinematic genre and cinematic *techne* generally.

Genre and Parody as Cultural Critique

> And suppose for a moment that it were impossible not to mix genres. What if there were, lodged with the heart of the law itself, a law of impurity or a principle of contamination? And suppose the condition for the possibility of the law were the *a priori* of a counter-law, an axiom of impossibility that would confound its sense, order and reason?
>
> Jacques Derrida, 'The Law of Genre' (57)

> From its earliest days Hollywood has made films about itself and the process of film-making, usually with a comic tone. The self-consciousness of high art tends to be the self-consciousness of *the presence of the creator*; the self-consciousness of a genre film is of *the continuity of a historical method and form*.
>
> Leo Braudy, *The World in a Frame* (114)

Linda Hutcheon describes parody as something more complex than a simple imitation of another piece of art (or art form) for the sake of ridicule or amusement. She returns usefully to the Greek etymology of 'parody' as a combination of the prefix '*para*' and the root noun '*oedi*', yielding a song (GK. *oedi*) sung alongside (GK. *para*) the main song. In doing so, she looks forward and backward – that is, to the past usage of the term and its current/future uses – to articulate the historicity of the term in its more pejorative forms, as well as to account for its increasingly expanded and expansive current usage. 'In fact, what is remarkable about modern parody', she writes, 'is its range of intent – from the ironic and playful to the scornful and ridiculing. Parody, therefore, is a form of imitation, but imitation characterized by ironic inversion, not always at the expense of the parodied text' (6). Harries notes that 'para-' in Greek can also mean 'against' or 'counter', which connects parody to its more common usage as a mode of expression that spoofs or mocks another mode or person or text (5). The tension between a song sung alongside the main song and which comments upon it and one that mocks the main song allows us to understand film parody as potentially operating in either register, or both, at any given moment: commentary and agonism operating in tandem or separately within the same text.

The affix 'para-' has also come to be used to indicate an ancillary or supportive function of a more highly developed or trained professional function, as in the term 'paralegal', thus contributing to the generally received sense that parody is derivative of the main song, even parasitic of it, rather than being equal to the main song. As an ancillary to the main song, then, the parody underlines its relation to the ode as supplement, thus providing further credence to the interpretation of parody as bolstering rather than challenging the main form. Also, of course, 'para-' can mean 'beyond' or 'outside', as it is used in 'paranormal' phenomena. This last sense can be productive for considering film parody in so far as it indicates a departure from the norm (that is, cinematic convention and genre expectations) by underscoring the prevalence of the norm, and perhaps by bringing the norm to its logical conclusions, which is the failure of its operation. This kind of parody thus reveals the mechanistic repetitions operative in any form that can be identified as the norm or as being normative. The norm, then, might well be linked to genre, one readily recognisable in its contours and conventions, but also with parody as already engendered in the workings of the genre's mechanistic operation.

Derrida, in his examination of the law of genre (as well as the law *as* genre), writes of this lurking or ineluctably nascent 'para-' when he states

> what interests me is that this re-mark – ever possible for every text, for every corpus of traces – is absolutely necessary for and constitutive of what we call art, poetry, or literature. It underwrites the eruption of *techne,* which is never long in coming. (64)

All works operate with the mark of genre, he continues, but the mark of genre also bears its machinic underpinnings that simultaneously allow it to be identified and transgressed. Because parody depends as much on similarity as difference between the para-ode and the ode, then, 'reiteration' becomes important: repetition of elements, props, *mise-en-scène*, lines, actions, movements, characters and so on in the parodic text, borrowed from the parodied text in a modified, inverted, exaggerated fashion or exactly repeated (Harries 43–54). In such a manner, the machinic mark of the genre that reveals itself as genre becomes easy fodder for parodic commentary. Hutcheon's attention to difference in parody thus must rely structurally on heavy lashings of similarity and repetition within the parodic text for the difference to become one that makes a difference and is thus identifiable as such.

Genre and parody might, therefore, be almost unavoidably linked, in that the ode for which a parody provides commentary (is sung alongside) resides in the generic example of a genre, with the text for our discussion being the generic or genre film. With genre film parody, we might indeed find the purest form of parody, in that parody targets aesthetic conventions and stylistic devices operative in a dominant mode of expression or medium. Parody, in this instance, seemingly reaches Baudrillard's final stage of the image, which is the simulacrum, for it has essentially relinquished any referent to the real or the regime of representation at all. Serge Daney called the same phenomenon of images only referencing other images 'mannerism', which has an evocative appeal related to ideas of intertextuality and the closed circuitry of representational reference. The reference of the parody, the main ode, is simply a Hollywood genre, itself stylised to such an extent that it too is virtually bereft of any external referent. The image in the parody, as it is within the genre film, relates solely to its predecessors, which does not mean that there is no innovation – far from it. Rather, the hermetic nature of parody, as with the genre, allows for questioning the conditions of its existence, its aesthetic forms, its easily telegraphed messages to its audience versed in the literacy of the genre, and the technological forces (material and immaterial) that constitute its existence.

Like the genre film, parody is inherently self-reflexive, aware of its status as cultural production, product, medium and tempero-historical placement. The parodic modality depends heavily on audience literacy in the genre being parodied and in parody itself (though the same thing can be said for the genre film generally and for all of comedic film). As with irony, if the audience does not know that the parody is, in fact, parodic, then the parody fails. Indeed, this doubling is true of comedy generally, as previously discussed, relying on its dual-focused assumptions about audience knowledge and awareness. The converse, though, is also true, for a failed articulation in one genre or another might be valued for its unintentional (or unconscious) parodic qualities, and with aficionados of camp or schlock, often is.

This point is the fulcrum around which turns Mel Brooks's most famous film, now ironically or parodically a stage hit as well as *another* film, *The Producers* (1968). The plot centres on a failed theatre producer who bilks little old ladies out of their savings to fund his flops. An accountant tosses out the idle thought that if one were a fraud and willing to oversell shares in a play, then a flop could earn more than a success. The two unlikely partners pursue this illicit path. In order for the fraud to work, though, the play must fail. To safeguard their plan, the producers acquire the most egregious play they can – a musical entitled 'Springtime for Hitler' – and support it by hiring the worst director they can find, along with the most horrendous casting possible. Their plan is too carefully crafted and the results too actively bad, and the play reaches the tipping point. The audience is horrified and flabbergasted, at first, and then believe this grand failure not to be a failure at all but a parody. Those who had initially started to leave in disgust return to their seats in gales of laughter. The play thus becomes an accidental hit; too much of a bad thing becomes a good thing. At the heart of the first film is an examination of art and its potential, indeed inherent, possibility for parody (intentional or otherwise). With the musical about a musical (from a film), which Brooks first staged in 2001, and then with the film version of a musical from a film (2005), Brooks has made of his trajectory of avatars a palimpsest of parody and self-referentiality. Rather, it is a Möbius strip of intertextuality and medium engagement, in which there is truly 'no outside the text'. When we add Larry David's hilarious and touching, season-long tribute to the many forms of *The Producers* in his TV series 'Curb Your Enthusiasm', then the text, or ode, that is *The Producers* apparently has no end – rather like the series of Rocky films.

Leo Braudy's influential critical re-examinations of genre follow the lead of the French New Wave directors' unabashed embrace of Hollywood genre films to argue that they both appropriate and subvert tradition, convention and audience expectations (that genre is, in other words, variations on a familiar theme), and his writings anticipate some of the discussions about parody found in Hutcheon and Harries. Braudy writes that genre films 'can potentially criticize the present, because it too automatically *accepts* the standards of the past, to build subversion within received forms and thereby to criticize the forms instead of only setting up an alternative vision' (111, emphasis in the original). Other than converting a temporal moment into an actor with agency, Braudy's analysis vitally links up genre with its own potentials for subversion, rather like the argument made by Derrida. Braudy's assertions can be usefully extended to parody as that potentially disruptive dimension resident within genre films. If we recast Braudy's statement slightly to put 'automatically' in italics rather than 'accepts', then *techne* becomes the central operating factor in genre, cinematic production, and audience reception or expectation. As Hutcheon and others claim, parody posits within itself both 'a law' (the tradition, the form, content, the ode and so on) *and* its transgression (the parody). The *techne* that makes the cinematic work possible at material and immaterial levels also erupts, as Derrida calls it, in the disruption of its operation: the failure of the machine in the logic of its production.

To follow Eco's critique of the carnivalesque mentioned earlier, how might this inherently divided and doubled nature of genre film – as well as parody – be problematic for cinema in particular and popular culture in general? Bakhtin understands and anticipates Eco's concerns by arguing for a deep kind of carnivalesque, one with potentially revolutionary possibility. The genre film and parody, however, seem to elude these more transformative possibilities of inversion because of their essential dependence upon the ode. Bahkhtin's claims for a carnivalesque (read as genre and/or parody here) would demand that the work or act transcend the conditions of its existence, which seems impossible if we are to follow Derrida's point that all works of art, of necessity, partake of genre. In addition to the unavoidable role of the ode in the problems facing parody (or genre film) as cultural critique, though, we can add the sources, contexts and conditions of production, as Adorno and Horkheimer reminded us back in the 1940s. For these two Frankfurt School theorists living reluctantly in the US, popular culture was no different from cars or weapons (the two US products they cite) in their complicity with the production of consumer culture, and thus popular culture products are unable to be either 'Art' or revolutionary. Lucid and prescient though their argument remains, Adorno and Horkheimer maintain stark divisions between high art and popular culture such that no Hollywood production could breech, thus rendering all such films unredeemable.

However, the line tracked by Derrida, Braudy, Hutcheon, Harris and others in relation to parody and genre returns us to the interpretive aporia of any text: its simultaneous and unavoidable participation in intertextuality and its ineluctable transgression of the same (its failure to conform completely to its genre). Parody can, from such a position, be understood as a collective and dispersed enunciative modality, one that leads us to a meditation, intentional or not, on the various *techne* that makes film possible at all. To form a sense of how parody operates with and in relation to the genre (ode) it comments upon – the *techne* of genre and of cinema properly – we can return to Keaton's *Sherlock Jr.*, discussed in the second chapter.

If parody takes aim at an aesthetic form, then it need not be tethered solely to one medium. Keaton's film works through a few different genres and several different media, though the main parodic target is cinema and the *techne* of its narrative/genre teleologies. With a few decades of audience literacy and knowledge of shared codes and conventions to draw on, the 1924 film is clearly a movie about movies, about how cinematic illusion and lived existence influence one another, commenting (the para-ode) on both art and existence. But Keaton's starting point for a parodic examination of how various media mediate our lives is literary, drawing on its primacy in the creation of 'the detective', whom Edgar Allan Poe invents in the 1840s. Poe's Dupin led to Sir Arthur Conan Doyle's Sherlock Holmes, who has thrived in novels, short stories, radio plays, theatre, TV and cinema up to the present. Poe's detective tales and his detective Dupin simultaneously set the mould for the detective and break it, for Dupin is omniscient, and his analytical skills become increasingly hilarious and parodic as he moves from insight to insight, making Holmes seem a bumbler by comparison. As the hero of the movie that his dream-mind generates (and that *is* a movie, not a dream), he evades every trap through skill, intelligence and sheer luck (the phrase a near-homophone with

Sherlock). In real life (that is, the diegetic world within the film narrative), the girl solves the crime with her own intelligence and initiative. In spite of the title, Dupin appears to be the immediate parodic target in the film because Keaton's cinematic dream detective possesses the same ludicrous omniscience and skill.

Keaton's parodies of the genre conventions of the novel and popular fiction lead to another genre, the 'how to' or 'do-it-yourself' texts, which influence the lead character prior to his involvement in the 'dream screen'. The first sight the audience has of Keaton's character is a shot of the book 'How to Be a Detective', before the camera pulls back to reveal Keaton reading the work, indicating that the book precedes the character-qua-person. That he takes instruction from the book and takes it well becomes a plot device, but more importantly sets up the 'happy ending' of the film, in which he takes his cues on romantic reconciliation directly from the screen action of the romantic drama he is projecting in the cinema. His waking state equals cinema-as-guide as much as how-to-book-as-guide. Cinema pervades his conscious mind as easily and as readily as it does his unconscious mind, with the conventions of genre novels and films ticking over like clockwork.

The dream film, or dream-as-film, contains many of the conventional detective tropes and objects but also provides a pointed parody of dramatic and action films by spoofing a chase scene (much as the Keystone Kops did), coupled with a parody of D. W. Griffith's stock last-minute rescue. Keaton trots out Griffith's staple, complete with cross-cutting and rhythmic editing, thus mixing the cinematic genres he is parodying even further. Perhaps the darkest and most savage parody of Griffith's last-minute rescue comes from the anti-Griffith Erich von Stroheim, in his exquisitely dark comedy and heaping slice of naturalism, *Greed* (1924). In von Stroheim's ending, he relies on *mise-en-scène* and little editing as the two protagonists, chained to each other, fight to the death in the desert over a chunk of gold they can never spend. There is no last-minute rescue, only death in the desert, and thus this is the complete opposite of Griffiths's standard heroic feats (even if the 'heroes' are the Ku Klux Klan). Keaton's parody is more directly repetitive of Griffith's style and narrative results. His eponymous detective eludes numerous near-accidents as he races solo on the handlebars of a motorcycle, with cuts to the cabin where the female lead trembles before a leering fiend bent on assaulting her virtue. Sherlock Jr. arrives at the cabin, crashes into a log, flies off the handlebars through an open window and knocks the villain senseless. Just when the audience thinks the day is saved and when the normal two-reeler would have ended, Keaton exaggerates the danger and the chase continues anew with the villain's gang turning up. Keaton revelled in film parodies but cast his net widely here to play with the conventions of editing (including getting caught in the machinery of editing in the dream film), the goal-oriented trajectory of narrative closure (which he reaches twice before the final fadeout, and even then the character is left confused), and the stereotyped last-minute rescue as happy ending, amongst other conventions codified strongly by the early 1920s.

Sherlock Jr. serves as a forerunner for films produced in the late Seventies and Eighties, such as *Airplane* and the *Naked Gun* series by Zucker, Abrahams and Zucker, who had their first hit in the form of an intermedial parody of TV called *The Groove Tube*. In the Nineties and Noughts, film parody seemingly telescoped solely to being interested in satirising genres or specific films, including the spoof of *Gladiator* and *300* called *Meet the Spartans*, the *Twilight*/Anne Rice/vampire parodies, horror films such as the *Scary Movie* series (which already parody themselves in George Romero's films and *Texas Chainsaw Massacre*), and *Not Another X Movie*, in which X equals teenage, gay or independent. In a sense, these films are probably more akin to pastiche than parody, as Fredric Jameson has argued the difference, in that there is little acknowledgement of or interaction with cultural history or established forms but more simply 'a random cannibalization' of styles or specific films, though fully with the intent to mock (18).

Although many of these might well be ephemera and are simply daft films designed for teens so that they can laugh at rude jokes or reinforce their identity through allegiances against certain popular cultural phenomena, they reinforce genre audiences and hone their tastes. Thus teenage boys laugh at the *Twilight* parody, *Vampires Suck*, because the target films (the ode) largely appeal to teenage girls. The attack on genre in these instances serves to reinforce genre directly and indirectly as audience diversification and targeting become increasingly splintered and specific, securing one sector of an audience in its collective disdain of films designed for other demographics. The larger machinery of genre and parody reveals multiple effects in narrative expectation, audience formation and the enunciative modality of parody, one largely shorn of content and solely operating with regard to *techne*.

The US as Western: Mel Brooks's *Blazing Saddles* (1974)

Most of the immigrants came from Italy and Eastern Europe . . . They were filthy and illiterate. They stank of fish and garlic. They had running sores. They had no honor and worked for next to nothing. They raped their own daughters. They killed each other casually. Among those who despised them the most were the second-generation Irish, whose fathers had been guilty of the same crimes.

E. L. Doctorow, *Ragtime* (15–16)

Well, if that don't beat all. Here we take the good time and trouble to slaughter every last Indian in the West, and for what? So they can appoint a sheriff that is blacker than any Indian. I *am* depressed.

Taggert, in *Blazing Saddles* (played by Slim Pickens)

Appropriately and literally linking parody to its root, *odein*, meaning 'song', *Blazing Saddles*' use of music provides a key to interpreting its parodic concerns on multiple levels. Deploying music as a source for critical engagement from the very start, the film features Frankie Laine singing the title song, thus drawing on his fame as a singer of themes for westerns ranging from 'Rawhide' to 'Mule Drive'. Both of these tracks, which helped make Laine famous, are invoked with the crack of a whip, as one might imagine hearing on the (cinematic) trails of the Wild West, and the whip cracks loudly to herald the lyrics, themselves a mishmash of good and evil binarisms and heroic stances for the just and the right, embodied by the noble sheriff immortalised in the song. A similar kind of mock-song is provided by the character Lilli von Shtupp, based on Marlene Dietrich's turn as a fatal temptress in *The Blue Angel* (Josef von Sternberg, 1930) and her role as a saloon singer in *Destry Rides Again* (George Marshall, 1939). (Interestingly enough, Dietrich parodied herself as the singing femme fatale in Hitchcock's terrific film *Stage Fright* (1950), and thus opens Madeline Kahn's hilarious performance to several inter-textual references.)

Some of Brooks's more subtle musical allusions operate in a self-referential manner. One of these is the moment in which Bart's death sentence has been rescinded and he is, at the same time, made sheriff of Rock Ridge, becoming the first African-American lawman in the West. As we see Bart decked out from hat to saddlebag in Gucci designer leather, the non-diegetic music is as anachronistic as his costume: Count Basie and his orchestra belting out a swinging version of the jazz standard 'April in Paris'. However, the music turns out to be diegetic after all, as Bart rides through the desert and up to Count Basie himself, referencing Basie's then-contemporary gigs in the desert oasis known as Las Vegas. The desert as the visual setting that most evokes the West-as-frontier within the western genre here becomes fully commodified in the form of desert-as-playground, putting a new spin on the 'wild' of the Wild West.

However, the most intricate of music-based parodic elements comes in the first sequence of the film, a complex set of references related to the West, race, slavery and their manifestations in the earliest emergence of US popular culture. The scene opens with a point-of-view shot on a railroad cart (an apparatus often used for tracking shots and thus twigging the audience to the many meta-fictional elements of the film). The head of the railroad work crew jumps from the cart and chides the group of blacks laying track in the blazing sun for not singing while they worked. 'When you was slaves', he goads them, 'you used to sing like birds. Now give us a good coon song.' Coon songs as a form of popular music swept through the Reconstruction-era US, improbably helping to link the recently war-torn but now reunited states of America in a celebration of race known as minstrelsy or blackface performance. Coon songs were a staple of such shows, which became the forerunners of vaudeville (and which lived on much longer in the UK and its colonies, so much so that one could buy 'Darkie' toothpaste in Singapore and Malaysia into the 1990s, complete with a top-hatted, blackface visage). The workers react badly but Bart (the black sheriff-to-be) calms them and whispers to them a plan for a song. Rather than a coon song, the work foreman and his crew receive a sophisticated *a capella* arrangement of Cole Porter's 'I Get a Kick Out of You'. The song is brought to an untimely close by the foreman, who says, 'What the hell is that shit? I mean a song, a real song,' which he exemplifies as gospel tunes or Stephen Foster songs. The songs written by Foster made him the first composer of country-wide hits in an emergent popular culture form on a national scale, and many were indeed coon songs, including 'De Camptown Races', the song that the foreman and his crew enthusiastically start singing and dancing about to, much to the amusement of Bart and his labourer friends.

In this one opening moment (along with the movie's title track), Brooks establishes the main parodic target of his film: the performative dimensions of race as an integral source of US popular culture since its advent in post-Civil War America. The western might well have proved itself the genre of Hollywood cinema that was the least self-reflexive regarding the racial dimensions of its mythic status, its reclamation of white US culture advancing on the empty (though occupied) and dangerous (because of the anger of those occupying the land that the whites perceived as empty) space. When race plays a role in the western, it is usually in relation to the Native Americans that the white settlers had to fight, and, in some of the more enlightened films, a grudging respect between combatants occurs or a minor inter-racial love interest might emerge. However, the role of blacks in representations of the West, much less the western as a genre, is virtually non-existent. Rather, as the so-called empty space of the frontier was indeed populated with indigenous populations, so the white civilisation advancing through the West was actually a good deal more hetero-geneous than popular culture depicts. This fact reflects the racial turmoil that continued at the time that Brooks was making the film, thus laying the foundations for his parodic work: a western filtered through post-Civil Rights American sensibilities.

The Western and Why it is Useful to Parody it

The existence of an area of free land, its continuous recession, and the advance of American settlement, explain American development.
>   Fredrick Jackson Turner, *The Frontier in American History* (1)

Not long after Fredrick Jackson Turner's 'The Significance of the Frontier in American History' (1893) had established the myth of the American frontier as a site for individual spiritual, economic and almost exclusively masculine renewal, as well as a site for starting life anew, the West as central to the collective US psyche was taken up by Hollywood. Through methodological moves that became familiar to cultural studies many decades later, Turner examines the roles of 'high' literature and popular culture (the 'penny dreadfuls' of the mid-1800s and the 'dime novels' of the late 1800s), as well as the Wild West shows, to argue that a shared consciousness had been established by these forms of representation sur-rounding the centrality of the West in the auto-generated definition of the US. The power of the West in various media staked claims widely, including Franz Kafka's imaginary trip to Oklahoma in his novel *Amerika*, lending some credence to Turner's central, if somewhat reductive, thesis. A substantial body of critical work has been carried out on the western genre as an active site for nostalgic US myth-making, from the 'dime novel' to the Wild West show to radio to cinema to TV. A knowing example of the genre revisited with embedded parody can be found in the Coen Brothers' remake of *True Grit* (2010). Their version ends with the elderly protagonist performing his earlier life in a Wild West show: the immediate conversion of actual agonism to spectacle and performance for profit, hence parody.

The explanatory power of Turner's analysis grows exponentially when coupled with the concept of 'Manifest Destiny' that coincided with the roiling growth of the US population and the desire for land acquisition prevalent in the early part of the nineteenth century. The belief that the US was ordained by history and/or God to spread the ideals upon which the republic had supposedly been founded to the entire breadth of the continent was widely if not universally held, despite its (always problematic) Universalist claims. As famously articulated in an editorial by John L. O'Sullivan, who first used the phrase 'Manifest Destiny', certain influential sectors of the US saw the nation as one disconnected from the tyrannies of the past and leading all other nations to a future in which the virtues of the US nation would be emulated throughout the world. These virtues, enshrined in the nation's founding documents, institutionalised Enlightenment ideals, and those who believed in Manifest Destiny believed these ideals to be universally held – values such as equality, democracy and freedom. Never mind the fact that the nation still allowed slavery, a paradox that would tear the country asunder. The fact that Manifest Destiny meant closing the frontier is but another irony. The widespread displacement of indigenous Americans, if not their outright slaughter, in the name of advancing the greater brotherhood of nations and steering a futural trajectory for a nation of immigrants fleeing oppression and genocide in Europe makes for an even greater irony. Yet it is out of the loss of the frontier and its mythical possibilities, especially with the advancement of 'civilisation' and legal institutions, that the western as a genre in literature, and later radio and cinema, emerged, especially in the naïve glorification of the frontier.

The cry 'Go West, young man!' accords with the ideal of the frontier as *tabula rasa*. Similarly, the desire for spaces free for human self-fulfilment emerges from specific Enlightenment ideals, ones even carried into the Romantic critique of the assumptions underlying Universalist claims. Goethe's final manifestation of Faust is essentially as a land developer, as Marshall Berman persuasively argues, reclaiming land from the sea through ruthlessly organised intensive labour. Faust, giddy with pride and accomplishment at resculpting the earth, knows it has come at a cost: 'Human sacrifices bled / Tortured screams pierced the night' (11127–8). All of it, though, is meant for the greater good, for freedom – for life on a scale greater than that of the individual found in the masses. His is a site that will 'open up space for many millions / To live, not securely, but free for action . . . To walk on free ground with people who are free!' (11563–4; 11580). Faust's geographical imagination accords with the frontier in that it is one especially formed for specific types of individuals and not others, despite claims for universal values. The myth of the frontier as blank slate clearly articulates a racial ideal related to empire and colonialism (for example, the 'discovery' and naming of places with the aid of native guides). The western genre has largely and unreflexively participated in this myth, perpetuating the tropes and discursive practices that show how, as John Beck writes, 'a vocabulary of vacancy and always already wastedness is put to the service in the erasure of temporal con-

nections between violent conquest and its retelling as creation myth'
(56).

The famous penultimate line of Mark Twain's *Adventures of Huckleberry Finn* find Huck expressing his desire 'to light out for the territory' (that is, the Indian territories) because he wishes to be free of the meddling ways of society and institutions. He wants his own frontier experience, a place where there are no rules and the white male can test his mettle against nature, not social formations and constraints (265). It is worth noting that Huck is a mere boy, one who has been taught some important lessons about and by others, lessons about alterity, the lives of women and slaves, choice and possibility. With such a social arrangement built on power, violence and suppression, it is no wonder that Huck yearns for a Faustian open space such as the frontier. However, Twain is clearly mocking the adolescent belief in the existence of just such a space free from history, control and authority, a childish yearning that underpins an important and lasting American self-image and mythos – for in order to obtain this kind of ahistorical space free of ideology and history, it means clearing the history and occupants of the land: an impossible and self-defeating task. And yet the western continues to tell this story time and again through numerous shining heroes – all white, all male, all good (or mostly good).

Standing in the way of the frontier's regenerative potential for the nation as a whole was slavery, and in this manner, the pegging of geographical space to ideological imaginary is radically altered by shifting attention away from a North–South divide to a settled–'free' dichotomy (here demarcated as the frontier) as determinant of US collective visions of itself. Henry Nash Smith, in a famous essay on (and critique of) the frontier thesis, claims Turner focused, successfully and persuasively in Smith's view, more on the West, rather than the pro-slavery South or anti-slavery North, for a geographical significance in US history. Brooks, in an almost Swiftian move, combines them both in *Blazing Saddles* to show that the savagery of one geographical ideal (antebellum South) accorded with another (the frontier West), with no slippage as to whose ideal this was and for whom it was shaped, no matter where it manifested itself.

In fact, even though the 'closing of the frontier' in the post-1849 Gold Rush period also closed off elements of Manifest Destiny, the supposedly inexorable march of US values as universal was resurrected and exported in the explicit US imperialism that emerged at the end of the nineteenth century, just as the nascent film industry was getting under way. In the run-up to what became the Spanish–American War, William James famously said that imperialism was tantamount to the country 'puking up its ancient soul'. Noble (and colourful) though the sentiment might be, it belies a self-delusion about the frontier, the West, Manifest Destiny and the nation's (then very recent) history, even in the better angels of the country's soul. Still within the West as frontier after the Civil War, as the US worked to drive off Native Americans and settle the territory (thus hastening the demise of the frontier in the realisation of Manifest Destiny within the continent), amongst those who worked as actual cowboys on the actual frontier was a disproportionately large number of African-Americans, especially runaway slaves or the children of runaway slaves who found no place in 'free' US society, North or South, for a black man. This particular scenario led to Bob Marley's famous song 'Buffalo Soldiers', about the first all-black cavalry units, composed of ex-cowboys and slaves, such as the 10th Calvary Regiment formed in 1866 in Fort Leavenworth, Kansas. Marley's song comments on the divide-and-conquer strategy of the US government, in which blacks were used to wage the Indian Wars (wars on Native Americans, as well as on their buffalo, which meant killing off that which sustained the tribes). With this form of intranational imperial strategy, then, no matter who dies, white power is served, for the combatants on both sides are essentially undesirable in the dominant vision of the nation's future.

Returning to the importation of Manifest Destiny elsewhere, these units went on to fight the next step of American expansion in the Spanish–American–Cuban–Filipino War of 1897. The continuity of the missions on the Western frontier and the Filipino archipelago led to a discourse of the frontier being used in the later quasi-imperial (if not fully imperial) Vietnam War, in that land held by the Viet Cong military was called 'Indian Territory'; at the same time, the cavalry units were converted into helicopter units, their sources of mobility and attack shifting from horses to airborne machines. Made at a moment when the Vietnam War, though nearing exhaustion, none the less continued through an escalation of the US presence and of violence, *Blazing Saddles* takes on the frontier mythos at home and abroad, but most especially within the film industry's romanticisation of the expansion of the US in the form of the lone, white male confronting savagery on the edge of the frontier and learning existential, moral, metaphysical lessons of manhood and nationhood in the process.

To do this, Brooks engages in meta-cinematic gestures from the outset, as we have heard in relation to the film's title song. This is followed by the first shot of the film: a tracking shot on a railroad cart running along the kinds of tracks that are used for tracking shots, such as the one that opens the film. A hermetically sealed sense of the film-as-film emerges in this sequence. The railway proves important for the plot, as it did for the rapid settlement of the West and the end of the frontier, not to mention for the establishment of cinema as an early reproductive technology. In the opening of the film, it provides a means of highlighting the fact that this is a film about films, especially but not exclusively the western. The handcart is used for another gag that is dependent on the camera's ability to move, or not, to narrate and enframe the audience's vision. In this instance, two of the African-American labourers are sent on the cart to look for quicksand that might spoil the route laid out for the train tracks. As they hit a spot in the track and stop, the two labourers begin to sink, slowly sliding out of the bottom of the frame until a cut reveals that they are indeed caught in that topographic morass and they scream 'Quicksand!' The effect alludes to Robert Paul's similarly comic still camera in his 1903 *A Chess Dispute*, in which the brawlers have fallen out of the frame, allowing the audience to catch but glimpses of the fracas: body parts in violent motion, clothing, extreme gestures of mayhem, all popping up into the frame from just below the static camera's view. The awareness of the camera eye equalling the audience's eye, as well as the comic potential of action taking place outside the enframed eye, makes the cinematic frame work by actually not working – an excellent example of the gag tapping into the comedic operation of failure.

If the opening provides meta-cinematic moments reliant on framing, the ending reveals a sustained sequence of breaking one formal cinematic frame after another, at the level of narrative, genre, set, screening and film history. At the same time that Sam Peckinpah was making his westerns, which became explorations of 'closed space and shrunken time', as Sean Cubitt evocatively describes them (215), Brooks explodes the genre in terms of space and time by systematically delaying and deferring the film's closure, with each denouement leading to another stock but false ending and thus revealing its artifice at every turn. Although one can read a temporal–spatial implosion in Peckinpah's early 1970s westerns, one finds in Brooks the western as the venue not of elegiac loss but of utter absurdist relevance for a dynamic and expansive presence, one not containable by cinema as a whole, much less the western genre.

A sequence near the diegetic ending of the film exemplifies Brooks's explosive (literally) take on the genre and the medium. The Rock Ridge townsfolk's ruse to take 'the bad guys' by surprise entails their building a mock version of their town laden with dynamite. The audience then sees their handiwork from a distance: a simulation of the town that is actually the set of Rock Ridge used in the film. The simulated town is the 'real' town when perceived diegetically by the film audience. Not only is the diegetic reality of the visual surface of the town revealed for what it is (a film location set), but this is done in such a fashion that it becomes, through yet another sleight of cinematic hand, something else: a fake version of the town. The inability to contain even the set within the parameters of film convention is an initial step in the direction of a cinema of the absurd that is absurd because it is about cinema, one that involves consistent unfoldings of cinematic boundaries. The ruse works and a large fight between the combined forces of the Rock Ridge citizens, the disenfranchised railway workers and the massive array of 'bad guys', including Nazis and Ku Klux Klan members (anachronistic but ideologically appropriate for the frontier), literally spills out of the confines of the western genre into a musical. The film suddenly cuts from the fight to a sound stage for a large musical number reminiscent of MGM's golden era. As the fight swells on the musical set, it too spills out into the film lot, where the movie is being made. Not even the large sound stage can contain Brooks's assault. The fight continues in the actors' canteen, thus involving all manner of film character types recognisable by their respective genres. When the villain of the film emerges not in the nineteenth-century West but from the 1970s canteen bathroom, he encounters the large-scale, cross-genre brawl and flees the studio. There he hails a cab and, in another kind of reversal of Keaton's dream sequence in *Sherlock Jr.*, asks the taxi driver to take him off the picture.

The film's many allusions to Keaton further the meta-cinematic concerns of the parodic engagements, especially in the film's so-called conclusion. Just as Keaton's character in *Sherlock Jr.* is caught in the compulsion of narrative closure found in Classic Hollywood Cinema and, in fact, turns to cinema for a sense of how narrative closure might work in his own life, so some of those in Brooks's film are driven (literally) to the cinema to see how the film they are in ends. They go to Grauman's Chinese Theater, where the film *Blazing Saddles* is showing. Evil to the end, the villain tries to get in with a student discount, though he is clearly middle-aged. When the heroes, Sheriff Bart and the Waco Kid, enter the cinema, they are laden with concession stand goodies, and the Waco Kid expresses his hope for a happy ending because he (as does the larger Hollywood audience) loves a happy ending. The film, then, cannot be contained in the western genre or in its diegetic setting, which is revealed as a set. Next, it cannot be contained in another sound studio and moves inexorably, like the US through the frontier and beyond, into the entire studio lot and beyond film production to film distribution and projection. The final gunfight takes place outside the cinema, with the villain falling on the famed Walk of the Stars that has the handprints and footprints of Hollywood legends embedded in cement. To find out if there is indeed a happy ending, the heroes return inside to watch the end of the picture. With the diegetic frame restored (for the moment), the end entails a stereotypical farewell speech by Bart (which is greeted by all the Rock Ridge citizens and their new neighbours from the railway, who respond in unison with 'Bullshit!'). Then he and the Waco Kid ride off, the closing soundtrack tugging at the emotions, only to have them dismount and ride off in the sunset together in a stretch limo, as befits Hollywood stars, if not Hollywood heroes.

'Genre enclosure', argues Braudy, 'enforces the happy ending as both a formal necessity and a false thematic summary' (121). The inexorable trajectory of narrative closure becomes the fodder of Brooks's manic parodic moves, an ironic capitulation to the conventions of the happy ending making such an ending impossible. Again, the nod to Keaton's *Sherlock Jr.* and his parody of Griffiths helps reinforce the historicity of and explicit engagement with film parody. Indeed, the teleology of the parodic object – the West, the frontier and Manifest Destiny, as glorified in an exemplary US popular culture genre – finds an analogy in the teleology of narrative demands in Classic Hollywood Narrative. The machinic drive to settle the West is parodied in its representational twin: the western film. The same willed naïveté that finds a populated land empty, believes its values to be universal and possesses faith in its nation as the culmination of historical teleology (for example, the goal or end of history) also operates in the demand to have plots not only neatly concluded but endowed with happy endings too: the teleology of plot and narrative. However, with a parody of a genre film, such as one finds in *Blazing Saddles*, the diegetic narrative has no real purchase, only becoming a stock frame upon which to hang Brooks's parodic interventions and play. Thus the always problematic dimensions of generic endings become foregrounded, but in so doing, when the main song or ode is that of Manifest Destiny (and/or the future of the US nation, shed of its violent and racist past and present), then the role of cinema in the machinic demands, delights and disappointments of generic narrative and film becomes the more pertinent object of inquiry as Hollywood returns, yet again, to meditate on its mediations.

Team America versus the Axis of Evil (and Hollywood Cinema)

> Team America has once again pissed off the entire world by blowing up half of Cairo.
>
> News reporter, in *Team America*

> America, fuck yeah! Freedom, it's the only way.
>
> From the title song for *Team America*

I've always acted alone. Americans admire that enormously. Americans admire the cowboy leading the caravan alone astride his horse, the cowboy entering the village or the city alone on his horse. Without even a pistol maybe, because he does not go in for shooting. He acts, that's all, aiming at the right spot at the right time. A Wild West tale, if you like.

Henry Kissinger, in an interview with Oriana Fallaci from 1972

As Tom Englehardt has persuasively argued in his book *The End of Victory Culture*, US popular culture embraced the western anew during the advent of the Cold War, and in greater volume due to its ubiquity on TV. The 1960s and 1970s, though, found Hollywood struggling to maintain the standard Hollywood heroic western, as Sam Peckinpah, Sergio Leone, Arthur Penn and others created anti-heroic westerns. These mirrored events and concerns about potential expansion on the part of the nation further into 'Indian Territory', as exemplified by Vietnam, and the tropes of the genre failed to hold. It was not too long before the frontier of the West yielded to the frontier of space, as the Cold War grew increasingly entrenched, with the deeply ironic success of *Star Wars* (George Lucas, 1977) leading the way. Englehardt documents, charts and argues for an intimate linkage between predominant genres in Hollywood production and geopolitical policy, with an ebb and flow between the two (as exemplified by Reagan dubbing the Strategic Defense Initiative 'Star Wars'). The 1980s and 1990s saw the emergence of the action picture as a dominant genre, with films such as *Top Gun* and the *Die Hard* series, as well as *Rambo* (which aided a sense of individual victory after collective defeat). When the War on Terror emerged after the 9/11 attacks, the Bush administration drew upon a number of tropes ranging from the western to the action film, the latter taking centre-stage at the now-infamous public relations snafu of 'Mission Accomplished'. With the 'golden hour' sunlight hitting the deck of an aircraft carrier, the President dusted off his flying skills (sort of) to land a jet fighter on the deck and to swagger out and claim premature victory in Iraq in 2004 (Englehardt 305–33).

The *longue durée* of American empire obliquely alluded to in *Blazing Saddles* finds the frontier being exported within the colonial impulse. This yields to the global intervention of the Truman Doctrine, which stated that any act anywhere in the world could be interpreted as bearing upon US sovereignty and security. As a result, the US conflates with and becomes the global, its interests reflected everywhere. This sense of Cold War surveillance and action is resurrected in the War on Terror, and we find them marked in Hollywood genre shifts from the western to the action film. Trey Parker's film, *Team America: World Police*, as its title indicates, broadly and widely parodies the deep connections between various Hollywood genres, American geopolitical strategy and the reductive US public discourse that reflects both. The film clearly parodies action films (what Parker called 'Jerry Bruckheimer films') while simultaneously mocking the interventions undertaken by US geopolitical strategy that had been justified by the invocation of 'freedom', showing how clearly the two complement and reflect one another. As with their TV show 'South Park', Parker and his co-writer, Matt Stone, blend strong political parody and satire with adolescent, indeed suspect, humour – all of it very silly, childish, angry and pointed.

The virtuosic opening sequence neatly parodies 'the grabber' that opens almost all Hollywood action films, a large-scale action sequence that grips the audience by the eyeballs and ears with its stunts and pyrotechnic display, while providing a glimpse of the lead characters doing what they do best: action – and, as in the western, subduing 'bad guys'. At the same time, the film foregrounds its primary political parodic target: US desires to police / control the world, to act like real-life action heroes, and therefore reap the gratitude of those in any locale where US intervention occurs. *Team America*'s grabber performs the parody that runs through the entire film, that of revealing the difficulty of separating Hollywood film from US policy and the public discursive beliefs that underpin them. By setting the sequence in Paris, Parker and Stone provide the kind of global urban locale filled with icons that action films almost always deploy (even if for the opening sequence only), while also poking fun at the anger generated toward France when it refused to participate in Bush's 'Coalition of the Willing' – the name his administration gave to the nations that agreed to act under the auspices of the United Nations and participate in the invasion of Iraq. France's refusal to participate generated much ire and grandstanding in the US, as members of Congress engaged in gestures of 'patriotism' by denouncing the French, the silliest of these coming when Republican representative Bob Ney, who controlled the House of Representatives' cafeterias, changed the menu and offered 'Freedom Fries' rather than 'French Fries'. (A joke from the same time claimed that, in France, American cheese became known as 'Idiot Cheese'.)

The action-film qualities of the movie are beautifully staged in this sequence, with cinematographer Bill Pope drawing on his experience of having shot several Matrix and Spiderman films. The sequence opens with a rather crude demonstration of puppeteering, tricking the audience into believing that the 'B-grade' quality of the cinematic performance on display in the shot and relished by kitsch aficionados everywhere is what the viewers have in store – rather like 'South Park's low-tech animation practices. The shot pulls back, though, to show that this expectation is created and determined by the camera's frame as it reveals a marionette operating the strings of the puppet we initially see. This initial shot pulls still further back to reveal a highly polished marionette-populated evocation of a Parisian street scene, complete with street vendors, a mime, birds flitting about and gardens complete with topiary poodles. The entire effect is one of clashing skill levels, as the puppetry (no matter how skilled) rends the sleek surface of the action film. Further, the entire shot, coupled with the marionettes, compels audiences to see the artifice of the film and that it is film.

With all the subtlety of an action film, Parker and Stone show the tranquility of daily life disrupted by the presence of evil: thawb- and turban-wearing men with beards. We meet them when a small French boy, who is happily eating an ice cream and singing 'Frère Jacques' (the only French song many Americans know), stops dead in his tracks when confronted with the villainy of these Middle Eastern men; here we see the innocence of a child awed by the evil the men incarnate within the action film world, an insight the audience gains through both the stereotyped representation of 'terrorists' in the Noughts and the stereotyped Middle Eastern music that plays when the men appear. Parker and Stone pull out all the stereotyping and reductive stops to display the ways in which Hollywood telegraphs genre conventions and audience reactions to them, the latter being ever receptive.

The sequence ripples with the kind of action hero quips and one-liners in the midst of flamboyant violence made famous by Clint Eastwood in cop movies but taken to a new level in Arnold Schwarzenegger action films. Here the lines include: 'Why can't they ever do this the easy way?' and 'Hey terrorist, terrorize this.' The cracks in the dialogue show when the Team identifies the terrorist threat posed by the men who scare the boy, and they announce from a helicopter hovering over Paris, 'You in the robes, put down that weapon of mass destruction and get on the ground. You are under arrest.' The lines reveal the naïveté of US interventionism that works with and emerges from cultural ignorance and a belief that the entire planet is under US jurisdiction. When the men bolt and action is required to stop them, machine guns blaze and there is more collateral damage than in most live-action action films. One of the Team members pulls out a ground-to-air missile that he fires at an escaping terrorist. The shot misses its mark and hits the Eiffel Tower, which topples over, hitting the Arc de Triomphe, which explodes rather than collapses. The hilarious compression of the iconic cityscape further reinforces the stereotyped views of Paris that many Americans hold, but more so the cinematic shorthand from which this knowledge is derived. The fleeing terrorist with bomb in hand seeks refuge in the Louvre but he has been spotted with visual tele-technologies by another Team America member in a jet fighter. The pilot locks on to I. M. Pei's pyramid in front of the building (perhaps never more ironic or parodic itself than in its invocation here) and fires a missile into the museum. Bits of burning rubble fly as yet another landmark is destroyed in the quest for justice in the name of global (read as US) security. Rooted to the spot amidst the destruction are the Parisians, agape in shock as the Team celebrates the shot. The Americans turn to the assembled and traumatised crowd, to have one Team member announce in mangled, Frenchified English, 'Bonjour everyone. Don't worry. Everything is bon. We stopped the terrorists.' Adding further insult to massive injury but again skewering the unstinting belief in the correctness of US action and its being desired by the rest of the world, the team says upon departing, 'You're welcome, Paris,' the tourist/cinema portion of which there is precious little left.

Even before we reach the opening action sequence, the titles indicate the tripartite topoi of parodic intervention. The camera moves through the name of the film's studio, Paramount Pictures, as if the chirographic representation were composed of massive three-dimensional metallic slabs hovering over an image of the earth seen from space. The studio's name recedes so it can be contained within the frame (and thus read), before receding further into space and exploding. The film's title emerges in the same manner, the camera seemingly pulling back through the words 'Team America World Police', also rendered in giant steel letters and hovering in space above the earth. The film's title then blows up, leaving just the earth as seen from a distant spot in space. Then the earth too explodes.

In this concise title sequence, Parker and Stone have managed to link action film parody to Hollywood global hegemony and iconography, as well as to the evidently self-destructive nature of US geopolitics, intended, in the Cold War policing and surveillance words of General Douglas MacArthur, 'to defend everywhere'. The simple escalation of adrenaline and testosterone-driven hyperbole that constitutes the action film's tone of self-import to the display of Hollywood's power and then to US global military might and desire provides a synecdoche of the consistent set of parodic critiques that run throughout the entire film, in that these three dimensions, or targets, are inextricably intertwined and inter-related. Just as the film parodies military overkill with regard to weapons overkill in US operations, it also parodies the action genre and cinematic overkill. An arty and artful example of the latter can be found in Coppola's *Apocalypse Now* (1979). Writing of the director's massively influential Vietnam-era recasting of Conrad's *Heart of Darkness*, Baudrillard argues that 'the war became film, the film becomes war, the two are joined by their common hemorrhage into technology' (60). Baudrillard's argument that the US makes film the way it makes war is echoed and expanded parodically in Parker and Stone's film to include not only geopolitics and cinema but also the public discursive ideology of the nation's position in the world and the nature of its relationship to the globe, as found and formed in cinema.

The inordinate truncating of the different languages used in the film (French, Arabic, Korean) also reflects both US geopolitical and Hollywood myopia. Thus all locations in the film are identified by their distance or relation to the US (for example, 'Paris, 2,258 miles from America'; Panama is indicated as 'south from the real America'), and all the locales are visualised as US clichés and stereotypes of them. The language of the terrorists is almost solely comprised of gibberish and repetitions of 'derka, derka, Mohammed jihad', alluding to both Hollywood's indifference to languages other than English and the same lack of curiosity or knowledge on the part of much of the US citizenry. French comes in for similar treatment in the opening sequence. As with *Blazing Saddles*, the use of linguistic stereotypes often corresponds with ethnic and national stereotypes, as when Spottswoode, the head of Team America, realises he has placed the blame for the threat that is central to the film's thin plot in the wrong part of the world:

> Team, this is all my fault. I was overzealous in Cairo. I let racism cloud my judgment. I was so sure the ultimate terrorist was Middle Eastern, but I didn't realize he was a goddamn Gook. I'll never be a racist again.

The language of a certain ethnic stance vis-à-vis the US vision of itself, as found on the Western frontier and parodied by Brooks, is found on the global frontier, fighting terrorism and parodied by Parker and Stone.

The self-reflexive opening shot of the puppeteer draws attention to cinematic artifice in animating images and creating the illusion of movement. When the shot pulls back to reveal that it is actually a French puppeteer operating within a film composed of far superior, though still rather crude, puppets, the film opens up a regression of self-reflexivity that reminds audiences that action film heroes are 'meat puppets' for the film genre they occupy and not actors in a political arena outside the film frame (if one can be said to exist). The puppets in the film are not 'uncanny' or *unheimlich* at all; nor do they have the mimetic purchase of the computer-generated animation that has swamped traditional animated film. Nor are these puppets the beautiful stop-action claymation work found in Nick Parks's 'Wallace and Gromit' shorts or Tim Burton's *The Nightmare*

Before Christmas (1993). They owe more to those cheesy animations found throughout the history of cinema, in Willis H. O'Brien's *The Lost World* (1925) and *King Kong* (1933) or Ray Harryhausen camp classics such as *The Seventh Voyage of Sinbad* (1958). However, the puppets used here are more directly related, of course, to the children's supermarionation adventure TV series *Thunderbirds*, which ran on British television in the 1960s. The basic premise of the show echoes elements found in *Team America*: a global group of action heroes called 'International Rescue' that saved the world from various forms of evil. Parker and Stone simply swap the Tracey family and its international friends for a national team with a supposedly international agenda, while having them occupy a present that looks much like the 2060s future of the TV series in terms of high-tech gadgetry for dealing with international undesirables. With its artifice fully on display in the form of marionettes animated by puppeteers during real-time filming, as opposed to stop-action, *Team America* literally shows the filmmakers pulling the strings of the action, dissolving audience capacity for entering the diegetic world of the narrative and thus serving as a reminder of the many ways in which cinema cannot be contained within its frame.

A key parodic target of the film is Hollywood's fetishisation of actors and stars, especially the position of celebrity actors with explicit political agendas. The puppet of Janeane Garofalo mocks this self-importance by participating in it and claiming that, 'As actors, it is our responsibility to read the newspapers, and then say what we read on television like it's our own opinion.' The role of actors in the political domain is echoed by the need to recruit an actor (Gary) for the team. The actors' collective action replicates, though from a different part of the political spectrum, the kind of naïve US interventionism found in the War on Terror and enacted by Team America as metonymic of adventure film heroes. In an especially adolescent joke, the Screen Actors Guild becomes the Film Actors Guild, in order to yield the acronym F.A.G. Yet, in a different register, we find a quotation outside the Film Actors Guild building from the eighteenth-century satirist, Alexander Pope: 'Act well your part, there all honour lies' (74). The combination of high-school derision and sophisticated literary allusion becomes a less jarring juxtaposition when one remembers (as Parker and Stone clearly do) the scatological nature of Pope's more barbed social satires, and that, when the quotation from his 'An Essay on Man' is returned to its context, it reveals itself as a bitter riposte to governments that use ideals relating to human equality as an excuse to ignore conditions of social inequity, for 'honour and shame from no condition rise' (74). Returning to Hollywood proper, Parker and Stone remind us of the nature of the industry on all sides, including that of the altruistic and 'politicised' actors, by having the palm trees outside the F.A.G. building bear fronds crafted of US paper currency. Not to ignore the geopolitical domain and the massive financial influence of the military, the filmmakers have the male members of Team America sport buckles made from the 'tails' side of Susan B. Anthony dollar coins.

As with *Blazing Saddles*, music and songs play important parodic roles in the film, and with some of the same topics of parody at stake. Once again, the parody is literally a song sung alongside and commenting on the main song (ode) of Hollywood cinema, as well as genre demands and effects. After the opening action film sequence, the title song comes roaring in on the machismo–laden, hard-rock guitar chords of US triumphalism, with the assertive first line, 'America', belted out in a baritone, followed by the song's background refrain that punctuates most of its declarations: 'Fuck yeah!' Drawing on a war lineage that takes into account both World Wars but which continues to have resonance with US audiences into the twenty-first century, the lyrics continue, 'Here we come again to save the motherfucking day.' The rationale for global interventionism emerges in a quieter, almost elegiac bridge, the lyrics of which assert, 'It's the dream that we all share. It's the dream of tomorrow. (Fuck yeah!),' parodying the conflation of the US point of view with that of the world's, in which the 'I' becomes, if not a Royal, then an imperial 'we'. The same conflation occurs with the beautifully oxymoronic line, one that appears in the song but could just as easily be heard in a jingoistic speech by a politician or read on a placard at a political rally: 'Freedom: it's the only way.' Parker and Stone get the skewed logic of Pax Americana down into one logically self-defeating statement. The title song continues with a list of qualities meant to justify US geopolitical power, as well as the superiority of its culture and history. The list, with the lyric punctuation following each item, combines elements from fast food to fast technologies and more: 'McDonalds! (Fuck yeah!) Wal Mart! (Fuck yeah!) Gap! (Fuck yeah!) Baseball! (Fuck yeah!) NFL! (Fuck yeah!) Rock 'n' roll! (Fuck yeah!) Internet! (Fuck yeah!) Slavery! (Fuck yeah!).' With the last item, the assertions about 'freedom' that littered the War on Terror rhetoric wear more than a patina of hypocrisy, leading us back to the issues in Brooks's western, made in an age just following the Civil Rights movement and the associated internal, racially motivated violence. Such historical echoes, at a time when Guantánamo Bay was in full operation, are not lost on the rest of the world, though the US population might miss the ironies.

Just as the title song parodies the kind of hard-rock song indicative of certain action films, a ballad from the film about 'the costs of freedom' sends up trite patriotic music that, though probably sincere, often seems simply to trade in cheap Pavlovian patriotism. The same lyric register operative in the theme song functions in this one: that of sentimental nationalist moment (a trait encountered in Barry Levinson's *Wag the Dog*, addressed in the next chapter). Songs such as Toby Keith's 'Courtesy of the Red, White and Blue', the Merle Haggard Vietnam-era 'The Fightin' Side of Me', Brooks and Dunn's anthemic 'Only in America' or Alan Jackson's 9/11 elegy 'Where Were You (When the World Stopped Turning)?' all play to a level of knee-jerk sentimentality – just the kind of fare ripe for Parker and Stone. So they offer the song 'Freedom Isn't Free', a patriotic slogan that is actually bandied about. With lines like those found in Keith's 9/11 revenge song, 'And the eagle will fly and its gonna be hell / when you hear Mother Freedom start ringing her bell,' or his words 'My daddy served in the army where he lost his right eye / But he flew a flag in our yard until the day he died. / He wanted my mother, my brother, my sister and me / To grow up and live happy in the land of the free,' the parodic mode is almost already invoked within the genre, as these kinds of lyrics tread the thin line between sentiment and the parody of sentimentality.

Parker and Stone offer 'Freedom isn't free / it costs folks like you and me. / And if we all don't chip in / We'll never pay that bill.' The chorus continues with another in a series of questions addressed in the second person directly to the listener; 'And if you don't throw in your buck o' five, who will?' Taking the colloquial 'buck o' five' a bit farther, they have the singer intone, 'Freedom costs a buck o' five.' This bit of play provides an answer to the question that arises from the statement 'freedom isn't free.' The earlier answer, 'it costs folks like you and me,' gives way to a minimal sum, rather as lives in battle throughout the centuries were held as worthless – the cannon fodder of World War I or Thomas Hardy's Drummer Hodge. The lower classes served up to war's machinery, especially in the history of the twentieth century, were disproportionately represented in Vietnam and in the current 'volunteer military' in the US. The song within the narrative carries the immediate parodic task of linking action-film deaths on the US side to country-song sentimentality, but includes the resonance of a longer story in which sacrifice has been asked (as the song does) of a specific class in far greater numbers and percentages (the class that, ironically, also comprises the bulk of the audience for patriotic country songs) than of others, especially those that occupy positions in government.

Music and songs in the film also work at more self-reflexive, meta-cinematic levels. The love ballad is called '*Pearl Harbor* Sucked, and

I Miss You,' aimed directly at Michael Bey's romantic World War II drama. The intertextual cinematic reference pertains to a film that is also apparently cashing in on post-9/11 heroic representations based on another historical moment when the US was the victim of a 'surprise attack'. Using the directly mocking mode of parody, as does this entire film, the lyrics say that the protagonist misses his love interest as much as that movie 'missed the point, and that's an awful lot, girl'. The more interesting meta-cinematic piece, though, is a song about montage and how it operates within Hollywood cinematic narratives. As with the theme song to the meta-television series 'It's the Garry Shandling Show', which begins with the line 'This is the theme to Gary's show,' the montage song uses film construction and convention as content:

> The hour's approaching to give it your best
> And you've got to reach your prime
> That's when you need to put yourself to the test
> And show us the passage of time
> We're gonna need a montage
> Ooh, it takes a montage
> Show a lot of things happening at once
> Remind everyone of what's going on
> In every shot, show a little improvement
> To show it all would take too long
> That's called a montage
> Girl, we want a montage
> In anything, if you want to go
> From just a beginner to a pro
> You need a montage
> Even Rocky had a montage
> Always fade out in a montage
> If you fade out it seems like more time has passed in a montage . . .

The joke clearly comes from having the narrative and editing techniques operative in montage serve as the lyric content. Through the meta-cinematic move with the song (not to mention the puppets), during which an actor trains to become part of the 'world police' team, Parker and Stone return us to the mechanistic nature of genre film to reveal its formulaic organisation. In this instance, the machinery of the action film reveals, in parodied moments, its deep affiliations with the more mechanistic dimensions of patriotism and nationalism, as articulated in geopolitical policy and public discourse during the War on Terror. To the filmmakers' credit, the parodic reach is such that it takes aim at all elements complicit in the momentum of audience expectation working in tandem with blink-ered political actions. Their film is by no means limited to the moment of its production, working on the heady mix of popular culture forms and jingoistic sabre-rattling that has spoken to the US populace (and increasingly the world's) for more than a century, certainly back to Hearst and Pulitzer and their role in that pivotal expansionist move that resulted in the Spanish–American War discussed earlier.

Some elements of the film are very much of the moment, however metonymic of specific processes they might be. For example, when Spottswoode realises that the Team's computer has given them incorrect information, he reprimands it. The smart machine that serves as technological source and guide for Team America's missions and intelligence gathering is, appropriately enough, named I.N.T.E.L.L.I.G.E.N.C.E. (though just what the acronym means is never made clear). Spottswoode scolds the computer as one would a beloved pet dog, saying 'That was bad, I.N.T.E.L.L.I.G.E.N.C.E. Bad I.N.T.E.L.L.I.G.E.N.C.E.,' mocking the excuse of 'bad intelligence' that some in the Bush administration and the Pentagon claimed led them to undertake the war in Iraq, which proved so ill fated. The rush to police the world failed, so some of these people claimed, due to faulty information gathered through various intelligence sources. Other than the humorous use of linguistic play to convert information into a subject with agency, the implicit reliance on high-tech that has so determined military engagement since the advent of the Cold War becomes, in parodic light, an opportunity to consider the large-scale effects of consistently removing 'the human element' from military operations and even governmental decision-making, all of which take place in the name of speed and efficiency. The art of the motor, as Virilio calls it, that resides at the centre of Western historical change manifests itself in the immaterial elements of ideology and the material effects and causes of cultural production and consumption, including, profoundly, the cinema camera.

In Brian Henderson's reading of the centrality of the 'cartoon' (read here as puppet or flat) figure in the work of Preston Sturges, he argues that, though cartoonish, these characters need to be taken seriously. He likens this to a proliferation of such paradoxical situations in the post-World War II comedy of Joseph Heller, Terry Southern and Stanley Kubrick, to name a few. Henderson attributes the proliferation to the larger social forces of 'total mobilization' that so determined and stereotyped lives in the US during the war and into the postwar period (170–1). This mechanistic dimension of existence, linked to the totalising technologies of warfare, industrial production and cultural production, and resulting in the narrowing of individual horizons and the types of lives that Sturges and others address, repeats itself in larger and grander ways as the country hurtles through the century, a technicity with a momentum of its own, repeating and intensifying along the way. Parker and Stone's parody of action films and US geopolitical strategy, as well as US public discourse about both (that results from and in both), stages this momentum . . . with marionettes.

Team America's Uncanny Other in Gameland – a Coda

In a very brief sequence from Sacha Baron Cohen's 2012 political satire *The Dictator*, we see the despot of the film's title playing a Wii game on a wall-sized screen. The tele-haptic game in this case is called 'Wii Terrorist 2K12' and includes the following levels: Kabul Kidnap, Tokyo Subway, Munich Games, Car Bombing, London Underground and Achille Lauro. Proleptically anticipating the next chapter, this satirical segment shows comedy's capacity to address that which is unspeakable in the public discursive sphere. Several of the specific incidents – the Munich Games and the Achille Lauro, for example – have been the subject matter of cultural productions already: a film by Stephen Spielberg and an opera by John Adams, respectively. The trick here is to convert the horrific into the comic to highlight the horror rather than attempt to replicate it. To do so, Cohen translates the humour on to the cinematic anxiety about film as a distinct medium in the early twenty-first-century media landscape and thus plays up cinema's ineluctably intermedial nature. Indeed, the screen in the movie on which the game is shown might well be as large as, if not larger than, many screens on which this film will actually play in many a mall cineplex, and will almost certainly be a good deal more 'cinematic' than the majority of screens on which the film will be consumed, ranging from portable DVD players to laptop computers to hand-held devices.

As with *Bowling for Columbine*, the ever-growing ubiquity of screen culture becomes part of the joke as the computer game enters cinema. Similarly, CCTV camera footage enters computer games after the Colorado shooting. The same cute Anime graphics aesthetic that one finds in the Columbine computer game appears in Cohen's game, whether it is for the third-person clip of a beheading or the first-person shooter of the Munich Games level. The game looks as if it has been designed for children, creating a disparity between game content and graphic aesthetic. With Cohen's incorporation of Wii technology into the film, the tele-haptic wand is variously wielded as a sword, a gun and shovel digging mass graves (complete with blade striking the earth sound effects) in this grimly hilarious throwaway segment. The satire here revolves around the ways in which media reinforce power structures rather than resisting them. In the Columbine computer game, we have unrealistic computer game graphics and aesthetics that seek to defuse the realism and hyper-realism of computer games (such as first-person shooters) in order to deflect the blame being levelled against the gaming industry for adversely affecting the Columbine shooters. With the Wii Terrorist 2K12, the graphics satirically reveal the violent medial fantasies that computer games gratuitously traffic in, as well as the overtly realistic graphic aesthetics they deploy. The sequence reminds audiences that, in addition to being multibillion-dollar entertainment industry products, these games are also US military recruitment and training tools. Similarly, those groups that the US military targets use videotapes and DVDs to recruit and train their members. The stakes represented by these vision machines, as Virilio and others have pointed out, are high. But then again, they always have been. The complementary scopic legacies of culture and the military have antecedents that reach back to antiquity, and Cohen's satiric snippet indicates this genealogy in some of its current guises.

Works Cited

Achebe, Chinua. *No Longer at Ease*. New York: Knopf–Doubleday, 2011.

Baudrillard, Jean. *Simulacra and Simulation*, Sheila Faria Glaser (trans.). Ann Arbor: University of Michigan Press, 1994.

Beck, John. *Dirty Wars: Landscape, Power and Waste in Western American Literature*. Lincoln, NB, and London: University of Nebraska Press, 2009.

Benjamin, Walter. 'The Work of Art in the Age of Its Technological Reproducibility', in *The Work of Art in the Age of Its Technological Reproducibility and Other Writings on Media*, William Jennings, et al. (eds). Cambridge, MA, and London: Harvard University Press, 2008, pp. 19–55.

Berman, Marshall. *All that is Solid Melts into Air: The Experience of Modernity*. New York: Vintage, 1982.

Braudy, Leo. *The World in a Frame: What We See in Films*, 25th anniversary edn. Chicago: University of Chicago Press, 2002.

Cubitt, Sean. *The Cinema Effect*. Cambridge, MA, and London: MIT Press, 2004.

Daney, Serge. *Cine-journal 1981–1986*. Paris: Cahiers du Cinéma, 1986.

Derrida, Jacques. 'The Law of Genre', Avital Ronnell (trans.). *Critical Inquiry*, 7:1, 1980, pp. 55–81.

Doctorow, E. L. *Ragtime*. New York: Fawcett–Crest, 1974.

Eco, Umberto. *Carnival!*, Monica Rector (trans.). Berlin and New York: Mouton, 1984.

Englehardt, Tom. *The End of Victory Culture*. Amherst: University of Massachusetts Press, 2007.

Fallaci, Oriana. *Interview with History*. New York: Houghton–Mifflin, 1977.

Goethe, Johann Wolfgang von. *Faust*, Walter Kauffmann (trans.). New York: Anchor, 1962.

Harries, Dan. *Film Parody*. London: BFI, 2000.

Henderson, Brian. 'Cartoon and Narrative', in Andrew Horton (ed.), *Comedy / Cinema / Theory*. Berkeley: University of California Press, 1991, pp. 153–73.

Hutcheon, Linda. *A Theory of Parody*. Urbana and Chicago: University of Illinois Press, 2000.

James, William. Quoted in George Tindall and David Shi, *America: A Narrative History*, vol. II, 4th edn. New York: W. W. Norton, 1984, p. 989.

Jameson, Fredric. *Postmodernism, or The Cultural Logic of Late Capitalism*. Durham, NC: Duke University Press, 1991.

Janko, Richard. *Aristotle on Comedy: Towards a Reconstruction of Poetics II*. London: Duckworth, 2006.

Joyce, Simon. 'Genre Parody and Comedic Burlesque: Keystone's Meta-cinematic Satires', in *Slapstick Comedy*, Tom Paulus and Rob King (eds). New York and London: Routledge, 2010.

King, Geoff. *Film Comedy*. New York and London: Wallflower, 2010.

Pope, Alexander. *Essay on Man and Other Poems*. New York: Dover, 1994.

Smith, Henry Nash. *Virgin Land: The American West as Symbol and Myth*. Cambridge, MA: Harvard University Press, 1974.

Twain, Mark. *The Adventures of Huckleberry Finn*. Boston: Bedford, 1995.

Turner, Fredrick Jackson. *The Frontier in American History*. Available at http://xroads.virginia.edu/~hyper/turner/ 1893.

Virilio, Paul. *The Art of the Motor*, Julie Rose (trans.). Minneapolis: University of Minnesota Press, 1995.

CHAPTER 5

The Unspeakable and Political Satire: Performance, Perception and Technology

Other dogs bite their enemies. I bite my friends to save them.

Diogenes of Sinope

'Jack, Jack,' I said. 'You don't want to do it. Remember what happened to the guy who dropped the bomb on Hiroshima? He went crazy!'

'That asshole? He was not properly brainwashed. I,' he said with great pride, 'have been properly brainwashed.'

Spalding Gray, in Swimming to Cambodia

In the early part of the 1910s in the US, a small but influential movement to eliminate Darwinism and evolution from public education started to gain some legislative momentum, eventually resulting in laws forbidding such instruction and ending in one of the great trials of the century: the Scopes Trial of 1925. The trial became a radio and media spectacle featuring two of the best-known orators of the age: populist and perennial presidential nominee William Jennings Bryan and legal star for civil and constitutional rights Clarence Darrow. The two adversaries had once been friends and colleagues but fell out primarily over their religious views. Bryan famously took a swipe at geology, Charles Lyell, what his scientific investigations wrought in relation to the age of the earth, and Church dogma on the matter by saying, 'Better to trust in the Rock of Ages than to know the age of rocks.' The trial became a circus, in spite of the seriousness of the legal issues at stake, open-air tents containing preachers contending with hawkers of everything from food to cloth to special occasion goods. In Zelig-like fashion, stores began selling simian-themed items, including the 'monkey fizz' drink. Radio and newsreels, in a media frenzy indicative of the age, circulated the entire event. Additionally on offer was a Coney Island sideshow freak with a conical skull named Zip (an obvious reference to the minstrel character, Zip Coon), who was put forward as 'the Missing Link'.

The missing link in the Great Chain of Being leading from animals to humans became, in the early part of the twentieth century, a source of speculation in popular culture. Willis H. O'Brien, who later did clay animation work for Edison, created the socio-political claymation satire *The Dinosaur vs. the Missing Link: A Prehistoric Tragedy* in 1915, poking fun at the evolutionary issues at play in the public discursive sphere with his witty tale of love and hunting (or rather love as hunting) in the prehistoric era. Wild Willie, the missing link, is a precursor for the larger monkey named King Kong that would terrorise New York, also rendered by O'Brien. Wild Willie's own stomping grounds and victims had a much smaller reach than did the giant ape, but he looks like a miniature version of his iconic avatar. In a Spenserian 'survival of the fittest fashion', Wild Willie meets his end when he mistakes a dinosaur's tail for a snake (snakes were on the menu for his dinner that night) and tries to kill and eat the tail. In the battle between two symbols of a prehistoric past that counters Biblical timescales – the dinosaur and the missing link – the former comes out on top. The 'hero' of the tale, though, takes credit for the dinosaur's deed and, by so doing, secures the hand of the love interest, who has the best line in this silent film. When her many Stone Age suitors turn up at her cave, she says via intertitle to the eventual mock link-slayer, 'Won't you come into the drawing room? I should offer you tea but unfortunately tea has not yet been discovered.' O'Brien became a specialist of claymation featuring dinosaurs and monstrous creatures, performing special effects for *The Lost World*, as well as *King Kong*; while making no claims to larger social or scientific theory, he was a canny satirist who took the pulse of the public at the time, anticipating the Scopes Trial's more farcical dimensions. Had he been around almost a century later, he would have found fodder for the same debates surrounding evolution, creationism and their place within US public education still circulating in the US. More importantly for our purposes, though, is the satirical subtitle that calls the film 'a prehistoric tragedy' because it reveals an awareness of the ways in which genres and aesthetic form reify content and ideas. O'Brien trawls the battles over scientific and religious speculations about the past and sees them as fodder for hucksterism, manipulation and political manœuvring, as well as earnest conflicts of ideological systems, while showing the role of the emergent medium of cinema in the perpetuation and dissemination of the reification of these contending views.

From elections to war to media manipulation, the satirical possibilities are many and varied, and US film comedy has often taken up political issues as the source for satirical engagement. Comic film, though, also pushes the boundaries of good taste and decorum in public discourse by asking if specific modes of gallows humour or satirical intent can be tolerated. Satire (as in the case of the films taken up in this chapter, as well as others such as *Dr. Strangelove* (Stanley Kubrick, 1964)), according to Linda Hutcheon, is didactic, with a clear, intentional lesson. In a strong sense, satire assumes and relies upon the efficacy of human agency, and therefore pertains to social or cultural critique. The satiric target lies, to a certain extent, outside of specific textual or aesthetic forms, though these too can be the objects of satire. Parody, on the other hand, demands and reflects a parallel text – or a set of texts that constitute a genre – and comments more on it. The ode, as it were, bears the load of parodic targeting.

Although satire is a literary form in and of itself, it can also comment upon, or be qualified by, other forms. Parody, then, can also be satirical. It can critique an aesthetic production for the purpose of explaining a moral, or satirical, position. So, parody might be satirical, but it need not be. Hutcheon's point about parody's prevalence in twentieth-century artistic production, though, indicates that there is almost always some satirical dimension to parody, if of nothing else than the conditions of possibility that allow for the work (both ode and para-ode) to exist at all. Parody necessarily involves imitation, quotation and alteration of a generic tradition or set of practices, while satire need not follow such intertextual references. The parodic target is the mode of representation as much as any other element, if not more so. Similarly, parody need not necessarily be attacking or critiquing the parodied text. For satire, a clear target for ridicule exists – an extra-textual target that might have to do with values, behaviour, societal norms, or injustices. The mode of satirising, its method of presentation and representation, need not be constrained by a textual set of practices (Rose 80–6). An important element of parody resides in its attempts to expose the machinations of realisation found in the parodied text, to thwart its coming to be, to make it impossible for the audience to suspend disbelief.

> While parody is in general a much more ambivalent form than satire, in that it makes its 'target' a part of its own work, when parody has been used in satire it has usually given the latter some of the ambivalence characteristic of parody, and helped to make new and multi-layered works of art from the process of satiric reduction. (83)

The satiric films taken up in this chapter all pertain to and relate to the intersection of warfare or militarisation and cinema, or some art form and / or set of technological practices that metonymically invoke cinema. In his groundbreaking work on the visual machines of the military and those of entertainment, *War and Cinema*, Paul Virilio states that, 'since the battlefield has always been a field of perception, the war machine appears to the military commander as an instrument of representation' (20). Virilio traces the emergence of cinema alongside and in dialogue with the emergence of an increasingly tele-technologised military apparatus, with an ebb and flow of influence and dependence. He further claims that a kind of homogeneity of the visual field existed prior to World War I, and that battle experience with more lethal ordnance resulted in further explosions of art and politics and the fracturing of the visual into a heterogeneity of visual and sensory fields. Cinema, with its myriad filmmakers leaving the trenches or the cockpits of World War I to enter film studios (and return to battle with World War II), played a central role in this fragmentation (20–2, and *Pure War* 45–56). The symbiotic relationship between military and cinematic visions that lasted over a century provides a pivotal and perhaps primary mode of technological momentum for shaping the image and how we engage it: 'the logistics of perception', as Virilio's subtitle puts it.

In some films addressed in this chapter, the war film genre as a codification of American unity and nationalism that came to underscore the US involvement in World War II becomes the site of satiric engagement. The war film as most manifestly codified emerges in the run-up to and through World War II. Although the war film seems to have congealed in a specifically nationalistic and patriotic model at this time as part of the overall war effort (somewhat akin to the strategy of 'total war', as articulated by Ernst Junger and other German political philosophers), its modes of enunciation remain solidly within the classical narrative film of Hollywood (Polan 45–100), with all of its fissures and gaps. The sense of continuity between, for example, the gangster film and a war film about the Axis forces meant that audiences need only shift their sympathies and antinomies slightly from one baddie to another, with the heroes equally self-evident and replaceable. Narrative film, even simplistically rendered, does not easily slide into propaganda per se due to its inherently polyvalent nature. That said, the slight change of key from one genre to the next could well result in an ease of representability of the war and war effort into the daily lives of US moviegoers (Polan 63).

Initially using two groups of two films each and then concluding with a briefer examination of a fifth film, this chapter first looks at the explicit content of the initial group as it pertains to the unspeakable, and then provides a critical engagement with the role of visual technology in the formation of propaganda through fiction film and the constitution of the Real for politically motivated aims. Each of the films discussed in this chapter uses, in some manner, other forms of performance and art than cinema to highlight simultaneously the limitations and efficacy of film's technics. Ernst

Lubitsch's 1942 film, *To Be or Not to Be*, clearly exemplifies the capacity of cinema to address the unspeakable, for it includes not only ridicule of the Nazis, who at the time were largely represented as thoroughly evil rather than potentially ridiculous, but also direct discussion of the operation of concentration camps at a time when the US government did not admit their very existence. Further, Lubitsch's desire to play with frames of reality and performance links directly to Keaton, while placing in question the veracity of political action. A few years earlier, Leo McCarey and the Marx Brothers used nineteenth-century operetta to ridicule the machinations of nationalism to set Europe once again on the rails to war. *Duck Soup* satirises the rush to war, war-profiteering and political intrigue at a time when Hollywood largely towed the Washington line.

The second group of films provides a transition from content in relation to the political as institutional parameter to the technology of vision, surveillance, and power of visual culture as the vehicles to enact politics. Jonathan Demme's film version of Spalding Gray's critical engagement with cinema and politics in *Swimming to Cambodia* uses theatrical monologue and various scales of intimacy operative within cinematic and theatre performance to supplement Hollywood's engagement with 'serious issues' in mainstream cinema. Barry Levinson's and David Mamet's *Wag the Dog* carries the idea further and foregrounds the technologies of cinema, television and surveillance to achieve Baudrillard's third level of simulation for political manipulation available in the 1990s. In this film, the entire store of visual memory available through photographic images (including satellite photos) becomes central to understanding the film's resonance with its present and past intertextuality, but more importantly, an uncanny prescience for its future. In concluding the chapter, Albert Brooks's satire of political do-goodism in *Looking for Comedy in the Muslim World* finds stand-up comedy to be one of the means through which the soft-power elements of the War on Terror could be pursued, and in so doing reveals the ethnocentrism that underscored so much of the public discourse around US policy in the post-9/11 moment.

With each of these films, as mentioned earlier, the satire employs cinema in conversation with or exploiting other modes of performance, such as vaudeville, operetta, theatre (including monologue), television, popular music or stand-up comedy. Parody depends directly on a form of representation and is bound by its generic demands, while satire can and does borrow from other representational modes for its enunciation, even incorporating those modes into itself. That cinema, rather like the novel, can easily embody and employ other representational strategies bespeaks its elasticity and, to a certain extent, its hegemony, for it is an art form (or business commodity, or technological concatenation) capable of incorporating resistance into its overall endeavour. The extent to which these capacities blunt the power of critique operative within satire, though, remains a subject of question and concern.

Satire and Dark Comedy Circa World War II: *Duck Soup* and *To Be or Not to Be*

After the First World War Paul Valéry said, 'Henceforth, civilizations knew that they were mortal.' After the Second World War, after Auschwitz and Hiroshima, we knew that henceforth they were dead. From then on we were post catastrophe civilizations, representations in light of catastrophe.

Jean Baudrillard, Hot Painting (23)

The transgression of taste and decorum, to say and do what cannot be said or done under the circumstances that prevail at any moment, is an integral aspect of comedy. One important dimension of this includes laughter and comedy themselves: what can be joked about and what cannot. Often, this has to do with power, but more frequently with the tragedy of daily life, of public or profound loss or violence that provides the comedic with the possibility for gallows humour. Every disaster, even a scrupulously planned disaster such as one finds with state-sponsored genocide, immediately generates a 'dark' comic response or utterance. This is not only the logic of the absurd at play – of pratfalls in the void – but also the logic of opening the ground of what can be addressed in the public domain to highlight what usually cannot be said. Such comedic utterances gesture toward what is allowed to transpire under the polite facade of keeping specific topics 'taboo' and off limits to decent human interaction. When the metaphysical level of mortality collides with the geopolitical or the nationally political, then the moment is ripe for such comedic interventions, and they always occur, despite their apparent futility and bravery, even if operating under the naïve assumption that transparency will lead to ethical behaviour. We can label all those areas demarcated by social, moral, political and even metaphysical censure the Unspeakable, and with the establishment of such a discursive space there has been an anarchic impulse to be the enunciator of the Unspeakable, which is essentially the thrust of the two films in this section: Leo McCarey's Marx Brothers satire from 1933, *Duck Soup*, and Ernst Lubitsch's 1942 satire of the Nazis, *To Be or Not to Be*.

Hail Freedonia! Duck Soup

We got guns. They got guns. All God's chilluns got guns.
> Minstrel moment in the going-to-war song sequence

If any form of pleasure is exhibited, report it to me and it will be prohibited. I'll put
my foot down, so it shall be. This is the Land of the Free.
> Rufus T. Firefly, singing about the laws of his administration

Like Keaton, the Marx Brothers were much loved and admired by the Surrealists, especially Dalí, who wrote a screenplay for them entitled 'Giraffes on Horseback Salad' (1937), drew pictures of Harpo complete with lobster headgear, and photographed the brothers. Dalí called the Marx Brothers films 'the summit of the evolution of comic cinema', after his sustained praise for Keaton and Mack Sennett, because their 'entertaining schizophrenias' led to a 'true and palpable lyrical amazement' (77). Antonin Artaud, Luis Buñuel and others sang their praises in early reviews of their films, recognising in the brothers kindred spirits in their shared assault on rationality, and an extension to the US of the kind of sensibilities found in the *fumisme* aesthetic practised in nineteenth-century France, which influenced the avant-garde (North 7–9). These sensibilities displayed an almost mechanical negation of artistic and communicative values, opting for maximum noise in the communications message, ridicule and nonsense.

The brothers' engagement with Surrealism is as much linguistic as it is visual. The Marx Brothers position themselves in an anarchic relationship to the dominant language of the US, and each provides a position along a continuum of undermining English and taking advantage of the general elasticity of language generally. Christopher Beach argues that each of the three comedic brothers stakes out a position within the immigrant's relation to the linguistic conformity (and thus to knowledge, per se) that all immigrants must endure (23–46). Groucho exemplifies the over-achieving and rapid-fire mastery of the language, Chico the inadvertently punning creole of mock Italian English, and Harpo the extreme position of silence, using gestures, noises and objects to communicate. To take Beach's argument a step further, each brother in his own way manifests, embodies and performs the unspeakable in a way that brings a larger political agenda to bear on their commitment to wholesale chaos. All meaning is undermined at every turn. Facile and eloquent as Groucho is, he generates non sequiturs and discursive leaps that make a mockery of mastery. In the famous opening sequence of *Duck Soup*, he enters as the newly appointed leader of the nation Freedonia and regales the woman

responsible for his appointment with a barrage of verbiage that adheres to
the associative logic of dreams:

> Mrs. Teasedale: As chairwoman of the reception committee, I welcome
> you with open arms.
>
> Groucho Marx as Rufus T. Firefly: Is that so? How late do you stay
> open?
>
> M.T.: I've sponsored your appointment because I think you are the
> most able statesman in all of Freedonia.
>
> R.T.F.: Well, that covers a lot of ground. Say, you cover a lot of ground
> yourself. You better beat it; I hear they're going to tear you down
> and put up an office building where you're standing. You can leave
> in a taxi. If you can't get a taxi, you can leave in a huff. If that's too
> soon, you can leave in a minute and a huff. You know, you haven't
> stopped talking since I came here. You must have been vaccinated
> with a phonograph needle.
>
> M.T.: The future of Freedonia rests on you. Promise me you'll follow
> in the footsteps of my husband.
>
> R.T.F.: How do you like that? I haven't been on the job five minutes
> and already she's making advances to me. Not that I care, but where
> is your husband anyway?
>
> M.T.: Why he's dead.
>
> R.T.F.: I'll bet he's just using that as an excuse.
>
> M.T.: I was with him to the end.
>
> R.T.F.: No wonder he passed away.
>
> M.T.: I held him in my arms and kissed him.
>
> R.T.F.: Oh, I see. Then it was murder. Will you marry me? Did he
> leave you any money? Answer the second question first.
>
> M.T.: He left me his entire fortune.
>
> R.T.F.: Is that so? Can't you see what I'm trying to tell you? I love
> you.
>
> M.T.: Oh, Your Excellency.
>
> R.T.F.: You're not so bad yourself.

Using the same kind of punning logic that Chico makes inadvertently
by confusing similar-sounding words, Groucho revels in the capacity
of language to undermine itself, to push dialogical interaction toward a
complete breakdown of meaning. Groucho's discursive torrents seemingly adhere to linguistic coherence but use the linking devices between
utterances to signal a failure of conversational or rhetorical progression.
Further, he falls prey to Chico's linguistic confusions and verifies them by

pushing them further than they might otherwise be taken, resulting in a symbiotic spiral of linguistic collapse.

R.T.F.: Now, what is it that has four pairs of pants, lives in Philadelphia, and it never rains but it pours?
Chico as Chicolini: Atsa a good one. I give you three guesses.
R.T.F.: Now let me see. Has four pair of pants, lives in Philadelphia . . . Is it male or female?
Chicolini: No, I no think so.
R.T.F.: Is he dead?
Chicolini: Who?
R.T.F.: I don't know. I give up.
Chicolini: I give up too.

At the seemingly more extreme end of the unspeakable is the mute, though highly articulate Harpo. With a coat filled with every item he might need to express himself, including his ubiquitous pair of scissors that he deploys on the ties of stuffed-shirt officials and blusterers, Harpo wields an array of meta-linguistic tools to overturn linguistic and social normalcy, including a bicycle horn that functions rather like Chaplin's kazoo-speaking politicians in *City Lights*. The Id with a trench coat of infinite capacity (which alludes to Felix the Cat's bag of tricks), Harpo spoke to the Surrealists in a way that the more linguistically tethered mayhem of Groucho and Chico could not. As silent film concentrated on the force and materiality of objects, Harpo, as the silent film presence in the brothers' sound-drenched cinematic world, made mute objects articulate, sometimes through their concreteness and other times through a kind of visual punning. Most eloquent of all is his eponymous harp, which captivates all who listen because of his musical virtuosity, rendering Harpo as *idiot savant*, as well as kind-hearted satyr.

Beach rightly argues that the Jewish and working-class backgrounds of the Marx Brothers inflect their personae and provide much of the bases for their humour, noting Groucho's many roles as the head of one institution or another, including a country in *Duck Soup*. He remarks further that there were no Jewish leaders of European nations in the early 1930s (34). Europe might not have had any Jewish leaders but Hollywood certainly did. And we can go further, to stress not only that were there no Jewish leaders in Europe, but also that Jews were being targeted and scapegoated (yet again), virulently so, as the rise of National Socialism indicates. The year 1933 sees Hitler become Chancellor of the Reich and the Marx Brothers release *Duck Soup*. The film transforms the theatre of politics into the vaudeville stage of the brothers' youth and the popular culture entertainment of Europe. Public entertainment and public discourse about the public sphere, or politics, take centre-stage, as the film plays with the artifice of its medium, as well with other performative genres, especially those that glorified political and knee-jerk nationalistic outpourings, such as are often found in operetta.

Originally a semi-libidinous theatrical form of light opera, operetta emerged, by the middle part of the nineteenth century, as the leading bourgeois art form, with the middle classes flocking to see semi-serious, tuneful works celebrating themselves and the political systems that secured their existence. In a vertiginous set of intertextual, parodic and satirical moves, *Duck Soup* follows the lead of many avant-garde modernists (such as Djuna Barnes with her stunning novel *Nightwood*) by sending up nineteenth-century operetta. The popularity of operettas was not confined to the stage; indeed, they became a staple of film in the first few decades of its existence. Directorial giants such as Lubitsch and von Stroheim made their international mark through film adaptations of immensely popular operettas. Henry Jenkins argues that *Duck Soup* satirises operetta as much as it does nationalistic films or US political positions in relation to the war clouds gathering over Europe (186). Jenkins is certainly right about the first point, but because he is, he blunts the sharper elements of the argument in the second, in that a critique of operetta (either on the stage or more pertinently in cinema) is in and of itself a critique and satire of nationalism writ large as a site of entertainment and celebration.

As with many emergent art forms, operetta often contained parodic and satiric engagements with its own form. Early operetta included heavy doses of satire and burlesque: for example, Johann Nestroy's immensely popular parodies of Wagnerian operas, one of which is labelled as a 'Comedy of the future with music of the past and current sets in 3 acts' (Crittenden 16). By the 1880s, the operetta had taken a more serious form, a popular cultural staging of the nation and its values, especially militarism. It began using idealised heroic types, as well as finding a new emphasis on and glorification of military power. In Vienna, the capital of empire and operetta, Austro–German nationalism became an increasingly dominant theme as the empire came under increasing pressure from its many ethnic groups (23–5). Johann Strauss's 1881 *Der lustige Krieg* (*The Merry War*), for example, as well as operettas by Millöcker from the same decade, indirectly and somewhat light-heartedly addressed issues of military responses to national pride. Even though operetta functioned in private theatres and formed an important portion of popular culture in nineteenth-century Austria, it was less subject to censorship and was given more licence than the official court theatre that hosted opera under the aegis of the Emperor. None the less, Franz Joseph often attended operettas and encouraged visiting dignitaries to do the same. That the art form could address issues such as war in a manner at once laudatory and light-hearted opens it to easy satirical engagement by those such as the Marx Brothers. It is far too short a step from nationalistic pomp to demonising pogrom, each cut from the same discursive, epistemic cloth.

As operettas contain celebratory elements of aristocratic rule and the fervent nationalism that helped foment World War I and its aftermath, *Duck Soup*, as a pre-World War II film (or even as a Weimar Republic riposte), satirises nationalism and war-mongering, as well as the art forms that perpetuate them. Nowhere is this more evident than in the musical extravaganza 'The Country's Going to War.' Starting with an insult from the Sylvanian ambassador to Freedonia that is actually the pure product of Groucho's projective imagination, the leader of Freedonia (that is, Groucho) sings, 'In case you haven't heard before, I think they think we're going to war.' The Prisoner's Dilemma of military brinkmanship – thinking that the enemy thinks that we are going to war so we should assume they are going to attack – and the pre-emptive strike makes Firefly's lyrical logic relevant for the remainder of the twentieth century and into the twenty-first. With the onset of the song, the film's action hurtles into a musical sequence combining word play, grave recitations of impending war, vaudeville parodies, spoof square dances and cod Americana music, including Stephen F. Foster (again). Reaching back to the Marx Brothers' vaudeville background, there is a Cab Calloway-ish 'hi-de-hi-de-ho' call-and-response sequence and a gospel-like imploring that eventually lead to a brief minstrel show sequence with the brothers in 'whiteface', shaking their hands like George Jessel or Eddie Cantor in 'blackface' and singing 'We got guns; they got guns. All God's chillun got guns.' By using a combination of early US popular culture in decline – one that was decidedly racist – and European popular culture in decline – ditto – to satirise the deadly alliance of nationalist and patriotic values mobilised as military action, the Marx Brothers hurl the audience into a hilariously horrific sequence that makes cinema the vehicle for exploding the deeply interdependent relationships between media, genres and nationalist agendas.

The opening sequence of the film announces Firefly's ascension to the seat of power and shows the formal occasion held to tell the public of the event. The gathering includes rows of armed soldiers, government dignitaries and young ballerinas strewing flower petals. The group extols Firefly's virtues in song, much as the late nineteenth-century Viennese operettas did for their heroes, leading to the anticipation of the new leader's arrival when 'the clock strikes ten.' When the magic hour arrives, the band and chorus sing the national anthem, which consists largely of 'Hail Freedonia! Land of the Brave and the Free!' But the hall remains anticlimactically empty, even after several rounds of the anthem, as if the singing will magically conjure up their leader. Such is the stuff of dreams, of operetta, of patriotism and, of course, satire.

Laughter at the Gates of Hell: the Unspeakable Death Camps and Lubitsch's To Be or Not to Be (1942)

I mentioned the war but I think I got away with it.
Basil Fawlty, in the BBC TV series *Fawlty Towers*

Thirty or so years after the end of World War II, John Cleese famously stages a confrontation between German tourists visiting the bed and breakfast, *Fawlty Towers*, and the deranged, xenophobic owner, Basil Fawlty, who reveals the taboo surrounding National Socialism as a site for comic commentary – though Mel Brooks had done so more flagrantly in the 1960s with *The Producers*. Still, this was broadcast television, a medium largely devoted to not pushing the boundaries of acceptable behaviour. As we know, though, even large-scale events of horror, such as the Holocaust, spawn jokes. On Larry David's television series 'Curb Your Enthusiasm', for example, he has a meeting with a Rabbi who will be coming to dinner later in the week. The Rabbi says he has a friend who is 'a survivor' and asks if he can bring him along. Larry agrees and then invites his elderly father and his friend, who survived the concentration camps. At dinner, it turns out that the Rabbi's friend was on the reality show, 'Survivor', and has had nothing to do with genocide. None the less an argument occurs as to who had it roughest: the reality show contestant or the Shoah victim. Comedy's capacity to speak what is unspeakable is important but danger-ous, or important because it is dangerous. And comedy's capacity to link the gravity of existence to the levity of shared misery means that comedy will forever be speaking the unspeakable.

Lubitsch's film *To Be or Not to Be* is made just before the US enters World War II, is released after the country has taken up arms, and comments, with and through humour, on the terrors being rendered in Central Europe. At a time when the US government rarely acknowledged the plight of internees under Nazi control, Lubitsch's film speaks openly about the existence of the camps and alludes to the atrocities committed there. Thomas Doherty notes that some comedies directly addressed the Jews as targets of Nazi ideological extermination, and one in particular,

Once Upon a Honeymoon (Leo McCarey, 1942), found Cary Grant and Ginger Rogers imprisoned in a concentration camp and threatened with sterilisation (126–31). Speaking the unspeakable led to controversy surrounding *To Be or Not to Be*, but not for references to the camps. Instead, Lubitsch was criticised for making the Nazis buffoonish and laughable – also, perhaps less apparently so, for making them complex, contradictory and human (though not sympathetic). Many at the time found the humour anti-Polish, but today this criticism hardly seems credible. If anything, Lubitsch perhaps transgressed the standard patriotic dimensions that so inflected US war films of the time, produced both before and during the war. Films made in 1941 included the wildly successful *Sergeant York* with Gary Cooper, the Marines drama *To the Shores of Tripoli*, and *Dive Bomber*. The standard Hollywood fare proved to be mostly vapid exercises in Manichean logic: patriotic, bland, predictable.

This film possesses none of these qualities. Indeed, Lubitsch skirts the US altogether, making the leads of the film a Polish theatre group resisting the Nazi invasion of their country. Writing in a letter to the *Philadelphia Enquirer* reviewer, Mildred Martin, about the controversy surrounding the release of the film, Lubitsch turned to its meta-cinematic and meta-theatrical qualities to explain its themes and positions:

> What I have satirized in this picture are the Nazis and their ridiculous ideology. I have also satirized the attitude of actors who always remain actors regardless how dangerous the situation might be, which I believe is a true observation. It can be argued if the tragedy of Poland realistically portrayed as in *To Be or Not to Be* can be merged with satire. I believe it can be and so do the audience which I observed during a screening of *To Be or Not to Be*; but this is a matter of debate and everyone is entitled to his point of view, but it is certainly a far cry from the Berlin-born director who finds fun in the bombing of Warsaw. (Quoted in Insdorf 67)

In his rhetorical move to double-satirise Nazis and actors, Lubitsch (somewhat) subtly links ideological fervour with performance, nationalism with play-acting, and violence/terror with laughter. The entire cinematic enterprise is thus put in a distinct context, one that suggests Albert Speer's modelling of the Nuremberg rallies on Hollywood musical sets, and how this revealed a relationship between the appeal of Fascism and the fascination of spectacle essential to cinema's affective power.

As with Keaton and *Sherlock Jr.*, *To Be or Not to Be* is very much about the thin line between art and actuality, linking, as it does, historical events, surreal interpretations of them and the role that theatre/cinema/acting/improvisation play in mediating between actual and imagined life (underscoring how the two influence and construct each other). The film foregrounds politics and performance, politics as performance and vice versa.

The play within a play (or play within cinema) that constitutes the opening sequences of the film reminds us of the other play within the film, the one invoked in its title and that also contains a play within a play: *Hamlet*. The use of the famous soliloquy in the film, repeated frequently and with increasing effect, is comic and absurd (with Jack Benny's character playing the title role of the tragedy), but also deeply pertinent to the political and military issues of the moment. The meditation on whether and how to exist in the world found in the soliloquy articulates not only the conditions of the characters in the film but also those of the audience, allowing the Möbius strip of the theatre-as-world and world-as-theatre to conflate in this instance into the technology of the cinema. As he did consistently in his early German films, Lubitsch plays with frames. In the teens and early Twenties, he frequently uses masks within the frame in a parody of Expressionist cinema, and in this war satire he uses frames to further the various themes: the frame of the camera as containing the real, the suspension of disbelief for the audience, and meta–cinema (meta–theatre), as with *Sherlock Jr*. He breaks the diegetic frame repeatedly, especially at the outset of the film, to reveal where and how we create such frames in our daily lives, serving then as a satirical meditation on subjectivity and perception, here cast in the conditions of occupied Poland under the Nazi regime.

When the Warsaw actors lose their stage, they are forced to rebuild it in the world of political action and intrigue for purposes of survival and resistance. Although both politics and theatre rely on the value of appearances, the stakes for the actors' success outside of the theatre carry a certain weight, one of which Lubitsch would have been all too keenly aware. Lubitsch had become a stage and screen star by acting in ethnic 'Jewish' comedies in his native Germany. Playing up and relying on one's Jewishness in Weimar Germany was a risky business, a point proven by the fact that his profile later appeared on Nazi posters explaining how to identify a Jew; rarely has the thin membrane between cinema and its context become more vague and rarely with more haunting resonance. In *To Be or Not to Be*, the actors are not known by their Nazi occupiers – despite Joseph Tura's frequent assertion of his fame as 'that great great actor'. As the worlds of ideological and theatrical performance blur, the actors have an advantage over the Nazis, for they know they are moving through, constructing and flaunting different layers of actuality. The actors are aware that they are acting; the Nazis are not, for they are not acting (or so they believe). The highlighting of unintentional performance as both performance and unintentional – knowledge of which the actors use to their advantage – obviously underscores the *techne* of ideology and how it functions in the world as transparent, real and natural: simply the way things are. In other words, the actors furnish us with a vehicle that epitomises the purpose of comedic inquiry into social and cultural formations. The actors further provide us with a critical take on the technique and technologies that help these social and cultural formations to be realised as the Real.

In this sense, an exceptionally optimistic sense, theatre/performance has the upper hand on politics and raw power. The laughter of the film replicates, to an extent, the mode of resistance that the actors within it display. The film operates as a kind of gallows humour that allows us to confront horror or terror without necessarily succumbing to it. But the experience of the war itself reminds us that the comedic or absurdist view, while richly productive and powerful, can do little in the face of tanks, aerial bombings and systematic genocide. This film speaks of concentration camps while they were in operation and converts them into a joke surrounding the life-and-death performance of the actors. None the less, the camps persisted and even became elided from the public sphere in the US for a few years after the film's initial screening.

In his elegy for Yeats, Auden famously asserts 'Poetry makes nothing happen.' If poetry can be read as a metonym for all the arts, including cinema, then the issue becomes one of representation and which forms might effect some change and which maintain a dangerous status quo, rather like that rendered heroic and light in the operettas satirised by the Marx Brothers. Some thirteen years after this film was made, the Swiss playwright Friedrich Dürrenmatt wrote, in his 1954 essay 'Theatre Problems', that drama was dead because there was no individual guilt any more, only collective guilt; similarly, there is no individual agency or responsibility any more, only horrific events orchestrated by faceless bureaucratic machines. Thus, for Dürrenmatt, only *grotesque* comedy suits the dire paradoxes of our historical condition. This, indeed, is a position articulated not only by such absurdist and tragicomic postwar writers as Samuel Beckett, but also by that Central European sensibility we find prior to the war in the Marx Brothers and in Lubitsch's existential, meta-theatrical/meta-cinematic work in *To Be or Not to Be*, suggesting a strain of the grotesque suitable for most times. Almost completely lacking the 'Lubitsch touch' of deftly layered visuals and dialogue, as well as the droll sophistication that Adorno and Horkheimer criticise, this film's odd mix of genres and surprising combination of high and low humour place its conversations about the camps within the camp of those who understand comedic intervention as potentially revolutionary, barely effective and virtually an automatic default mode.

Spuddy Gray's Talking Cure: Genocide and Satire as Supplement in *Swimming to Cambodia* (Jonathan Demme, 1987)

> In peace, sons bury their fathers; in war, fathers bury their sons.
>
> Herodotus

> Perhaps an invisible cloud of evil that circles the earth and lands at random places like Iran, Beirut, Cambodia, America, set the Khmer Rouge out to commit the worst auto-homeo-genocide in modern history.
>
> Spalding Gray, in *Swimming to Cambodia*

> There are no American combat troops in Cambodia. There are no American combat advisers in Cambodia. There will be no American combat troops or advisers in Cambodia. We will aid Cambodia. Cambodia is the Nixon doctrine in its purest form.
>
> President Richard M. Nixon, November 1971

> This is exactly what is so uncanny, that everything is functioning and that the functioning drives us more and more to even further functioning, and that technology tears men loose from the earth and uproots them. I do not know whether you were frightened, but I at any rate was frightened when I saw pictures coming from the moon to the earth. We don't need any atom bomb. The uprooting of man has already taken place. The only thing we have left is purely technological relationships.
>
> Martin Heidegger, *Der Spiegel*, in a 1966 interview

Swimming to Cambodia documents, though in an understated filmic fashion, Spalding Gray's monologue of the same name. Gray's performance provides a supplement to the film that resides at the centre of the performance: Roland Joffé's hugely successful film about the horrors perpetrated by the Khmer Rouge, *The Killing Fields* (1984), in which Gray plays a US embassy official in Cambodia at the time of the coup and the US departure. *The Killing Fields* is itself a supplement to another film, *Apocalypse Now*, providing the Cambodian dimension to the Vietnam War and affording that troubled nation its cinematic due. Gray uses the high-profile status of *The Killing Fields* and his tiny role in it to his advantage, commenting on Hollywood's relationship to history, politics and the technologies of filmmaking. *Swimming to Cambodia* supplements and therefore renders problematic the heroic tale told in *The Killing Fields*, the kind of high-minded film that Hollywood produces to show that it takes itself seriously as an influential participant in the public discursive sphere.

This film of a performance supplements a film that is meant to supplement not only another film but also print coverage of events in Cambodia under the Khmer Rouge, or rather to reveal the lack of the story in print, despite *The Killing Fields*' lead character being a *New York Times* reporter and being based on historical events. In this sense, Demme's film anticipates David O. Russell's wonderful parody of the action film and war film genres, *Three Kings* (1999), which supplements the TV coverage of the first Iraqi war through a series of unveilings regarding what lay beneath the surface of the TV reportage. In so doing, Gray's performance asks a useful question: what is the public space of cinema, especially in relation to the live event (whether it be performance or war or genocide)? To begin thinking through that question as a supplement to *The Killing Fields* and as a type of counter-history, *Swimming to Cambodia* works with memory and history, ignorance and forgetting, and how they operate in ambivalent though structurally necessary ways with one another. It is a self-aware film about film's capacity to document events, as well as to show us one way that technologies of memory (of the external storage of memory) operate: they allow us to forget.

The Heidegger quotation that serves as an epigraph for this section comes from an interview with *Der Spiegel* and is a response to a question about what might be lacking in the materialistically secure moment of Germany circa 1966. Heidegger's answer takes us back to his dictum on technology's essence as an enframing or emplacement of the mind. Gray's performance foregrounds cinema *as* one of the technologies that Heidegger discusses: a televisual and teleaural technology that delivers the intimacy of his performance from a spatial and temporal distance. Gray's monologue might be read as an attempt to halt the uprooting Heidegger evokes and ground us again in human intimacy, as the philosopher might well wish. But the attempt is caught in the anti-humanist paradox of using the film medium to query and critique film as a medium and what its mediation achieves. Rather like Plato's critique of the technology of writing in his *Phaedrus* and 'The Seventh Letter', in which he uses the written word to criticise writing and thus blunts his argument, Demme's film of Gray's performance offers a deeply paradoxical relationship to the medium. The film shows a pronounced ambivalence towards its subject matter, its means of production and the grounds out of which it emerged and is able to be reproduced. That Gray called himself 'a crusader for the live event' and said that, if one has only seen the Demme film, then one has not experienced the performance, does little to erase the film's medial examinations, its cinematic qualities or its complex filmic intertextuality and commentary.

Gray's monologue is an example of the performance art scene that flourished in the 1980s, including artists such as Laurie Anderson (who provided the music for a few of Gray's pieces, including this one), Ann Magnuson, Eric Bogosian and others. The 1980s performance art scene owed a debt to the Dada and Futurist performances in the early part of the twentieth century that were responses to World War I and the techno-political conditions that led up to it and resulted from it. These in turn are revived in the 1960s, influenced and performed by artists such as Yoko Ono and others from the Fluxus group. Sometimes called 'events' or 'happenings', these too were meant to explore the relationships between sound, light, space and duration in times of war, as well as being a response to conflict. Each moment of performance art, from Dada to the Eighties, took humour as the subversive base of the performances. All of these performance art traditions have connections with the avant-garde, and in this manner Gray updates, personalises (while destroying individuality) and renders intimate avant-garde performance, thus gesturing to the critical performative possibilities explored by Chaplin and Keaton that so captivated the continental avant-garde as well as the large cinema-going audience, as discussed earlier. Cinema and its ability to capture performance are on display in Demme's film, as is the near-impossibility of never being able simply to document what transpires before the camera, adding its own mediation. When editing, camera positions, close-ups – the entire filmic lexicon – enter the mix, as they do here, the impact of direct access results from cinema's visual techniques and their invisible operation. At the same time, the film also offers the promise of performance and protest, as well as performance as protest. Performances of this kind explore public space as a site of protest and did so after harrowing displays of the same by Buddhist monks who, in the early 1960s, engaged in self-immolation on the busy streets of Saigon to protest against the policies of the Diem regime and its cooperation with the US in the conduct of the war with the north. Thus Gray (along with Demme) returns us to the question of cinema's public space and its level of address.

Gray's performance technique and site of enunciation is essentially that of Marlow in Conrad's *Heart of Darkness*, and thus that of Willard's in *Apocalypse Now*. Marlow's direct audience is 'the Company' and Gray's is his New York-based audience, themselves metonymic of the US (which, by the latter half of the twentieth century, arguably could be read as a company). The indirect audiences, the reading and viewing audiences, hear a long narrative of the atrocities committed so that they may enjoy the comforts of being at the distance provided through reading and viewing. Similarly, Willard is to the US as Spalding Gray is to the US (and to us, as audience): a witness to the US military presence and activities in Southeast Asia. Willard witnesses Kurtz in Cambodia, who, in Coppola's version of the Conrad novel, evokes the entire set of US covert and horrifying engagements inside Cambodia, a nation with which it was not at war. Gray witnesses Hollywood in Cambodia, with Thailand filling in as its neighbour's stunt double, as Hollywood tries to evoke the genocidal horrors that transpired with the aid of US missteps (to put it mildly). If *Apocalypse Now* gives one version of the US covert war in Cambodia, then *The Killing Fields* tells another . . . and *Swimming to Cambodia* yet another, the latter concentrating on the filmic mediation of the events that transpired there as offered through both of the former films, as well as filling in some of those elements glossed over by the other films (and the mass media generally).

The secret and illegal bombing of Cambodia during the Vietnam War was intended to disrupt supply lines for the North Vietnamese along the Ho Chi Minh Trail, and the raids killed approximately 600,000 to 800,000 civilians. Despite having signed a peace treaty with the Cambodians, the US, from as early 1964 but with massive intensification from 1969 to 1975, still bombed its territories. The covert bombings occurred despite the explicit withdrawal of support by the US Congress for the use of air power in Laos or Cambodia and resulted in over 230,000 sorties, dropping nearly 3 million tons of ordnance. The US supported the Sihanouk government in Cambodia and its troops to fight against the Viet Cong. The Khmer Rouge, led by Pol Pot, worked with the Viet Cong to fight against the US. Ostensibly and publicly supporting Sihanouk, the US covertly supported a coup led by the army general Lon Nol (supported, most believe, by the CIA). The palindrome-named Lon Nol, in turn, aided the US invasion of Cambodia to fight the North Vietnamese. As with Diem in Vietnam, support for Sihanouk was withdrawn by the US and a violent coup ensued, leaving the political situation open for Pol Pot, who had been strongly influenced by Mao and the Cultural Revolution. Under the guise of an agrarian and anti-urban peasant revolution, Pol Pot and the Khmer Rouge swept to power, toppling Lon Nol. The US fled, and as Pol Pot decreed the calendar 'Year Zero' and initiated 'the purifying of Cambodian society', genocide followed, with the civilian death toll reaching approximately 2 million. Coppola allegorically tells the story up to the ascendancy of Pol Pot and the Khmer Rouge, suggesting in the figure of Kurtz the sowing of the seeds of the bloody coup and genocide through US interventions in the region. Joffé takes over the story from there to reveal the genocide itself and its individual human toll.

Joffé's film follows Sidney Schanberg, a New York Times reporter who covered the Khmer Rouge entering Phnom Penh, but who did not break the news of the illegal and secret bombing of Cambodia. He covered one minor incident, the accidental bombing of a Cambodian village, while ignoring the large-scale and illegal bombing of the Cambodian and Lao countryside. Although Schanberg was lauded as a 'voice of conscience' because of *The Killing Fields*, the left in the US (for example, Noam Chomsky) excoriated him. Schanberg stayed after the fall of the government in 1975 and was one of the few US reporters on the ground there at the time. His guide in the Khmer Rouge era became a Cambodian reporter named Dith Pran, played by Haing S. Ngor, a Cambodian doctor whose wife died in the genocide. As the Khmer Rouge targeted intellectuals for purification, Ngor's medical training had to be hidden when he was taken to a work camp, and when his wife began to miscarry, he could not save her without imperilling them all. Pran similarly had to hide his educational credentials when sent to the labour camps for four years, nearly starving to death in the process. The film, rather like the film version of *Sophie's Choice* (Alan Pakula, 1982) uses historical trauma almost as backdrop for individual suffering and moral choice as Pran takes Schanberg through the killing fields of the Khmer Rouge after their defeat in 1979. And this opens up a specific dimension of Gray's satirical engagement with the film, for if *The Killing Fields* counts as 'politically engaged cinema', Gray seems to imply, what hope exists for Hollywood cinema as political engagement in the public sphere?

As with Willard's journey, Gray's working film junket becomes a vehicle for learning and remembering with regard to the collective ignorance and forgetting of US history as it pertains to US influence in Southeast Asia during the Vietnam War. By implication, of course, what pertains to the specific chronotope of Southeast Asia in the 1960s and 1970s might well pertain to other sites and times, allowing Gray to suggest this as but one of many such spots around the world, and also to imply that perhaps we only consider its shadowy nature due to the harshly angled light cast upon it by Hollywood. Gray's monologue is part lecture and part *apologia* for his ignorance, as revealed each time he repeats the line about his sessions with Joffé: 'Leave it to a Brit to explain your own history to you.' Gray is self-indulgent but the self-indulgence is meant to underline the familiar character-driven cinematic experience while subverting the desire for character in the process, satirising its narrative comfort for most moviegoers. The self he stages – the persona – is not an individual self, despite the tales of his search for work, good stories, 'the perfect moment' and other seemingly solipsistic, self-involved pursuits. Rather, the self on stage that Gray offers is a fully mediated subjectivity produced through a series of US institutions, including cinema, media and government – technologically traced and stored. Gray's persona is, on the one hand, entirely egoistical (all about the self) and, on the other, completely egoless (all about others), in order to stage the ineluctable scene of mutual dependence between self and other as unavoidably dependent – despite Heidegger's fears – on technological relationships: which is the scene of his performance.

In this manner, the film and performance evoke many of the means through which the contestation and traffic between humans and machines have served as foundational elements of comedy since Bergson and have been admirably unfolded by Michael North. From a latent humanist perspective that Gray both embraces and eschews, we have ceded something essentially and fundamentally human to machines, and in this case it is collective memory and knowledge, which have been relinquished to cinema as well as other prosthetic storage devices. If history is usually written by the victors, whose story of authority to author the history text is told in the historical and heroic narrative they write, then Gray's history is that of the defeated that marks the post-Vietnam War era in America. According to the eighteenth-century rhetorician and historiographer Giambattista Vico, the accounts of the losers (the counter-history) remain in less authoritative sources: jokes, songs and oral tales. Gray's monologue is a studied exercise in counter-history as he uses these Vichian forms to evoke the larger issues of historicity and memory. His film is story telling as performance, and it harkens back to the oldest canonical work in the Western literary tradition – a tale of war that includes honourable defeat and yet more honourable victory, *The Iliad*. Demme's film leaves us a long way from the war films of the World War II era, in which Hollywood served as a virtual extension of the Defense Department through numerous fiction films and directly provided propaganda for the Pentagon through Frank Capra's 'Why We Fight' series. Films such as *Apocalypse Now* and *The Killing Fields* foreground ambivalence toward and critique of this past, as they explicitly perform a cinematic rethinking of cinema's long relationship with war and the nation-state, especially in the US. But this tradition is not the satirical target of Gray's bile. That target is Joffé's film, no matter how well intentioned – and, in fact, because of its good intentions.

Through Gray's monologue, which makes his film not really a film in some important ways while reaffirming cinematic experience and technics in others, he provides his satiric engagement with the Joffé film in which he performed. Cinema as concealer and revealer becomes contrasted with performance as revealer, though Gray would never be naïve enough to believe performance is that alone. His supplement would require, following the logic of the supplement, further supplementation. Such a demand is implied in the structure of his monologue, which is that of a spiral, taking a subject, going off on a tangent and then returning to the subject. The subjects and tangents emerge as variations on themes *and* scenes. Gray's scenes in the film *The Killing Fields* become a site and strategy for thinking about scenes generally and what they stage (for example, the scene of war, or performance, or technology, or human understanding, or historical memory and so on), and he returns to these again and again. Gray claimed that the stream-of-consciousness writing found in James Joyce's *Ulysses* and Virginia Woolf's *To the Lighthouse* influenced his monologues, but their structure and performative mode seem more fundamentally indebted to Samuel Beckett's plays. The monologue foregrounds the voice to such an extent that the body and face can disappear with minimal lighting shifts. The voice – the ceaseless voice – continues, through the tape recorder in *Krapp's Last Tape* and the cinema camera in *Swimming to Cambodia*, and it 'runs on in silence' (Beckett 28); the machine of reproduction, on to which humans record thoughts, history and life, runs on machinically but also in silence. A machinic propulsion, a story-telling deluge of industrial prodigiousness, marks Gray's performance. Also like Beckett, he turns his individual pain into laughter, his despair into comedy, the greatest joke being that the individual suffering the pain is anything but an individual. The monologue is by turns arch, sardonic, touching, spleen-venting and hilarious as he converts his stories about being on the set or at cast parties or at sessions with Joffé into a national accountability for collective memory. If the performance serves as a revelation of neuroses and anxieties – an example of Freud's 'talking cure' – then it is a talking cure for the nation: a purge of repressed national trauma lost to the mechanistic white noise of cinematic narrative expectation.

All of Gray's monologues, many of which were filmed, have the same spare table, tabletop microphone, notepad (rarely used) and glass of water. The stage techniques and filmed versions of them are decidedly low-tech, in the standard way of using the phrase, but they are not 'no-tech'. The film's *techne* starts with its very format, which foregrounds the functionality of non-fiction film by documenting a performance in a film. The Möbius strip of *techne* operative in representation comes to the fore and thus forces the cinema audience to consider critically the mediation of cinema generally, as this film offers subtle, seemingly direct, access to a performer's skills. As discussed earlier in relation to Chaplin and Keaton, cinema as documentation affords a record of virtuosic performers and performances, and Gray's monologue falls into that camp. Keaton and

Chaplin are kinetic and silent while Gray is still and talking, with the virtuosity being found in the voice, the telling and the stage/film punctuations: the lighting, Laurie Anderson's minimal but effective music, the props (a map and pointer), and camera cross-cutting and – most especially – the close-up. As with the theatrical cameras of Méliès and Chaplin, the effectiveness of the close-up and its utterly inescapable cinematic qualities break the frame of performance, the illusion of presence and witnessing, to plunge viewers deep into the frame that constitutes the cinematic moving image and obfuscates its transparent operation.

The close-up might well be cinema at its most expressively powerful and intimate, given an abstracted and anonymous audience. It clearly contrasts in specific ways with the intimacy of a performance before a live audience, especially one as close to the stage and as small in number as with Gray's monologue. Gray is interested in this intimacy – the intimacy of story telling and human connection – but also in the lack of intimacy and connection, whether in performance or in the cinema, as technologies of representation (either language or cinema) distance and connect simultaneously. He wishes to explore how distance emerges from and through the means of bringing things and people closer together. Through the mediation that allows for connections, these media reveal the distance between people (spatial and temporal) that exist in order for the media to function at all. Other and new kinds of intimacy occur through such media, though. For example, cinema's capacity to record ephemera, elements of a moment of performance, creates a kind of cross-temporal intimacy: the evanescence of performance captured and preserved on film, as with Demme's picture. As such, Gray's decision to film his performance highlights his monologue's themes of memory, forgetting, witnessing – and the technologies that deliver them. Cinema is indeed capable of providing access to amazingly moving moments, to which the camera offers a kind of one-eyed and limited guide. Such a moment occurs in Robert Drew's *cinéma vérité* film, *On the Road with Duke Ellington* (1967), when the camera films Ellington and a small number of musicians playing before the open coffin of his long-time collaborator, Billy Strayhorn. The images, framing and sound become shockingly intimate, tragic and beautiful. But the intimacy excludes the audience, though they are allowed to witness it at a distance that is rendered all the more distant by its apparent intimacy. This situation, as with Gray's performance, and more importantly the subject of his satiric attack and its medium, displays the impossibility of cinematic witnessing due to the very conditions that make the witnessing possible.

Gray's monologue/performance/film does not necessarily satirise Joffé or the intentions of those who worked on and made the film in which he took part (and thus himself). Rather he satirises the entire Hollywood apparatus, machinery, hubris and technicity surrounding an 'important political' film, and the efficacy of such a project, from such an industry with such reproductive technologies and media. The entire confluence required to deliver such a film militates against its stated goals. Similarly, Gray does not satirise *The Killing Fields*' inability to address the unspeakable, but rather its capitulation to the unsaid of its historical topic and subject, those concerns about which it chooses to remain mute, and being mute is never an option for Gray.

Proleptic Renderings of Media *Mise-en-abîme*: *Wag the Dog* (1997)

There's a great difference between the event that happens (happened) in historical time and the event that happens in the real time of information. To the pure management of flows and markets under the banner of planetary deregulation, there corresponds the 'global' event – or rather the globalized non-event: the French victory in the World Cup, the year 2000, the death of Diana, *The Matrix*, etc. Whether or not these events are manufactured, they are orchestrated by the silent epidemic of the information networks. Fake events.

> Jean Baudrillard, *The Intelligence of Evil* (124)

That's not the way the world really works anymore. We're an empire now, and when we act, we create our own reality.

> Quotation attributed to Karl Rove, Senior Advisor and Deputy Chief of Staff to George W. Bush, by Ron Susskind, *New York Times Magazine*

We're not going to have a war; we're going to have the appearance of a war.

> Conrad Brean, in *Wag the Dog*

Billed as 'A comedy about truth, justice and other special effects', Barry Levinson's 1997 film of Hilary Henkin and David Mamet's screenplay provides something akin to an updated version of the 'actualities' of early cinema to explore and satirise the relationship between media, modes of representation and politics. Just as the 'actualities' played fast and loose with 'actual' footage and staged reconstruction to provide a seamless sequence of events as unmanipulated by the camera in its address to the audience, so this film explores the irrelevance of truth or reality to short-term political goals and agendas caught in the maws of media news cycles, resulting in a Möbius strip of media and the actual with no inside or outside verifiable as such. Very much an intertextual result, as well as perpetuator, of the *mise-en-abîme* of IT and media interactions, the film reveals its satirical concerns at the outset, showing, via closed-circuit video screens, the movement of political consultant Conrad Brean into and through the White House. All of the audience's initial views of the film and its lead protagonist come from shots of a screen and, as with *Bowling for Columbine*, of screens endlessly repeating and broadcasting other screens. The first diegetic shot of Brean — that is, one that stages the invisible image of the traditional realist camera point of view — occurs in a White House seminar room, where the President's election committee chairs have met to stave off a scandalous news story just about to hit the news media. Brean's role is to prevent the media from focusing on the scandal for long enough to make it through the imminent presidential elections. A nice insider joke works with Brean's name, which is a homonym of one of the two major Hollywood censors, Joseph Breen, who controlled what Hollywood could show from 1930 to 1968. Just as Joseph Breen was tasked with keeping the moral codes of the Hollywood product up to scratch and not offending the nation's sensibilities by what was shown on screen, so Conrad Brean is asked to keep political smut out of the media, not for the sake of moral decency but for political gain. Whether it is fictional or actual smut matters not; whether it appears on screen or not does. And just as nature abhors a vacuum, so does a screen, especially in the 24/7 real-time news cycle.

The direct political target of the satire is a Bill Clinton-like figure, constructed in this instance prior to the Monica Lewinsky scandal, though the film proved prescient in that regard as it emerged almost simultaneously with the scandal. The oblique but more sustained target of the film's satire resides in the media, yet again thematised by cinema to reveal its capacity to coordinate, contain, disseminate and proliferate all other media. In this and other ways — at the levels of technology and media manufacturing of the Real — the film proves even more prescient, exacting and funny. The film appeared after the US invasion of Grenada and the Gulf War, but before the Iraq War, making it difficult to avoid interpreting it as more productive today than when it was made.

The US invasion of the small Marxist Caribbean island of Grenada on trumped-up issues can be and has been interpreted, rightly or wrongly, as an attempt to deflect media (and public) attention away from the devastating terrorist attack on US marines in Lebanon that occurred two days prior to the invasion. Whether or not Reagan launched the invasion to distract the public, his administration certainly made much media hay out of its relatively easy success, and thus helped eliminate the deaths of 241 marines from the main focus of the public sphere. Similarly, the Gulf War has been interpreted as the result of repeatedly baiting Saddam Hussein and providing easy political gain for Bush Senior when his presidency was at a low ebb. Incidents such as these and the Jessica Lynch episode in the Iraq invasion, which will be discussed later, help to keep this film increasingly contemporary and current, as examples of the medial manufacture of events for political advantage proliferate like so many cable news talk shows.

To help Brean divert public attention from the sex scandal involving a minor in the Oval Office, Brean enlists the aid of a Hollywood producer, Stanley Motss, to help him generate a fake war: a simulated conflict staged solely through the mass media and broadcast in the press. To convince Motss of the import of such an effort, as well as to underscore the efficacy of such endeavours in the past, Brean discusses the famous shots taken during the Gulf War by guided 'smart' missiles flying down the smoke stacks of a strategically targeted factory.

> Conrad Brean: What's the thing people remember about the Gulf War? A bomb falling down a chimney. Let me tell you something: I was in the building where we filmed that with a 10–inch model made out of Legos.
> Stanley Motss: Is that true?
> Conrad Brean: Who the hell's to say?

This example of frequently repeated footage from the first real-time, televised war seemingly shows precision technology at work, and the government, mass media and military celebrated it as such. In the post–Cold War moment, precision technology could allow the US military to strike with conventional weapons, even in urban sites, with minimal loss of life, and thus wage war in a manner that kept US soldiers out of harm's way while assuaging the public conscience because civilians too are made safer. This was the spin at the time and remains a default discursive mode when addressing military technology and action abroad, especially when such strikes are addressed on TV news shows.

A singularly important element, though, is the clip's point of view, which is machinic. The missile itself delivered the image to TV screens worldwide, as well as delivering the payload and its destruction. The weapon produces a moving image and destroys the object produced in the image. The guided missile also watches or reads its own film of the terrain in which the target is embedded. So it not only sees and projects from machine to machine, but it also views and reads what other machines have generated. As with the CCTV camera shots and screens that follow Brean through the White House back corridors and underground hallways, or the point-of-view shots of trains from the first decades of film, this image seemingly provides unfettered (by human intervention) access to the actual. Brean asserts that the images were faked and shot in a US studio, but his point is a larger one: the media's repetition of the clip helps to constitute it as the Real.

For us, though, it is not so much a matter of the media duping the American public, which seems to be the film's satiric and didactic point, but rather how the Real is technologically constituted, regardless of its relationship to the actual. The film's critique, therefore, operates on Baudrillard's second level of simulation, in which the simulation stands in for the real in a manner that distorts it. What is more relevant for the analysis at hand, though, is the third level of simulation, in which the simulation and the real are no longer separable, thus forming the Real. The shot of the missile flying down the chimney in the Gulf War is but one of the many machinic visual objects whose cumulative effect is to construct an archive of the Real that visual culture and media generally have been compulsively generating and compiling for over a century and which can be drawn on (consciously or not) for rhetorical, ideological or political purposes. The repetition of these images creates the Real, thus exemplifying Baudrillard's 'hyper-reality' and pushing us toward a mediated image archaeology, through which we can critically consider how the reproducible images of the past haunt and are used by the evanescence of present visual technologies – the externalised medial store of collective historical memory.

Wag the Dog proleptically gestures toward this mediated image archaeology, as the Iraq War and the case made for waging it reveal. Colin Powell's speech to the UN (televised, of course) about weapons in Iraq, used to justify military intervention – a speech that squandered all of Powell's credibility in one fell swoop – proves heavily reliant on visual evidence that deploys both a duplicitous mode of media manipulation, as with *Wag the Dog*, and one reliant on the kind of mediated image collective history that constitute Baudrillard's third level of simulation. Powell's presentation of the 'proof' of the existence of illegal weapons of mass destruction, chemical weapons stockpiles and nuclear weapons consisted primarily of aerial surveillance photographs of Iraq, annotated with descriptions and identifying markers. Not only did Powell borrow the forum of his speech from the powerful presentation made by Adlai Stevenson at the UN arguing that Soviet nuclear missiles were being delivered and installed in Cuba, but he also borrowed the visual rhetoric. With its specific presentation of satellite photo imagery, the Bush administration used simulated analogue images, poster boards and annotated images. In fact, the rather crude imagery looked at the time more like 1962 than early twenty-first century, and thus seems calculated to invoke in the minds of TV viewers the Kennedy administration's famous speech and its articulation of imminent danger.

Relying upon an aesthetic of verity and a common collective archive of the visual imagination operating with regard to truth, reality and indexicality (analogous to the documentary aesthetic), the photos Powell presented of the so-called 'mobile chemical labs' and 'weapons storage sites' used technologies, framings, formats and image qualities that replicated explicitly the same kinds of evidence provided by the Kennedy administration. This manipulation of images sought to evoke a collective archival past of the Kennedy/Stevenson images and thus to persuade us that the situations and threats were analogous, the analytical images of each providing a visual reiteration intended to mirror the gravity of the threat at each moment. The exploiting of our scopic/visual memory and history is not necessarily where the satire in *Wag the Dog* resides, but it is the next step in simulation analysis. The film, however, does explore the effects of this kind of image manipulation within media and politics, equating politics with Hollywood productions. The trite affect of film becomes the trite affect of politics. When Motss tries out his Hollywood-inflected speech for the President on a test group of secretarial staff in the White House, they emerge deeply moved and there is not a dry eye in the place. 'Cue the tears' works the same in Hollywood and Washington; in fact, it is the same medial imperative. The test audience is also, of course, the movie's audience, or us, as the film's address to the audience makes abundantly clear. However, this message is subverted by the film's level of address, the conditions of its articulation. Because the tale is one of media manipulation of audience perception and reality, the film's thematising of media and cinema's power over the political system, as well as the corruption involved, undermines its argument. The picture says the media and cinema deceive, although this film tells the truth about deception.

The film further invokes a mediated audience dumbed down by its engagement with the media, especially in relation to its general knowledge about the world; hence the choice of Albania as the site for and combatant in the manufactured, simulated media war that Brean and Motss wage. Albania proves a useful choice because of the Enver Hoxa regime and *its* manufactured extension of World War II, which it used to frighten and pacify its citizenry (in a way that evokes Emir Kusturica's brilliant satire, *Underground* (1995)). Hoxa staged fake air raids by enemy forces for years after the end of the war to scare the population into following the government's rule. Albania, almost by default, becomes a stand-in for Iraq, given the film's appearance in between the two US attacks on and invasions of Saddam Hussein's former state. Thus it is difficult not to read *Wag the Dog* in light of Baudrillard's essays about the first Iraq War (the Gulf War) and the many echoes and intensifications of his arguments that pertain to the second. The eponymous titles of these essays – 'The Gulf War Will Not Take Place', 'Is It Really Taking Place?' and 'The Gulf War Did Not Take Place'– speak to the Albanian War in the film as much as they do to the two Iraq Wars on TV.

Baudrillard questioned the Gulf War's occurrence while it raged on TV screens, packaged by networks with their own theme music, slogans, titles, graphics and even sponsors. Then once a cessation of hostilities transpired, he asserted that the war had not taken place. Baudrillard argues that the Gulf War did not take place because the complete military, technological and visual control of the terrain made the outcome a foregone conclusion (something the US military asserted), thus making the conflict or war impossible because war has no predetermined ending. Further, and more provocatively, he asserted that the war was itself a simulation of future wars the US would fight, that it was all only ever an exercise, a military exercise or game, intended to ready forces to fight (for this was not a real fight) and to display (or advertise) US military technological superiority and weaponry (which is also, of course, one of the US's biggest export items). Many a commentator had fits of apoplexy about Baudrillard's sceptical and inflammatory rhetoric and wished to dismiss it by asserting that he was simply wrong, for the war had indeed actually transpired – a retort tantamount to the most naïve of empirical counters, which is to take his assertions in the most literal sense, and worse, to misunderstand fully Baudrillard's analyses.

Extending a conceit borrowed from François de Bernard, itself a continuation of his own conceit, Baudrillard writes that the Iraq War is a film: not *like* a film – not a simile – but film itself (rather as the Gulf War *is* TV). The Iraq War has a 'screenplay' that has to be fulfilled unerringly (Evil 124). Everything from technical to financial to materiel, including control of distribution (similar to Chaplin, Pickford and Fairbanks with their United Artists studio), has been mobilised for 'The Iraq War: The Film', which is rather like *Wag the Dog*'s 'The Albanian War: The TV Series', brought to us by Brean and Motss. Baudrillard argues that, 'in the end, operational war becomes an enormous special effect; cinema becomes the paradigm of warfare, and we can imagine it as "real," whereas it is merely the mirror of its cinematic being' (Evil 124). Baudrillard's argument aligns in an interesting manner with Gunning's suggestion that the advent of computer-generated imagery (CGI) and special effects-driven cinema means a kind of return to the 'cinema of attractions' found in the first decade of film history: contemporary warfare and cinema as CGI spectacle. However, Baudrillard's larger point concerns cinema's reach, or rather its absorption into and manufacture of those events that constitute history as it is commonly understood. There is no outside the cinematic text for Baudrillard, only cinema's protean productive capacity to generate the Real.

Wag the Dog anticipates the moments that arrived with the Iraq War, the second and third levels of simulation that first dupe viewers and then conflate reality and simulation, with reality being wholly generated by the simulation. A host of examples exist for analysis, including the toppling of Saddam's statue in Firdos Square – staged for TV by US forces, and not the spontaneous acts of citizens, as TV reported; or the Pat Tillman death by friendly fire, not in fact due to battlefield heroics, as the Pentagon announced through the press; or the Jessica Lynch routine return to her unit, and not her heroic rescue from vile enemy forces. Lynch became the poster child for Iraqi savagery and her rescue a pyrotechnic display worthy of an action film – or so the government and press represented events. Only later did the news emerge that Lynch had been well treated by the Iraqi medical staff after her capture and that her rescuers met no resistance at all. When Lynch later testified before Congress to set the story straight about how she had been used by the military and the media, the focus had long ago moved on and no one cared much. Lynch, of course, by then had landed a book deal and a made-for-TV movie deal, and hosted a website devoted to patriotic crafts that she and others manufactured, including an oil painting she made, 'America Loves Jessica Lynch' refrigerator magnets and Jessica Lynch soap boxes. Jessica Lynch became Zelig.

Perhaps the strangest moment of media-generated intertextuality, though, came with Bush's 'mission accomplished' appearance, a moment designed to evoke *Top Gun* (a movie made with generous support from the US navy). On 1 May 2003, Bush co-piloted a naval fighter jet on to the decks of the USS *Abraham Lincoln*, anchored off the coast of San Diego. Using the 'golden hour' burnish of dusk so beloved of cinematographers, the President emerged in full flight gear and strode on to a podium to deliver his speech. Behind him hung a large banner proclaiming 'Mission Accomplished'. There beneath the banner and bathed in the golden hue of sunset, Bush asserted that 'major combat operations have ended.' Citizens in the US, Iraq and Afghanistan to this day remain relieved and happy to know that hostilities ended officially on 1 May 2003, and that these countries are now free of violent engagements between combatant forces.

Bush's landing on the aircraft carrier lands us right back in *Wag the*

Dog territory. The frequent cinematic trope about the thin line between reality and fantasy, existence and its double, returns here with a vengeance because there clearly is no distinction; Hollywood becomes politics and reality. In the film, a manufactured and simulated war renders the US public as blank slates upon which the media write, complete with behaviourist responses to emotive patriotic cues. In the public sphere, further intermedial exchanges, some interesting and depressing side events related directly to the film and it diegetic content, transpired. In August 1998, just as Clinton needed to testify about a host of scandals (most sex-related, some not), he ordered attacks on two terrorist bases in two different countries. The first was in the Sudan, which turned out to be an aspirin factory. The Republican opposition seized on the sound-bite nature of media and used a film title to describe the President's decision, calling the military action 'Wagging the Dog'. A media reference to a media object intended for simplistic engagement with complex political and policy issues ensured that public discourse would be contained at the sound-bite level. The media firestorm whipped up, and Clinton decided it was best not to proceed with the second attack during that national political climate: the country, Afghanistan; the target: Osama bin Laden.

The Naïve and the *Haram*: Albert Brooks's *Looking for Comedy in the Muslim World* (2005)

Does Islam Have a Sense of Humor?
> Title of a BBC report (20 November 2007)

Albert Brooks can boast a relatively small but very high-quality body of film work, for which he is writer, director and actor. His comedy is self-deprecatory while also exploring chasms of misunderstanding and failures of communication, along with their resultant existential desperation. This particular film neatly combines the personal with the larger political frames in which a subject operates, and explicitly examines humour as a topic that has inherently political and social dimensions. One of the earliest comedic responses to the 9/11 attacks, *Looking* directly satirises American do-gooder naïveté and international meddling based on the certainty that the intervention will help all involved. The satire here is understated, and often articulated in an indirect, oblique or covert manner, so much so that the vast majority of critics and reviews seem to have missed much of what Brooks engages, along with the subtleties of the satirical attack.

Brooks's films often work on the theme of people who are self-absorbed (even narcissistic), individuals whose self-contained certainties about

the world and how things work within it run into evidence that refute
their viability; in this way, his protagonists are metonymic of the US
itself, which means he keeps good company with Spalding Gray and his
Swimming to Cambodia. In fact, many of the satirical targets in Gray's film
can be found here, updated and transposed to different conflicts, thus
revealing troubling repetitions and their even more troubling variations.
Much of the film's humour is self-deprecating, individually for Brooks
and collectively for the US. His character, a comedian named Albert
Brooks, embodies the somewhat widespread observation that the US was
poised at the start of the new millennium for a period of unprecedented
global control and yet was completely unprepared culturally and intel-
lectually for it. Having some knowledge of what it does not know, the US
government sends Brooks to India and Pakistan to find out 'what makes
Muslims laugh' and to write a 500–page report on the topic, for which he
is likely to receive the Medal of Freedom from President George W. Bush.

Clearly, the film is an invitation to think not just geopolitics but also
the micropolitics of daily life. At the geopolitical level, it requires a certain
amount of knowledge about the volatile relations between India and
Pakistan that Brooks's earnest character inadvertently unsettles. In the
background of his bumbling mission looms nearly a century of large-scale
religious violence, including the Partition that caused mass migrations
numbering in the millions and deaths in close to equal numbers. The
India–Pakistan conflict is frequently delineated, articulated and enacted
as religious in nature; hence the specificity of the site in which Brooks sets
the film. The mutual suspicions of the two countries are now counterbal-
anced and exacerbated by terrorist acts, as well as nuclear weapons on both
sides. It is one of the most combustible regions and borders in the world,
but Brooks's character knows not one whit about any of that. Instead, he
frets about the page count of his report like a deadline-frightened student
searching for filler in an essay lacking in substance. Throughout it all,
though, Brooks's character moves with sincerity and naïveté, lost in the
ignorant oblivion of the well-intentioned coupled with the self-involved
concerns of the solipsistic: a true innocent (which means American)
abroad.

Though he has been tasked with trying to discover what Muslims find
funny, as if such a massively heterogeneous, not to say internally riven
group could be reducible in such a fashion, Brooks's character decides
to forego the interviews he has been holding and instead conduct an
experiment using his older stand-up materials. As part of the wave of conceptual stand-up comedians that included Woody Allen, George Carlin,
Richard Pryor and Steve Martin, who eschewed traditional joke set-ups

and punch lines, Brooks' humor hardly constitutes the mainstream of American comedy in and of itself, operating as it does as a satire on show-business types and the formulae of comedy routines that he engages in meta-comedic fashion. Thus trying it out on an audience about whom he knows little provides a wonderful extension of Brooks's own humour with the additional layer of geopolitical critique: that whenever the US wishes to find out about the Other – friend or foe – it becomes a self-enclosed system of projection and discovery that only reveals US interests. The problem is not so much that Brooks's character does not know his audience, but rather that he believes that he himself is the key to discovering them. When his routine fails magnificently and hilariously (both in terms of its content and lack of efficacy for his Indian audience), the only adjustment he wants to make, when he decides he will give it all another try, is to the lighting.

His routine fares better when he illegally sneaks over to the Pakistani side of the border to meet covertly with a group of renegade stand-up comedians, who also happen to be stoned on powerful hash. His movements, though, cause alarm on both sides of the heavily monitored border, each suspecting with Cold War Manichean logic that he is working for the other. As Brooks's character heads home with the report negligibly written, he leaves the two countries hurtling toward armed conflict, for his actions have incited extant paranoiac thoughts and reactions on the part of both governments. The end of the film contains a very nice joke when his wife calls him 'the Henry Kissinger of Comedy'; in the background of the shot, the escalated tensions are being broadcast on TV, with Brooks's character unaware of the diplomatic and military fallout from his mission. This sly joke operates through a bit of general discursive knowledge, to the effect that Kissinger is known as 'a master diplomat' who won the Nobel Peace Prize, in contrast to Brooks's bumbling in India. The joke becomes funnier when we remember that, while winning the prize, Kissinger was also masterminding the secret and illegal bombing of Cambodia, which unwittingly helped bring Pol Pot and the Khmer Rouge to power. Similarly, Brooks's forays into Pakistan to speak to rogue stand-up comedians unwittingly unleash suspicions between the two enemy states and lead to clashes. The unintended consequences of US intervention, no matter how apparently benign, often leave the site far worse than it was previously, though those involved from the US believe themselves to have pulled off an utter and complete success. Brooks's little capstone joke contains multitudes of connections (including some to *Swimming to Cambodia*). And just as Gray becomes a metonym for the US, so too does Brooks, each performing his (and our) own intelligent and outraged failure.

A similarly deft and complex situation arises in the film when Brooks's character is informed that Al-Jazeera has heard that he was in the country and wish to meet him. Convinced that they know about his US-sponsored project, Brooks's character excitedly believes that the involvement of the global Arabic news channel will provide him with the key to writing his report (though not necessarily to discovering what he has been asked to analyse). But there has been a mistake, for the meeting is not with the news division but with Al-Jazeera's nascent, though growing entertainment division. The executives there wish to gauge his interest in starring in a new situation comedy set in a high-rise complex amidst a group of quirky and whacky neighbours, to be called 'That Darn Jew', Brooks to be cast in the title role. Brooks's character misses the obvious point that the show he is being pitched provides him with exactly what he is pursuing: an example of commodified entertainment designed to make Muslims laugh. Although we are not that far from the Lubitsch-graced posters explaining how to identify a Jew, the joke more importantly reminds us that a variation of 'That Darn Jew', with a Muslim as the butt of the reification and essentialism ('That Damned Muslim'), has been circulating for decades in the US and with whirlwind-like intensity post 9/11.

Brooks's character confuses entertainment media with news media, which makes him metonymic of the US audience once again. The film includes a good intertextual reference that highlights the seamless blend of media and politics, fiction and reality, and celebrity reminiscent of *Wag the Dog* and *Zelig*. The chair of the congressional panel in the film is Fred Thompson, who was a US senator before leaving the Senate to act in the TV series called 'Law and Order' which he left in turn to run for the Republican nomination for President in 2008. When that failed, he went back to acting. The revolving door of lobbying and politics, not to mention the Möbius strip of politics and media, is parodically enacted here as the revolving door of media personality and politician, now become not a door at all but a frame constituting the two as but one.

Coda: Satire and the Self of Cinema's Address

The films discussed in this chapter feature the deep and unavoidable ambivalence of satirical film comedy. The problems of satire and the unspeakable within cinema reside in the complex interaction of satire's dependence on the efficacy of human agency and the possibility of such agency in the face of, as well as through, the technical and machinic operations of film. The conditions of possibility that allow for the production of satirical films simultaneously circumscribe the capacity to enact the social and cultural change demanded of the didactic nature of the satire. That each of these films deploys another mode of artistic articulation or medium (vaudeville, theatre, operetta, television, performance art / monologue, and stand-up comedy) reveals the protean capacity of film to incorporate a range of media or performance modes while also domesticating these other forms or media through the generalised distributional and generic systems of mainstream cinema. Further, this incorporation of other performative forms or media draws attention to cinema's ever-uncertain ontological status within the larger media ecology and landscape of representational technologies (an issue explored more fully in the final chapter). For satire as a mode of address, the situation intensifies. With the increasing rise of political satire on television in the past decade within the US, as well as the increased role of peer-to-peer platforms such as YouTube for comedic engagement and general entertainment, cinema once again finds itself scrambling for both identity and purchase, caught as it is in the attributes that make it identifiable as a medium but at the same time delimited by them in terms of what it can produce.

Satire possesses a deep connection with the unspeakable, stating what cannot or should not be said within a specific cultural chronotope and its attendant value system. The films in this chapter bravely and compellingly take up the unspeakable, and in so doing, reveal yet another quandary, for their topics or issues or arguments actually are speakable, in that they have been spoken (as film). Regardless of the medium, the unspeakable of necessity must remain unarticulated. The unspeakable is not the potentially speakable but the absolute condition upon which speakability depends. Once uttered, then it is no longer unspeakable. Perhaps prior to these iterations, they were not speakable in these forums and media, but once realised, they only have the briefest taint of the taboo before that unique status passes. Their unspeakability becomes a kind of nostalgia or wish fulfilment for transgression that cinema facilitates in a moment of severely delimited capacity for the political subject to enact agency. Cinema's address, as usual, articulates its power to shape the audience and the world while remaining ambivalent about its status as a medium.

Works Cited

Barnes, Djuna. *Nightwood*. London: Faber & Faber, 2007.
Baudrillard, Jean. 'Hot Painting: The Inevitable Fate of the Image', in *Reconstructing Modernism: Art in New York, Paris and Montreal 1945–1964*,

Serge Guilbaut (ed.). Cambridge, MA: MIT Press, 1990, pp. 17–29.

Baudrillard, Jean. *The Gulf War Did Not Take Place*, Paul Patton (trans.). Bloomington: Indiana University Press, 1995.

Baudrillard, Jean. *The Intelligence of Evil, or the Lucidity Pact*, Chris Turner (trans.). Oxford and New York: Berg, 2005.

Beach, Christopher. *Class, Language, and American Film Comedy*. Cambridge: Cambridge University Press, 2005.

Beckett, Samuel. *Krapp's Last Tape and Other Dramatic Pieces*. New York: Grove, 1957.

Conrad, Joseph. *Heart of Darkness*. London: Penguin, 2007.

Crittenden, Camille. *Johann Strauss and Vienna: Operetta and the Politics of Popular Culture*. Cambridge and New York: Cambridge University Press, 2000.

Dalí, Salvador. 'Short Critical History of Cinema', in *Dali and Film*, Matthew Gale (ed.). London: Tate, 2007, pp. 75–7.

Doherty, Thomas. *Projections of War: Hollywood, American Culture and World War II*. New York: Columbia University Press, 1993.

Dürrenmatt, Friedrich. 'Theater Problems', *Selected Writings: Vol. 3 Essays*, Joel Ageed (trans.), Kenneth J. Northcott (ed.). Chicago and London: University of Chicago Press, 2006, pp. 137–62.

Gunning, Tom. 'The Cinema of Attractions: Early Film, its Spectator and the Avant-Garde', in *The Cinema of Attractions Reloaded*, Wanda Strauven (ed.). Amsterdam: Amsterdam University Press, 2006, pp. 381–8.

Heidegger, Martin. 1966 interview with *Der Spiegel*. Available at http://web.ics. purdue.edu/~other1/Heidegger%20Der%20Spiegel.pdf.

Insdorf, Annette. *Indelible Shadows: Film and the Holocaust*, 3rd edn. Cambridge and New York: Cambridge University Press, 2003.

Jenkins, Henry. *What Made Pistachio Nuts*. New York: Columbia University Press, 1992.

North, Michael. *Machine-Age Comedy*. Oxford and New York: Oxford University Press, 2009.

Polan, Dana. *Power and Paranoia: History, Narrative, and the American Cinema, 1940–1950*. New York: Columbia University Press, 1986.

Rose, Margaret A. *Parody: Ancient, Modern, and Post-modern*. Cambridge: Cambridge University Press, 1993.

Susskind, Ron. 'Without a Doubt: Faith, Certainty and the Presidency of George W. Bush', *The New York Times Magazine*, 17 October 2004.

Virilio, Paul. *War and Cinema: The Logistics of Perception*, Patrick Camiller (trans). London: Verso, 1989.

Virilio, Paul and Sylvère Lotringer. *Pure War*. Los Angeles: Semiotext(e), 2008.

CHAPTER 6

Conclusion: Between the Machine and the Event: Film Comedy

And on Fifth Avenue Harpo Marx has just lighted the fuse that projects from the behinds of a flock of expensive giraffes stuffed with dynamite. They run in all directions, sowing panic and obliging everyone to seek refuge pell-mell within the shops. All the fire-alarms of the city have just been turned on, but it is already too late. Boom! Boom! Boom! Boom! I salute you, explosive giraffes of New York, and all you fore-runners of the irrational – Mack Sennett, Harry Langdon, and you too, unforgettable Buster Keaton, tragic and delirious like my rotten and mystic donkeys, desert roses of Spain!

Salvador Dalí, *The Secret Life of Salvador Dalí* (332)

Where film cameras are involved – with the rider that there is strictly no difference between film and still cameras in the virtual world – then additional considerations are taken into account; for example, if a real camera movement is made using a physical 'rig' – as in a crane shot, or whatever – there will be an unavoidable degree of camera shake at the beginning and end of the movement. Software has been written to simulate that shake, which moreover allows the user to specify which particular film camera, and which type of rig, is being used. The prevailing standard of realism in computer modeling is not the world as such; it is rather the world as it appears to the camera. I believe that this is an ideological artifact of a period of historical transition, and will pass. In time we will forget how physical cameras showed the world, and we will adapt our supposedly 'natural' vision to the new standards.

Victor Burgin, in conversation with Ryan Bishop and Sean Cubitt

William Joyce and Brian Oldenberg's short animation film, *The Fantastic Flying Books of Mr. Morris Lessmore* (2011), provides a twenty-first-century mash-up ethos of aesthetic modes and media while also offering a whimsical, sentimental allegory of reading and a life of the imagination. A commentary on the power of narrative to aid one during the disasters of life, with oblique references to Hurricane Katrina serving as a metonym for our collective confrontation with individual mortality, the film proves useful for us, less with regard to the technics of narrative and more with regard to its profligate and skilled mobilising of an array of representational technologies. The animated short begins with the sound of a spring-driven gramophone's hand crank turn that leads to a thin and scratchy violin playing 'Pop Goes the Weasel'. The nostalgic and wistful tone of the entire short is set with this initial few seconds of sound that harkens back to an earlier moment of technological reproduction. As the tracking computer-animated shot moves in on the protagonist, the music becomes fuller with regard to instrumentation and cleaner with regard to audio fidelity, almost as if it were recreating the process of digitally remastering early sound recordings, with the tracking shot being a movement through the temporality of technological sound reproduction as much as through the urban space of the diegesis.

Deftly combining literary texts, flip action books, cinema, 2–D animation, miniatures, computer animation and other means for generating and reproducing stories, the short film exemplifies a meta-medial engagement akin to a media archaeology, with different temporal moments of technological production occupying the frame at the same moment. The literary texts, the books, act as both vehicles for story telling and as fantastical *dramatis personae*, as both delivery of narrative and characters within the film. The cinema allusions are numerous, Mr Morris Lessmore himself being an avatar of Keaton's silent persona, which also alludes to Buñuel and Dalí's lead in their classic, *Un Chien andalou*. The various medial references continually return to books and the written word as the source from which the other media have emerged. Literacy becomes a kind of salvation, literally bringing colour (and fulfilment) into the lives of characters, as, *Wizard of Oz*-like, the film combines black-and-white with colour images to underline specific thematic concerns. After surviving a natural disaster that has moved buildings and dropped houses from the sky, Morris Lessmore wanders through a paper-strewn black-and-white landscape. There he encounters a young woman being pulled through the sky by a flock of fluttering books. She leads him to a house teeming with tomes intelligently animated and in need of care, including feeding (alphabet cereal), clothing (book jackets), mending (book repair) and, most importantly, reading – without which the books will die. Lessmore provides this care for his grateful and playful, though very demanding charges. Here the protagonist lives out his days with his mobile and flying lettered friends, until he too must write 'The End' at the bottom of his life's journal or story.

A kind and sentimental reading of the film would hold that we are all dropped into a wondrous tradition of reading and learning that is handed down from generation to generation, here evoked by the young girl (who, we learn by the end of the film, has just died) who leads Morris Lessmore to the house of books, just as he will do with another young person (dwelling in black and white until the books bring colour to her world) after he too has passed on. A less sympathetic reading of the film can interpret the house of books, reading and learning as controlling the humans: that the humans live to serve the discourse networks and their technologies of delivery and circulation, not the other way around. (I think we can guess which reading Friedrich Kittler would prefer.) Kittler's interest in the materiality of the delivery systems of information and data effecting change on the body and mind of those who interact with these networks, and to which no human is immune, would read this animated short in a far less sentimental light. He would simply take Morris Lessmore as but one more (or less) node in literacy's external formation and construction of the human subject as a simple conduit of media and informational distribution and conveyance. Just as Derrida delineates a relationship to language that exists prior to us and which speaks through us, rather than us necessarily speaking it – summed up in the pithy formulation 'I have but one language – yet that language is not mine' (Other 1) – so Kittler argues that information systems and media create conditions, regimes of sensorial change and modes of thought to which we must accommodate ourselves in order to function. Benjamin makes a similar point in relation to cinema and industrialisation, as we have seen, and Kittler extends this to the materiality of mechanical and electronic media.

Although the short film uses the older technologies of the flip book to evoke early weddings of moving images and book materiality, the film as cultural and media object has also become an app for portable hand-held devices, a video game and a printed book, betraying its position within a vast twenty-first-century consumer culture and mediascape, as well as prompting some thought about the position of cinema historically and presently within interlocking, complementary and contradictory tech-nologies of aural–visual re-presentation. A sizeable body of current media scholarship, including cinematic theory, usefully explores this complex and productive terrain. For example, Siegfried Zielinski claims that cinema is but an 'intermezzo' in the longer trajectory of televisual technol-ogies (especially television), while William Uricchio has similarly called cinema a detour on the way to our current plethora of audiovisual devices, themselves also only stages for further media development and change. Tom Gunning, as we have noted, long ago made similar points, though with an assumption of a semi-secure ontological status of the cinematic medium. Film scholarship now is consistently in dialogue with a much larger set of sensorial extensions and manipulations, a long list of which is provided in Thomas Elsaesser's useful meditation, 'The New History of Cinema as Media Archaeology'. Kittler reminds us that the origins of film and the ability to identify film as something different from a host of other visual and audio tricks go back to the early part of the twentieth century, when Hugo Munsterberg, in 1916, asked a host of questions about the origins of an identifiable cinematic apparatus and states, 'it is arbitrary to say where the development of moving pictures began and it is impossible to foresee where it will lead' (quoted in Gramophone 117) Where cinema begins and where it leaves off is much fuzzier now than ever due to this scholarship, and that of many others, but clearly the intermedial nature of film has never been more certain than it is now, and therefore its status never more unstable (Parikka 8–14). Rather like a comedic unsettling of seemingly static categories, cinema, from the points of view articulated by and through this scholarship, emerges more as a process than as an object – thus undermining the very ontology of the object of inquiry.

This, as we have just noted, is an older point within film criticism than is often acknowledged. None the less, many cinema scholars have returned to André Bazin's famous and provocative question posed in the mid-twentieth century, 'What is cinema?', with variations of their own: perhaps a return to the ontological question Bazin poses, or a change in the status of the question itself, as in Thomas Elsaesser's media archaeology-driven 'When is Cinema?', which asks us to consider cinema's evanescent firming up as a recognisable medium within the larger flux of medial change and technological development, or in Victor Burgin's psychoana-lytically inspired 'Where is Cinema?' in *The Remembered Film*'s explora-tion of cinema as immaterial presence in memory and material influence in the phenomenology of daily life beyond the confines of the cinema. Others have essentially taken up 'How is Cinema?' and 'Why is Cinema?', but for this study any variation would necessitate the qualifying adjective 'comedic' that prompts 'What is comedic cinema?' – a question that brings to bear the immaterial, noetic systemic functioning of the material systems of cinematic production and reproduction within larger technological changes of culture by offering a critical engagement with, of and through them. The question further prompts us to ask how comedic cinema oper-ates and why the comedic is important (if at all). The crucial qualifying term aims to direct us toward thinking about the intimate linkages that mark the comedic as quintessentially cinematic and the cinematic as quintessentially comedic in so far as we can understand cinema's self-reflexive engagement with its own technics and effects, in epistemological and ontological senses. For cinema to work, something must fail (proper apperception being primary). For it to fail, as with the comedic and its dis-ruption and aesthetics of breakage, something also must work (comedy as self-apparently comic). The paradox of material and immaterial systems and technologies operating with regard to collective evaluations of success and failure resides at the heart of cultural critique.

The success and failure of systems and technologies, as well as the constraints and opportunities each affords us, connect with how we conceptualise the machine/machinic and the event –the former being associated with both success and the inorganic, and the latter being associated with failure and the organic. In the centuries of technological and electronic development and implementation, the organic yields to the inorganic in terms of organisation regimes. Whether it is a factory system or visual evidence in the laboratory or the courtroom, the machine (the technological) has the upper hand. In the essay 'Typewriter Ribbon', Derrida addresses these constants in the following manner:

> Will we one day be able to, and in a single gesture, to join the thinking of the event to the thinking of the machine? Will we be able to think, what is called thinking, at one and the same time, both what is happening (we call that an event) and the calculable programming of automatic repetition (we call that a machine). For that, it would be necessary in the future (but there will be no future except on this condition) to think both the event and the machine as two compatible or even in-dissociable concepts. Today they appear to us antinomic. (72)

Derrida's formulation speaks to the conditions that make thought and apperception possible. The role of cinema as a medium or distillation of various media at a specific cultural–historical moment embodies and reiterates this vexed antinomic relationship of machine and event while functioning as a heuristic for thinking the often-ignored interdependence to which Derrida alludes.

'[The machine] is destined, that is, to reproduce impassively, imperceptibly, without organ or organicity, the received commands. In a state of anesthesia, it would obey or command a calculable program without affect or auto–affection, like an indifferent automaton' (Typewriter 71). This quotation points toward the thinking together of the event, which might be recast therefore as organic and animate, along with the calculable programming of an automatic repetition (the inanimate, the machinic). Although we usually consider these qualities as antithetical, Derrida brings them together as necessary conditions for one another. The machinic is internal to irreplaceable singularity while remaining heterogeneous. The comedic impulse or eruption serves to bring these binaristic qualities together in one and the same moment, with the comic utterance showing the utter necessity and interdependence of the machine and the event for thought and interpretation of the world that erases easy or clear distinctions between subjects and objects, machines and nature, operation and failure, and exteriority and interiority. This comedic alchemy has long been projected on screens through cinematic technologies.

Video Dolls as Archaeology of the Present (Yet Again) – a Coda

'I am a real working video camera,' states the ad for the Barbie Video Girl, with the video girl commodity/toy/visual technology speaking to us in the first person through the written convention of direct quotation (http://www.barbie.com/videogirl/). The potential consumer of this hybrid entity is told directly, in the intimacy of the second person, 'record your own movies' and 'add your own special effects' – the potentialities of the product rendered in the form of imperatives. The doll has a camera lens in her chest and video screen in her back (for playback, editing and manipulation of the recorded image). The lens faces forward, the screen back, and the electronic reconfiguration and storage of sight, sound, time and space pass right through her chest cavity, constituting the core of the informational cyborg girl. No longer aspiring to be film, as with Virilio's analysis of online streaming, or the grainy video image of the Columbine shooters, as discussed earlier, but now aspiring to embody the recording and reproducing apparatus itself – to be the camera, the projector and the screen (the entire cinematic system at its most basic) – the Barbie Video Girl, as Vertov vestige and update, bespeaks mediation in a comedic register.

Her level of address to us, and within which is she is addressed as a child's role model, is undeniably cinematic and comic. As a toy with a didactic dimension attached and attributed to it – as most dolls possess – she clearly reveals an embrace of those external medial technics that inscribe us all and which she unironically and literally internalises. She states and celebrates that we are defined by the extent to which media shape, trace and archive us. She manifests an auto-referentiality of address that is only self-conscious at the level of consumer-directed advertising. As such, she draws attention not only to what she can potentially offer those who buy her – the capacity to make and alter movies – but also to the larger media in which the product partakes: the cinema. Her statement offers an evaluation of her message in relation to its addressees, one that proclaims an awareness of its supposed and stated positive attributes regarding how we position ourselves within and are positioned by medial networks, most readily articulated by cinema. The statement, though, is undermined through the comedic intervention of the Barbie Video Girl being a portable apparatus that serves as metonym of all those advances of audiovisual technology that threaten, if not actually end, cinema's status

– a status it might never have had, as Zielinski, Uricchio and others have argued.

Further, she tells us something about the future of viewers or spectators in relation to the camera as visual technological object and concept, articulated by Victor Burgin in the epigraph to this chapter. The digital camera's storage and reproduction of analogue camera effects and visions certainly entail a pause along the trajectory toward what 'the camera' will do to our capacity and expectations regarding technologies of sight. The Barbie Video Girl unsettles, comically, our sense of the visual and medial fields, rendering her one of the heirs apparent to Chaplin, Sennett, Harry Langdon, 'unforgettable' Keaton, and the Marx Brothers, as listed in Dalí's epigraph. Just as the fuse Harpo lit 'projects' like a film, so the Barbie Video Girl records and projects the future of the camera in its relation to those it engages. If Morris Lessmore is produced by and through literary modes of representation of the discourse and media networks of book technology, as well as others, the Barbie Video Girl whom we can find online is but another screen culture production, emanating light and projecting images and sounds. The fuse Harpo lights in the backsides of his expensive giraffes reminds us of the bodily manipulations of information technologies (including cinema, TV, books and so on), as well as of the comedic moment – a blast from this sublunary passageway – that unsettles, resists and alters the thorough working of these apparatuses. They would fail, anyway, in and of themselves, and the knowledge that they will is the comedic moment of fusing machine and event that film comedy stages for us each time we view the mechanistic operations of a film and marvel at the event of the laughter.

Works Cited

Barbie Video Girl. http://www.barbie.com/videogirl/; last accessed August 2012.

Burgin, Victor. *The Remembered Film*. London: Reaktion, 2004.

Burgin, Victor. 'Victor Burgin in Conversation with Ryan Bishop and Sean Cubitt', *Theory, Culture & Society*, 2013 (forthcoming).

Derrida, Jacques. *Monolingualism of the Other; or the Prosthesis of Origin*, Patrick Mensah (trans.). Stanford and London: Stanford University Press, 1998.

Derrida, Jacques. 'Typewriter Ribbon, Limited Ink (2)', in *Without Alibi*, Peggy Kamuf (ed. and trans.). Stanford and London: Stanford University Press, 2002, pp. 71–160.

Elsaesser, Thomas. 'The New History of Cinema as Media Archaeology', *Cinémas: revue d'études cinématographiques / Cinemas: Journal of Film Studies*, 14:2–3, 2004, pp. 75–117.

Gunning, Tom. 'The Cinema of Attractions: Early Film, its Spectator and the Avant-Garde', in *Early Cinema: Space, Frame, Narrative*, Thomas Elsaesser (ed.). London: BFI, 1990, pp. 56–62.

Huhtamo, Erkki and Jussi Parikka (eds). *Media Archaeology: Approaches, Applications, and Implications*. Berkeley and London: University of California Press, 2011.

Kittler, Friedrich. *Discourse Networks 1800/1900*, Michael Metteer (trans.). Stanford and London: Stanford University Press, 1990.

Kittler, Friedrich. *Gramophone, Film, Typewriter*, Geoffrey Winthrop-Young and Michael Wutz (trans.). Stanford and London: Stanford University Press, 1999.

Parikka, Jussi. *What is Media Archaeology?* Cambridge: Polity, 2012.

Uricchio, William. 'Cinema as Detour? Towards a Reconsideration of Moving Image Technology in the Late 19th Century', in *Der Film in der Geschichte*, K. Hickethier, E. Muller and R. Rother (eds). Berlin: Sigma, 1997, pp. 19–25.

Zielinski, Siegfried. *Audiovisions: Cinema and Television as Entr'actes in History*, Gloria Custance (trans.). Amsterdam: Amsterdam University Press, 1999.

Index